Randy Romero's Remarkable Ride

Also by Bill Heller

Obsession: Bill Musselman's Relentless Quest
Overlay, Overly
The Will to Win: The Ron Turcotte Story
Harness Overlays
Playing Tall: The Ten Shortest Players in NBA History
Travelin' Sam: America's Sports Ambassador
Exotic Overlays
Turf Overlays
Billy Haughton: The Master
Legends: Go for Wand
Legends: Forego
Legends: Personal Ensign
Run Baby Run
Graveyard of Champions
Go for the Green
A Good Day Has No Rain
Saratoga Tales
After the Finish Line: The Race to End Horse Slaughter in America
The Ten Commandments of Value
Howard Parker, a Saratoga Harness Legend

Randy Romero's
Remarkable Ride

BILL HELLER

PELICAN PUBLISHING COMPANY
GRETNA 2010

Library of Congress Cataloging-in-Publication Data

Heller, Bill.
  Randy Romero's remarkable ride / Bill Heller.
    p. cm.
  Includes index.
  ISBN 978-1-58980-752-5 (hardcover : alk. paper) 1. Jockeys—United States—
Biography. I. Romero, Randy, 1957- II. Title.
  SF336.R565H45 2010
  798.40092–dc22
  [B]

                              2010001478

Printed in the United States of America
Published by Pelican Publishing Company, Inc.
1000 Burmaster Street, Gretna, Louisiana 70053

To my precious granddaughter Mia.

Mia, you are my inspiration to live life. I love you and enjoy all the moments I spend with you. You brighten up my life in every way. You have brought such joy to me as your grandfather. Mia, let it be known that you should always follow your heart, even if it does not turn out for the best. There will be bumps and left-hand turns throughout life, but always remember that you must never give up. Mia, you mean so much to me and know in your heart that I will always love you.

Randy "Paw Paw" Romero

Contents

Acknowledgments

This is my twenty-first book, and I have never had more fun or more cooperation writing one. That's because of Randy, whom I am honored to now call a good friend, and his family. Not once in the ten-month process of writing his biography did he fail to return a phone call. Not once did he rule any topic taboo as he shared his life with me. And he and his lovely wife, Cricket, were kind enough to have me stay in their home in New Orleans for several days. Randy's older brother, Gerald, who lives in the same apartment complex with Randy, was also extremely helpful.

Randy's good friend Randy Gervais was responsible for beginning this process and I deeply thank him for that, as well as his assistant, Nicole.

Researching a biography is made infinitely easier if you have good sources, and I was blessed with two of the best, Cathy Schenck at the Keeneland Library in Lexington, Kentucky, and Allan Carter at the National Museum of Racing and Hall of Fame in Saratoga Springs, New York. Cathy saved me months of research by not only sending me hundreds of articles about Randy, but also dating and providing the source for each and every one of them. Allan repeatedly found obscure records and information that had escaped mainstream media. Thanks to both of them.

My good friend at the National Thoroughbred Racing Association, Joan Lawrence, provided Randy's year-by-year statistics as well as a chronological list of his hundreds of stakes winners, which are included in the appendix.

Charlie Hayward, the CEO of the New York Racing Association, was kind enough to read a first draft of the first chapter and offer his suggestions.

Charlotte Quinn of the New York Racing Association sent me valuable stories, and Jennifer Hancock of the American Quarter

Horse Association provided statistics and information about Randy's early years.

Kris Goddard of Home Box Office tracked down a copy of the HBO documentary "Jockeys" for my use. Ed McNamara's excellent book, *Cajun Racing*, was extremely helpful, and passages from it are cited in the book. More than that, his book helped capture the nature and spirit of Cajun racing, which helped me understand that very unique part of Randy's life.

My protégé and good friend Kim French read the manuscript and provided many useful suggestions.

My son, Benjamin, helped in a variety of ways, including reading the manuscript, fact-checking, proofreading, and compiling the index.

Lindsey Reynolds did a fine job editing the book.

I would especially like to thank all the people I interviewed for the book, many of whom I called unannounced. Thanks to Mark Guidry, Larry "Doc" Danner, Dallas Stewart, Shug McGaughey, Billy and Tina Mott, Ronnie Ebanks, Frankie Brothers, Neil Hopkins, Tommy Walters, Jimmy Lafont, Eddie Delahoussaye, Fred Aime, Bernie Flint, Todd Pletcher, Joe Riccelli, Kenny "Chopper" Bourque, Linda Wilson, Sturges Ducoing, Caroll Angelle, Ed Plesa, Pat Byrne, Mark Faden, and Joyce and Lloyd Romero, Randy's parents.

To anyone I've missed, I sincerely apologize.

Randy Romero's Remarkable Ride

1

Still Riding

Four horses headed off the Oklahoma Training Track on a mid-August morning in 2008 and walked back to barn 38, where their trainer, Dallas Stewart, was stabled for the six-week meet at Saratoga Race Course. Back at the barn, the riders dismounted and began putting away their equipment.

Three of the riders were young. The fourth, almost inconceivably, was Randy Romero. The fifty-year-old former jockey had nearly died in a Louisville, Kentucky, hospital six months earlier when his kidney was removed.

"His medical report would make a stunt man blush," Gerry Robichaux of the *Shreveport-Bossier City Times* once wrote of Randy. "He's broken a collarbone, a shoulder, ribs, his pelvis, a knee, a cheekbone, a thumb, his jaw and a toe. He's punctured a lung, his kidney and his spleen." Robichaux wrote that in 1980, nineteen years before Randy retired.

In April 1983, Randy was nearly burned alive in a freak accident in a sweatbox when a light bulb exploded and severely burned more than 60 percent of his body. His singed, bloody red torso was ghastly. Doctors gave him a 40 percent chance of living. He was back riding in three and a half months and won his first start back at Louisiana Downs on a horse trained by his older brother Gerald. Utterly exhausted in the winner's circle, Randy, who was wearing a pressure suit to protect his skin, could barely lift his arms.

Randy then not only captured his third riding title at the Fair Grounds the following spring, but also set a still-standing record at the New Orleans track with 181 victories, documenting his courage, determination, and, frankly, his stubbornness. "Randy put it all on the line," one of Randy's jockey agents, Larry "Doc" Danner, says. "There's never been a jockey with more desire or love of the game than Randy Romero."

But Randy couldn't stay out of harm's way. "My body is like a road map," Randy says. "I have scars all over the place." Less than a year after the burning incident, after riding an afternoon card at the Fair Grounds, he flew to a second Louisiana track, Delta Downs, to ride another horse that same night. The horse bolted and Randy jumped off, hitting the ground hard enough to break his femur. He also suffered cartilage damage in his knee, an injury that initially went undiagnosed. That cost him an additional four months. At the time he went down, he was the leading rider in the country by a margin of more than 40 victories. Despite missing four months in 1985, he still finished second in the country with 415 victories, 54 behind Chris Antley.

Randy came back and became the first jockey ever to win four stakes in a single afternoon, March 5, 1988, at Gulfstream Park, capped by long shot Brian's Time's victory in the Florida Derby.

Randy will be forever remembered for riding two outstanding fillies, Personal Ensign, the only undefeated major American Thoroughbred of the past one hundred years, and the brilliant Go for Wand. Personal Ensign overcame a broken pastern (ankle) as a two-year-old, an injury that would have ended most Thoroughbreds' careers. Benefiting from a flawless ride by Randy in the final race of her career, Personal Ensign preserved her legacy with a desperate rally to beat Kentucky Derby winner Winning Colors by a nose in the $1 million 1988 Breeders' Cup Distaff at Churchill Downs, a race that in 2008 was voted the greatest in the Breeders' Cup's twenty-five-year history.

Few dispute the worst Breeders' Cup race ever: when Go for Wand broke down just two years later in the final eighth of a mile in front of the grandstand in the Breeders' Cup Distaff at Belmont Park. Though seriously injured when thrown from the filly, Randy then rode Izvestia in the $3 million Breeders' Cup Classic, finishing sixth, before winding up in a familiar place: the hospital. He had suffered hairline fractures of his shoulder and eight ribs.

When he returned to ride the following spring at Gulfstream Park, he broke his elbow. The injury was misdiagnosed and wound up costing Randy more months of pain and lost time. Most importantly, it sapped his arm strength, so desperately needed when steering thousand-pound Thoroughbreds traveling forty miles per hour on ankles so narrow you can ring your fingers around them.

"I was never the same after that," he states.

Yet he endured. When he retired, he was the twenty-sixth leading riding ever with 4,294 victories. He won 25 riding titles. What would his numbers have been had he only suffered three horrific injuries instead of a dozen; if his number of surgeries was five instead of twenty-five; if his knee and elbow injuries had been correctly treated?

"He accomplished a lot; he would have accomplished more if he hadn't been injured," Hall of Fame jockey Angel Cordero, Jr, says. "He had the character of a champion. He went through a lot of accidents and the burn, and he never showed any fear. He just kept coming back. He came back like nothing happened. I liked that."

Randy knew no other way. "I was dedicated," he explains. "It's a gift that God gave me. It had to be because I sacrificed a lot in my life to be a jockey. I just couldn't get it out of my blood. That's all I wanted to do."

It showed.

Personal Ensign's Hall of Fame trainer, Claude "Shug" McGaughey, marveled at Randy's ability to recover from one injury after another. "You wouldn't think it could be done, but Randy would ride now if he could," McGaughey relates. "He was just like Cordero. He was born to ride."

After he stopped riding, Randy became a successful jockey agent until his deteriorating health intruded. In February 2002, he suffered kidney damage, nearly costing him his life. He needed a kidney transplant but was ineligible to receive one because doctors discovered he had Hepatitis C, a virus that causes chronic liver disease, a virus he may have caught from a tainted blood transfusion following his burns. They also discovered that only 25 percent of Randy's liver was functioning. Instead of performing a kidney transplant, doctors placed Randy on dialysis: three four-hour sessions per week that he will undergo for the rest of his life. Six years after that diagnosis, Randy's kidney was removed to stop internal bleeding. The kidney was so enlarged that doctors had to remove one of Randy's ribs to get to it. Randy recalls, "I was bleeding inside for like ten days. They had to take a kidney out and a rib. I got really, really sick, and I thought I was going to die."

Instead, he slowly recovered. Again.

He maintains a strict diet, which includes Himalayan GoChi juice, and daily exercise, mostly push-ups and sit-ups. Hall of Fame trainer Bill Mott's wife, Tina, introduced Randy to GoChi juice in 2005 and he believes it has made a huge difference in his health.

Randy might be healthier today had he not spent his entire riding career, and two years afterwards, "flipping" four or five times a day. Flipping is jockey slang for self-induced vomiting, a way for jockeys to keep their weight down. HBO featured Randy in its 2004 documentary on the issue.

None of that mattered at Saratoga in the summer of 2008. Randy—despite his draining dialysis treatments—exercised as many as eight horses every morning for Stewart, his former valet in the jockeys' room at the Fair Grounds and a close friend for years. "It was like Randy never left," Stewart says. "He never missed a beat. No fear and just glad to be on a horse."

Riding a horse, any horse, continues to give Randy the serenity he had found so early in his life. "Because you have no worries," he explains. "You don't worry about bills. You don't worry about pain. You don't worry about my son's having a problem, or my wife's having problems, or my brother's having problems. It's just me and the horse. And I'm focused on just that. I just block everything out of my mind. I feel like I have an instinct with a horse, and the horse feels it. The horse knows. He can read me and I can read him. It's true."

He can verify that by rolling up his pants leg. There is a souvenir from the very first time he mounted a horse, Belle, the paint his family owned on their farm in Erath, Louisiana. Belle correctly read that Randy, six years old at the time, was a little unsure of himself. She ran off with the boy. "I'll never forget it," Randy says. "I'm fifty-one years old now, and this scar on my right knee has been there ever since. She run off with me and I was scared to death. I was staying on the horse and she was running off with me full speed, and I couldn't stop her. I was small. I was six years old, seventy pounds probably at the most. I cried and I cried because I couldn't pull her up. Eventually she stopped." Randy's saddle had rubbed against his leg the entire ride, leaving a distinctive mark. "It hurt me for a long time," he remembers.

That did not preclude Randy from getting back on her that day. "They patched my leg, wrapped it up a little bit and I went back riding. I wasn't scared to get back on the same day. I was fearless. I liked it. I loved it."

The extraordinary natural talent he was born with only

accelerated Randy's drive to succeed, and he was riding in match races before he was ten years old. He was not alone. Adolescent boys who could ride a horse in Cajun country in rural Louisiana frequently found themselves competing in Saturday and Sunday match races at the wildly popular bush tracks prevalent in the 1930s through the 1960s before any of Louisiana's current racetracks west of the Fair Grounds in New Orleans opened. A slew of talented Cajun jockeys in addition to Randy—Eddie Delahoussaye, Kent Desormeaux, Mark Guidry, Robby Albarado, Shane Sellers, and Calvin Borel—built valuable foundations at the bush tracks. "The bush tracks were big," Randy's brother Gerald states. "It wasn't uncommon to have a thousand, two thousand people on a Sunday."

The less weight a horse had to carry in a match race the better, so the smaller the boy riding him, the better. Smaller usually meant younger, but few riders were younger than Randy. In his 2008 book, *Cajun Racing*, Ed McNamara wrote that Glynn "Tee Red" Bernis was credited with winning a 1953 match race at the age of five. Randy was slightly older when he trail rode his family's Shetland pony Flicka and discovered she was extremely fast and started match racing her against bigger horses.

Flicka's exploits were part of a movie very loosely based on Randy's family, *Casey's Shadow*, which came out in the late 1970s. In the movie, the Romeros bought a mare in foal who produced a fast quarter horse, Casey's Shadow, who qualified for the richest horse race in the country, the $1 million 1975 All-American Futurity at Ruidoso Downs in New Mexico. On the screen, Casey's Shadow won the race with Randy riding. In reality, Randy rode the family's horse Rocket's Magic and finished third. Randy was seventeen years old. Many good jockeys go their entire career without getting a mount in a million-dollar race.

The movie starred Walter Matthau, who played Randy's father, Lloyd, a former Marine and policeman who became a full-time trainer after a horrific automobile accident almost took his life. Matthau came across as a likeable curmudgeon in *Casey's Shadow,* as if he had Randy and his four brothers' best interests at heart. That was fiction. "My father was abusive, mentally and physically," Randy shares. "We used to go to school with black and blue marks on our legs. It wasn't only me. It was all my brothers." And their mom, too. "I just wanted to stay away from him," Randy says.

Randy's role model growing up was his grandfather, Henry "Rome" Romero, who lived just a mile away. He could not read or write and only spoke Cajun French, the language also spoken in Randy's house. "I loved to be around him," Randy remembers.

When Randy was sixteen and already a successful jockey at Evangeline Downs in Opelousas, Louisiana, he happened to spot one of his friends walking with the daughter of a trainer who used Randy on his horses. Randy insisted that his buddy introduce him to thirteen-year-old Cricket McKean. When he did, Randy told Cricket he was going to marry her. Less than three years later he did.

But when he was nineteen, he briefly experimented with cocaine. He got caught and was brought into jail in handcuffs. "I got busted," Randy says. "It is probably the best thing that ever happened. It would've gotten worse. It was going to mess up my career." And his marriage. Cricket stuck with her husband though, and she gave birth to their only child, Randy II. But Randy and Cricket eventually drifted apart and were divorced in 1984.

On the day his divorce became final, Randy called Cricket from the courthouse and told her, "I'll make it up to you." She received a dozen roses from him that day. Within a year, they were living together again and two years later were remarried in Saratoga Springs in upstate New York, not far from historic Saratoga Race Course.

Randy went on to compile an outstanding career, capturing twenty-five riding titles at ten different tracks: thirteen at Louisiana's five tracks, six at prestigious Keeneland in Kentucky, two apiece at Arlington Park in Chicago and Belmont Park in New York, and one each at Gulfstream Park and Hialeah in Florida. He still owns the record for most wins in a single meet at the Fair Grounds and for the spring meet at Keeneland.

He won nearly 4,300 races, including 342 stakes, and just under $75 million in earnings. Three times, he won six races in a single afternoon. He rode many of the greatest Thoroughbreds of the 1980s and '90s: twelve horses in addition to Personal Ensign and Go for Ward who were named champions.

The success did not affect Romero a bit. "One day in '90 or '91, Mrs. Payson [Virginia Payson, an owner] came up to me and said, 'With all the success your husband's had, he's never changed. It never went to his head,'" Cricket relates. She agrees: "Randy's never changed from the first time I met him."

His misfortunes did not change him either. "I didn't blame anybody when I fell and got hurt," Randy stresses. "I never have. You make the best out of it. You have to have a strong mind. You have to look forward. Never look backwards. Better yourself and make people proud of you."

Randy's attitude does not surprise trainer Mark Guidry, who retired as a jockey in 2008 after winning more than five thousand races. He has known Randy for forty years, ever since they rode against each other in match races in Louisiana. "He had a long, hard road," Guidry attests. "He was dealt a lot of bad cards, but he doesn't dwell on the negative. He's a fighter. He's going to keep on fighting until the day he dies."

Randy is well aware of the dear price he paid to be a successful jockey. He is still paying. Was it worth it? Randy pauses and sighs before saying quietly, "To me, it was. I loved it, man. I knew I was good. I knew I was one of the best."

2

Cajun Sensation

Most kids who want to earn a few extra bucks get a paper route or mow neighbors' lawns. Randy became a jockey. He was nine years old. "I grew up real fast," he states.

The Romero family's heritage traces back to southern Spain and two brothers who immigrated to the United States. Randy's great-grandfather Elie, one of the brothers' ten sons, settled in Erath, a one-red-light town of some two thousand people in Vermillion Parish in south-central Louisiana. "A country town," as Randy's older brother Gerald describes it.

Erath is the home of the Acadian Museum, which honors the French Canadians who settled in southern Louisiana. Originally called Acadians, they became known as Cajuns. The Cajuns love horse racing.

Erath had one combined school for elementary, junior, and high school students; a church; and two teenage hangouts, the Bobcat Inn and Tico's. "Young kids would hang out and dance at the Bobcat Inn," Randy recalls. "Tico's had ice cream and hot dogs and hamburgers." There was also Muno's, a saloon Randy's grandfather Henry frequented to play cards and talk about horses in Cajun French. The nearest movie theater was in Abbeville, ten miles away. Another one was in Lafayette, which was twenty miles farther.

Match races, a form of entertainment for the entire community, were held at Erath Downs on the town's outskirts, six miles from Randy's house. Elie Romero had raced quarter horses in match races throughout Louisiana. Elie's son, who was Randy's grandfather Henry, and Randy's father, Lloyd, continued their family's involvement in subsequent generations.

Lloyd, six feet and 180 pounds, served in the Marines then became a state trooper. He also trained horses. When a drunk driver hit his patrol car head on, he nearly lost his life. Lloyd suffered a broken back and neck, which left him disabled. After the accident he became a full-time trainer.

Randy's mother, Joyce Sonnier Romero, one of seven children, grew up in Youngsville, Louisiana, five miles from Erath, where her father owned a grocery store. "I took after her dad, Clement, who was small, about five-foot-four," Randy explains. Joyce herself is four-foot-eleven and 125 pounds. Both of Joyce's parents died from cancer when Randy was five years old.

Born December 22, 1957, Randy Paul Romero was the middle son of five boys. Both of Randy's older brothers, Gerald and Edward, and his younger brothers, Kenneth and John, were big, like their father. Randy was anything but. He was blessed with an angelic smile and a face framed by blond hair, which darkened as he got older.

The Romeros lived and worked on a one-hundred-acre farm owned by Randy's grandfather Henry, who lived a mile away. Lloyd, who had two sisters, was Henry's only son. Randy's house was small, with a sofa, television, garage, dining room, three bedrooms, and one bathroom for the family of seven. Randy's two older brothers shared a bunk bed in one room. Randy and his two younger brothers bunked in another. "I slept on the top," Randy says. "I liked to be riding high."

Randy describes his mother as a very good cook—his favorite dishes were gumbo, rice dressing, and tomato gravy—who liked a clean home. "The house was spotless," he says. "My mom cleaned all the time."

Randy adored his grandfather Henry. "He was a special man," Randy remarks. "I used to go to his house every night and sleep there. He was my idol. He and I were real tight." They would work together doing all the chores a farm requires a family to do. "I'd get up in the morning about 4:30 and go work in the fields. We had 150 hogs to slop and 30 cows [they would butcher one cow and one hog every winter for meat]. Wash the hogs and feed them and all that. Or, when I was a little younger, we'd pick up butter beans, corn, sweet potatoes, and sugar cane. Or bale hay. And I'd ride in the truck with my grandpa. We had a bunch of friends and cousins that worked together. We helped each other out on the farm. There was a lot of family there."

Randy guesses he was five when he began his daily chores on

Randy's grandfather, Henry, is pictured on the far right smoking a cigar. His father, Lloyd, stands next to Henry. Edward, Randy's brother, is standing just to the left of the horse Romero is astride.

the farm, which were done before and after school. Every day. His brothers, too. "Get ready to leave the fields for school by 7:30. Come home from school and go back in the fields. Work in the fields. We had two mules. They were named Dick and Red. We used to plow up the land. I rode with my grandpa in the wagon behind them. We had to take care of the hogs, and the chickens, too. We had everything. We had to feed them all, then we had dinner. Take a bath. Do your homework. Go to bed. Every day. We worked every day. I was never a kid. I told my brother Gerald, 'We've got to do something easier than this.'" But the work ethic was etched into his psyche and may explain why he has always been so driven. "I'm a workaholic," Randy states. "I didn't want vacations. We weren't raised that way."

Randy remembers how hard his grandfather worked: "He was big and strong. He worked his butt off. He had a damn stroke and he tried finishing a barn he was working on. He plowed the fields. He worked all the time. He'd get up there at 4:30 and work all day. I followed him everywhere."

Randy wasn't the only Romero brother who treasured his time

with Henry. "We were all close to our grandfather," Gerald says. "He was a very special person. He was a man of integrity. If he shook your hand, that was it. A hard worker. When he died, he had a hundred thousand dollars in the bank and all he could do was make an *X*. Our grandmother, Evelyn, was a special person too."

In a story by Gary McMillen in the February 1994 issue of *The Backstretch Magazine,* Gerald says of his grandfather, "He was always taking me and Randy to Evangeline Downs or to some match race. He loved the horses more than anything, and he taught us that honesty and respect fit right into the horse business like it fits everywhere else."

Although they both loved and respected their grandfather, Randy and Gerald, who left home at the age of seventeen to train horses at Delta Downs, could not get away from their abusive father soon enough. "Growing up was pretty tough," Gerald recalls. "He [their father] was a pretty rough character. We both got out of there as soon as we could."

Their mother could not leave and did not. Whether or not it had anything to do with the patriarchal nature of Cajun culture is conjecture. "The Cajun caste system is very different; Daddy was everything," Glenn Delahoussaye explains in Ed McNamara's book *Cajun Racing.* "He made all the decisions and controlled all the money. They didn't say 'the husband.' They said 'Daddy.' It was completely different from today. Although the woman was the main caretaker then and probably the most important part of the family, she was subordinate to Daddy."

It pains Randy to talk about it still. He cherishes a cross his mother gave him when he was nine and wears it daily. "She's a very good woman," he stresses. "She was ashamed. She didn't deserve that. No person deserved what she went through. She was very religious. She still is to this day. That's what keeps her going."

Randy talked to his grandfather, but nobody else, about the abuse handed out by his father. "He shook his head," Randy says. "He got on my dad's butt a lot, but he would still do it. We just figured that was the way things were."

Randy and Gerald were not alone. "That's all they knew, the Cajuns," says Ronnie Ebanks, a protégé of Randy's who became a highly successful jockey agent and Randy's long-time friend—despite beating him in a twenty-thousand-dollar match race. "My stepfather was the same way. We were tough, bad boys. It was a physical thing. I was used to getting beaten a lot. We always got our butt whipped. I came from the same strict environment."

There's a difference between discipline and abuse. "It was unbelievable what Gerald and Randy had to live with and the way they had to be raised," trainer Sturges Ducoing, a lifelong friend of Randy's, said in December 2008. "You hear about child abuse and things like that. There's physical abuse. There's mental abuse. There's total no-love abuse and these kids got all of it. I mean, Lloyd—forget about being a good father—he wasn't a good person. And what he did to those kids, they should have put him in jail for what went on. In those days, it was different. First of all, they didn't tell anybody it was happening. Randy and Gerald lived with it. We didn't find out about it until later in life. It's just unimaginable that human beings could not only do this to other human beings, but to human beings that are your children that you love more than life itself. I've got two boys and four grandchildren. And if anybody did that to anybody in my family, I'd kill him."

Regardless of how he treated his son, Lloyd recognized the incredible talent Randy had on a horse. "Randy was a natural," he said in October 2008. "Just like you put someone behind the wheel in a vehicle. He fit the saddle on any horse." His mother, Joyce, saw the talent too. "We could tell by the way he was riding," she says.

And Randy could not get enough of horses. "Everyone kept their horses by their houses, and we'd go on trail rides on weekends," he says. "There were only gravel roads, no blacktop. And on the trail rides, we used to race. My grandpa, he was in it a little bit when he was young, and he taught me a lot, my grandpa did. He told me how to lay down on my horse, how to use my legs and feet. Stuff like that."

Watching the 1968 Kentucky Derby on television with his brothers and friends, Randy proclaimed, "I want to be a jockey and I'm going to ride in the Kentucky Derby." He did. Nine times. His best finish was seventh. His most disappointing finish was on his brother Gerald's horse, Dixieland Heat, who was twelfth to Sea Hero in 1993.

Randy did better with Flicka, the Shetland pony he rode as a youngster. "She was fast," Randy says. "We started match racing her against bigger horses. She'd outrun 'em going short. I'd beat the big horses. I was nine years old at the most. I liked it. I loved the horse."

Randy on a horse at Hebert Downs in 1970. Randy's oldest brother, Gerald, stands in the back row at the far right. In the front row, standing in the middle and wearing a trench coat, is Randy's brother Kenneth.

Horses gave Randy a sense of freedom, a world away from schoolwork, his demanding chores, and his abusive father. And he was so good. "He was nine years and sixty-five pounds," his older brother Gerald says. "He was light, and he could ride. It was a great advantage for me when I trained. He rode match races for a serious amount of money. He was a very good rider coming out of the gate. They were quarter horses. You have to be quick out of the gate. Randy, his work ethic was his biggest asset. I drove him to the track in the mornings. He used to wake me up at 3:30 every morning to go to the track to work horses on other people's farms. He was eager. I said, 'Go back to sleep.'"

Once word spread of Randy's riding ability, he began exercising other people's horses before going to school. He'd get one dollar for galloping or exercising a horse, and he quickly became self-supporting. "I never asked my daddy and my momma, from the age of nine, for a dime," Randy states. "I bought my pencils and paper for school. I never asked them for nothing. I just saved it, and when I hit fifteen, I bought me a car and I kept working. By the time I was eighteen, I had twenty-eight thousand dollars saved, and I went on my own. I met Cricket and we got married. I gave my car to my brothers Edward and Kenneth and bought a new one."

The tracks used for match races were usually straightaways of 300, 400, or 440 yards, a quarter of a mile. Rails separated two paths, one for each horse. Randy was so small that his brother had to help him pull up his horse because he was not strong enough. Most tracks had a starting gate. A designated starter controlled a pulley with a rope which pulled the gate open. Riders would glance back at the starter. When both horses' assistant starters in the gate looked back at the starter at the same time, they started the race. Quarter horses leave little margin for error. "You can't make a mistake, because you can't recover from a mistake," Randy explains. "The distance is too short."

Randy would win a whole flock of races at the bush tracks, hundreds or more. Yet despite all his acumen, he did lose a match race to a chicken, not a game of chicken with another rider but a real, honest-to-goodness chicken.

"I never in my life figured I'd lose to a chicken," he laughs four decades later. "I'm looking for the horse's rider. I said, 'What the hell?'" When he stops laughing, he says, "It was embarrassing. I got in the gate . . ." And he starts laughing again. "I was waiting for the other rider." Instead, someone produced a bag and took out a live chicken. "I could hear the chicken screaming and hollering," Randy continues. "Then the horse comes in and they have this chicken tied down with wire and weighed down by empty beer cans with rocks in them and they tie it onto the other horse's girth. I thought there'd be a jockey on the horse. And there was a chicken. I said, 'That chicken ain't going to beat me.' Then they started the race, and the chicken started flapping his wings and scared my horse. My horse wasn't going to go past that thing. There was no way in the world. I just laughed. It was funny. It was hilarious. How the hell could anyone do something like that? That's pretty smart. The guy that beat me gave me five dollars, a jockey fee." And a story he could tell his kids and grandkids.

Randy rode in match races at Erath Downs, Cajun Downs (originally named Hebert Downs), Coteaux Downs, Broussard's Racetrack, the Quarter Pole, Plattman Racetrack, Derby Downs,

In 1970, at age thirteen, Randy weights just seventy pounds. He is riding Kurnis Jet at Patan's Race Track. The trainer, pictured, is Weasle Brusard.

and Carencro Racetrack. Match races on a typical summer Sunday began between 11 A.M. and noon. "You'll see lots of families, and the people with horses just bring them out and walk them around until they're ready to race," Randy described to Ed Munday in his February 28, 1991, story in *Racing Action.* "The tracks have concession stands set up where you can get barbecued chicken, pork chops, hamburgers, and they sell beer, too. Sometimes they have boudin [a sausage] and other food of the area."

A snapshot: October 3, 1971, at Hebert Downs. Randy, wearing a striped shirt, dungarees, and a helmet, is riding Vinny's Echo against Jet Star Flash in a match race. Behind the dueling horses is a parking lot full of cars and pickup tracks. Randy is about to win the race by 2½ lengths. He has perfect form atop his horse: his back nearly parallel to the horse's back, his body balanced. His right hand is extended, showing his horse the whip. It is a popular victory. There are forty-one people in the winner's circle, including the winning owners, Mr. and Mrs. G. Conner, and Randy. Most of the people are smiling. Randy, looking at the camera, appears indifferent, as if he's done this many times, as if he's saying, "What's next?"

Clement Hebert, whose family owned Cajun Downs, initially used Randy to exercise his horses then began using him in races. "He owned a slaughterhouse in Abbeville, right across the street from the racetrack," Randy says. "He had about thirty horses. His son, Doris, was the trainer for most of them. Clement trained also. He was a good-hearted man. He always tried to help other people."

He helped Randy in many ways. "He picked me up in his truck really early, about 4:30 A.M.," Randy recalls. "I was about eight or nine. After I exercised his horses—I'd ride six or seven—he dropped me off at school and gave me thirty-five cents for lunch." That didn't include the dollar Hebert paid Randy for each horse he exercised. "I loved the man," Randy says. "He was always joking. He told me to save my money."

When Cricket began dating Randy, Hebert had advice for her. Cricket remembers his words: "Let me tell you something; y'always make him walk a straight line." When reminded of it, Randy laughs. "He just wanted me to be a gentleman."

There were no limits on gambling at the bush tracks, and one of the biggest match races ever in Louisiana was at Cajun Downs in 1977. Each owner put up ten thousand dollars for a twenty-thousand-dollar pot. Randy, then nineteen, was already well on his way to a successful career riding Thoroughbreds. He was riding daily at Evangeline Downs in Lafayette when he was summoned for this match race to ride Pontiac, a gelding, who was owned by Albert LeBlanc, a prominent real estate dealer in Lafayette.

The opponent was a filly, Lil Keri, who was not allowed to run at recognized tracks because she had swamp fever, an equine disease, and could not pass the Coggins test required for every horse. The opposing rider was thirteen-year-old Ronnie Ebanks, who had learned to ride at Lloyd Romero's farm and idolized Randy. "When I was thirteen or fourteen, I was betting with both hands," Ebanks says in Ed McNamara's book *Cajun Racing*. "My mother had no idea how much I was betting. I got to know which trainers usually brought live horses, and I'd make a lot of money riding and betting."

The distance for this match race was a mere thirty-six feet, twelve yards. "It is two jumps," Randy says. LeBlanc paid Randy two thousand dollars for the race, with an extra one thousand dollars, which was 5 percent of the twenty-thousand-dollar purse, if he won. Randy decided he wanted to walk away with twenty-five hundred, so he propositioned his protégé after they weighed in, asking him if he wanted to split the thousand dollars so each rider would get half. "Randy said, 'You want to save?'" Ebanks tells in *Cajun Racing*. "I was just a kid, so I didn't know what he meant. He said, 'Let's split the $1,000 so win or lose we each get $500. I said, 'Okay.'"

Just before the start of the race, LeBlanc offered 3-2 odds on anybody who wanted to bet on Lil Keri. He had quite a few takers and the two horses walked in circles for a long time before the start, McNamara wrote. Ebanks, who became a jockey agent, won.

"My horse stumbled when he left the gate," Randy says. "He beat me easy. There must have been about a thousand people or more." Ebanks was obviously thrilled and in *Cajun Racing*, he says, "I was 13, and I thought I'd won the Kentucky Derby. I won, but Randy got his $2,000 guarantee plus the $500 for saving. When I got off my horse, he was waiting for his money, but his little protégé had kicked his ass." Randy told McNamara: "All true, all true. Ronnie got me that day, and I still love him like a little brother."

Most of Randy's match races had happier endings and he guesses he may have won more than six hundred of them. "It might be more than that," he adds. "I don't know. I could ride ten races a week and win three, four, or five every week."

Randy misses the bush tracks—"Those were good times"—but he misses the ride to the match races and back just as much. That was time spent with his grandfather. "He'd take me to the racing every Sunday. He enjoyed it and I enjoyed it too. I got close to my grandpa. Oh, what a good man he was. I loved to be around him. He was the person I really, really respected."

When he drove Randy to match races, Randy would give his grandfather five dollars. "He didn't want to take it, but I made him take it," Randy says. "It was for cigars, not for gas. He loved cigars, and he was always happy."

Happiness was not abundant in Randy's house. Randy's father kept a tight leash on good feelings. "All of us brothers are good boys, and he wanted to control our lives," Randy remarks. "He was in the Marine Corps. He came out of the service and became a cop. He was always right. He thought he was always right. What are you going to do? He's the dad. That was him. That's life. My mom was the sweetest person in the world. She worked through all that." Randy tried. "I was always scared of him and despised him," Randy states. "He was just a bad person. He was mean to all of us boys. And then, a minute later, he'd be nice to you."

Lloyd didn't want to loosen his hold on his sons as they grew up. As teenagers, they were allowed one evening out a week with an 11 P.M. curfew. "He wanted to control our lives," Randy says, "and he thought he could rule our lives after we were eighteen. That wasn't going to happen. I left home at eighteen. I got the hell out of there and I thank God I did."

3

The Art of Living Dangerously

There is an art to living dangerously. Jockeys know they risk injury and death every time they get on a horse. They know they may never come back the same, if they come back at all. And they take that knowledge and store it in the back of their minds. Because if they didn't, they would never be able to get on a thousand-pound Thoroughbred traveling forty miles per hour in tight quarters during a race five, six, or seven times a day.

Randy used that same coping mechanism with all his injuries. How can you ride well today if you are worrying about an injury that happened months ago? So he never worried. He moved on. Always, even when he knew he shouldn't. After all, he knew he shouldn't be flipping—jockey slang for self-induced vomiting—but he did that several times a day too.

Jockeys must keep their weight to an absolute minimum to meet the assigned weight for each horse they ride in a race. The usual minimum is 116 pounds. Jockeys who fail to make weight quickly lose their business. Maintaining the least weight possible while not compromising the physical strength required to handle a Thoroughbred is a dicey proposition jockeys face daily. They go to ridiculous degrees to shed pounds, be it in a sauna or sweatbox or by flipping.

While he was riding, Randy flipped as many as five times a day to maintain his weight of 114 pounds on his five-foot-three frame. Even while doing that, he still had to sit in a sauna or a sweatbox almost every day he rode. When he retired in 1999, it took him an additional two years to stop flipping. "It's a sickness," Randy admits. "It's a disease. It's just like a crack addict or a tobacco addict. You need to be strong in your mind to quit or you need help. But I did it on my own."

He guesses he was fourteen when he saw pieces of hot dog

33

floating in the bathroom toilet in his house. At the time, Gerald was riding quarter horses and had not yet turned to training.

Randy yelled: "Gerald, you sick?"

"No."

"What's this?"

"I threw up my food."

"What the hell you doing that for?"

"To keep my weight down."

Randy began flipping two years later. "Since I was sixteen. It gives you the taste of food, and you fill up, and you drink a lot of fluids, and you throw it back up. You can do it by sticking your finger down your throat, but I had trained my stomach to do it any time I wanted to. Four or five times a day. Every day."

He was asked how he could live that way. "I couldn't," he says. "It works on your mind, your nervous system. It works on your body. It eats your muscles. It's terrible, terrible. It's not good at all."

He continued flipping even when he had breaks from riding. When Randy was recuperating from injuries and unable to ride, he almost always stayed with his best friend, Jimmy Lafont, one of nine commissioners of the Greater Lafourche Port Commission, and Lafont's mother in Cutoff, Louisiana. "He's like a brother to me," Randy says.

Lafont tells the story: "He was staying in my house, and my mom was making red beans on the stove. She didn't know that he flipped. And there was a drugstore about two blocks away from my house. He went to the drugstore to buy candy bars. I think he bought every one. [Randy admits to eating ten of them.] Then my momma called me on the phone, crying. She said, 'Something isn't right. I'm worried. He's got a hole somewhere. I can't fill him up. He ate up every candy bar they had and half a pot of my red beans.' I explained it to my mom. She didn't believe it. She thought people don't do that."

Lafont had another story about preparing for a hunting trip with Randy. The first stop was a grocery store for provisions. "Cricket said, 'Good luck,' and I didn't know what she meant. Randy ran up a three-hundred-dollar bill for groceries at Piggly Wiggly's. He ate everything we had. He had all this corn, the best corn I ever had. I seen it. I knew it was because of his job, but I didn't realize the extent of it. I remember one year when I wanted to do that [flipping] to lose weight. He looked at me straight in the eye and said, 'I wouldn't teach it to a dog.'"

Randy, though, was hardly alone. Jockeys flip so routinely that many jockey rooms once featured a purging bowl in one of the toilet stalls. "There's none of us that didn't have to do it," explains trainer and former jockey Mark Guidry. "It's a sad situation in the racing game. They took out the purging bowls, but the riders just go into the stalls. It's sad. Sure I did it, like everybody else."

Guidry estimates that he flipped for seven years before stopping. "When I stopped, it was rough for the first three or four weeks. But once my stomach shrunk, it was easy then." The difference between Guidry and Randy is their eating habits after they stopped riding. Guidry eats normally. Randy, who maintains a strict diet, does not. "Now I don't hardly eat anymore," Randy says. "I've been watching what I eat now."

In addition to the stress of such a lifestyle on the jockey himself, a jockey's life is difficult for his family. "It's a lot of glory; it's a lot of excitement; it's a lot of worry," Randy's wife Cricket shares. "It was hard because you feared for him. I can't speak for everybody, but for me to know that's he's happy doing what he loves, you put that fear behind you. When he'd come home, I'd ask him how he did. He'd say, 'I came back safe.' Not everyone can handle it. It's ruined a lot of marriages. People would say to me, especially on weekends, 'Are you sure you're married?'"

Her trepidation endures even though her husband has retired. "Even now, I never turn my phone off. Now it's a different worry with him doing dialysis. Even now, in case anybody has to get hold of me. The worry is still there. To be honest with you, the worry is more now than when he was riding."

Randy's son, Randy II, now twenty-eight, was at the track when his father suffered many of his most serious injuries. "It was scary," he states. "It was tough. It was awesome what he did, but I knew how dangerous it was."

He also knows how hard his father worked to achieve success. "He's never changed," Randy II affirms. "He was the leading rider in the country and he got up at four in the morning everyday and went to the barns to hustle mounts. He still gets up every morning with the same attitude: go get it."

And Randy could not wait to get started. Anxious to begin his official jockey career, Randy forged his birth date, saying he was sixteen instead of fifteen in order to receive his Louisiana state license a year early. That allowed him to ride both quarter horses and Thoroughbreds at Evangeline Downs in Opelousas, forty-five miles southeast of Erath, which, like Delta Downs in Vinton, ninety miles north of Erath, ran mixed meets of both breeds.

Evangeline Downs opened in Carencro, just north of Lafayette, on April 28, 1966. Randy, who was eight and a half years old at the time, would not ride in a race at Evangeline Downs for seven years. But when he did, he had already been riding in match races for six years, an apprenticeship that offered him a solid foundation few young jockeys enjoy when they begin their careers.

In Thoroughbred racing, apprentice riders receive a weight allowance of ten pounds initially, then seven, and finally five pounds until the one-year anniversary of their fifth winner (except in Louisiana, where the initial weight allowance is only five pounds). Any apprentice with even a hint of ability attracts trainers who are anxious to have their horses carry less weight in a race. Riding with that weight allowance—known as the "bug," which the asterisk indicating it in the racing program resembles—must have made Randy feel as if he were cheating, as he was already a proven rider when he received his weight allowance, which only increased his appeal to trainers.

Nevertheless, Randy still had much to learn. Only quarter horses were used in match races, so Randy had to learn the nuances of riding Thoroughbreds at Evangeline Downs. "I used to send my horses to the lead because I was riding quarter horses but they weren't finishing," Randy says. "I had to learn patience and pace."

It did not take long for Randy's talent to become apparent. Randy won his first race on his ninth attempt on Jody's Lad, May 18, 1973. Owned by Cyr Daigle and trained by Alphie Peltier, Jody's Lad defeated Tagaree by three lengths, covering six and a half furlongs in 1:22⅗. The winner's circle was jammed with family and friends. Randy journeyed to Columbus Race Course in Columbus, Texas, to win a quarter horse futurity on Easy Greasy by a neck, then rode Vince Bar King to win a seventy-five-thousand-dollar quarter horse futurity at Goliad, Texas. Back at Evangeline Downs, from July 14 through July 27, he rode ten winners, taking two apiece on Co Co Masco, who was trained by

"EASY GREASY"
R. RAMERO UP- 250YDS. COLUMBUS RACE COURSE: COLUMBUS, TEX. 6/29/73
OWNER: MANUEL FREDRICK & JOE LANLANDE   TRAINER: M. FREDRICK
2ND. SWORDS DREAM   3RD. JET YET APRIL

COLUMBUS RACE COURSE

Randy aboard Easy Greasy, owned by Joe Lanlande, in 1973. The trainer, Manuel
Fredrick, holds the horse. Randy's father, Lloyd, stands to the left of Frederick.

Family portrait of Randy's family at the Carencro Raceways. His brother Gerald is astride the horse, Co Co Masco. Randy sits to the left of his brother Edward, pictured on the far right in the front row. Their mother, Joyce, is in the second row, fifth from the right. Randy's brother Kenneth kneels fifth from the right in the first row.

his father, Lloyd; Certified Copy, who was owned and trained by Clement Hebert; and Aqua Doll.

Randy seemed to have all the momentum in the world when he went down at Evangeline Downs. That happened repeatedly throughout his career. In the first race of a Thursday evening card, riding a horse for his father named Grand Pro Man, Randy was near the five-eighths pole when another horse came over into his path. "The jockey came over too quickly, and I fell," he says. "What I can recall is that I just covered my head." Randy's head hit the track hard, and he was trampled by several horses while he lay unconscious on the ground. He was unconscious for two days. He had punctured his lung, liver, and kidney, and doctors had to remove his spleen. He underwent four hours of surgery.

When he regained consciousness in Lafayette General Hospital, his mother begged him to give up riding. "My momma wanted me to quit," Randy says. "I said, 'Momma, I want to be a jockey.'" Thirty-five years later, his mother acknowledges, "I discouraged him to ride. I thought his life was better than his career, but he wanted to ride. I said, 'Do what you have to do.'" Randy returned to the track.

"Ninety percent of people would have quit after that accident," Randy's older brother Gerald says. "Not a lot of riders can handle those kind of spills and come back. They lose their nerve. He never did. He was the same rider from the day he started until the day he retired."

Randy never even considered quitting: "I had the desire and drive to be a jockey; that's all I can say. I just wanted to ride. I had a gift and I wanted to use it. Most other people would have quit. I was fearless. I wasn't scared. I'm fifty-one now and I'm still not scared today."

He had already learned how to come back from surgery. At the age of thirteen, he fell when he was working a horse and broke his kneecap. He was back riding in eight weeks. "I rushed back too early from every accident I had," Randy admits. But that is the way he has lived: take what obstacles life gives you and move on. Always move ahead. Randy was out for three months after his frightening accident, then began taking over Evangeline Downs. "When I came back, I kicked their butt," he proclaims. "I started doing really well. I won a lot of races. I became a little star in Louisiana."

He had no idea how big a star he would be. But he knew whom he wanted to share his life with. He was sixteen when he met Cricket McKean. She was thirteen. Randy was riding horses for her father, Clyde McKean, who was a leading trainer at Evangeline Downs and Delta Downs. "He trained horses for twenty-something years," Cricket says. "He was successful, but he never really wanted to go big time because he didn't want to travel. He broke Wild Again [who won the 1984 Breeders' Cup Classic at odds of 31-1] for owner Bill Allen." In a 1980 story by Gerry Robichaux in the *Shreveport-Bossier City Times,* Randy spoke of Clyde McKean's influence on his career: "He showed me a lot. He taught me to rate a horse, to make it run when you want to, not when it wants to."

Cricket's uncle Eddie Holdsworth owned Oak Downs, one of the biggest bush tracks, in Pearl River, Louisiana. Cricket, whose real name is Cindy, grew up in Slidell, Louisiana, twenty-five miles north of New Orleans (a five-hour drive from Erath), with her older brother Clyde, Jr., who was better known as "Rusty" and became a trainer, and younger sister Candice. Her brother gave her the nickname Cricket. The reason? When their mother, Shirley Walden, was pregnant with Cricket, Rusty watched the Roy Rogers television show, which featured a young girl named Cricket. It stuck. "Nobody calls me Cindy," Cricket says.

During the summer of her thirteenth year, the summer she met Randy, Cricket had decided to earn spending money by scrubbing food buckets for her father, who would pass away in 1988. One night at Evangeline Downs, her path crossed that of Randy's. "I met him on the front side one night," Cricket recalls. "You had to be eighteen to go into the racetrack. We sat in lawn chairs out in the parking lot. There was this area near the jockeys' room to get food and drinks."

Randy was walking out of the jockeys' room when he spotted Kenny Fabre, an exercise rider for Cricket's father, walking with Cricket. He called Kenny over. "I'll never forget it," Randy says. "I says, 'Kenny, who's that?' He said, 'Clyde's daughter.' I said, 'Introduce me to her.'" So he did. Kenny said, "Cricket, this is Randy." Randy said, "Hi, Cricket. I'm Randy. I'm going to marry you." Cricket started laughing. "I was goo-goo eyed," she confesses. "I was thirteen. It was really funny. I thought he was cute."

Cricket's father had given her just one simple rule about dating: "No jockeys." Except this one. "He loved Randy like he was his own son," Cricket says.

Randy's pickup line was either the best or worst of all time. Asked why he would say something so outrageous, Randy replies, "I don't know. She was just beautiful, beautiful. And she had a pretty smile. And she was young, thirteen years old. I was sixteen. I was really young."

They made plans for a first date on a Sunday, when racing was held in the afternoon. Three nights before their first date, Randy went down again, and a horse stepped on his face, breaking his cheekbone and jaw. "I had to go see him in the hospital," Cricket says. "That was our first date."

They would have many more and were married by a justice of the peace on July 19, 1976, eight days after Cricket's sixteenth birthday. Randy was thrilled: "I wanted to get married. I wanted to be with her. I was in love."

Lloyd Romero wanted nothing to do with his daughter-in-law. "He didn't like me or my family," Cricket explains. "His father is a sick control freak. With five boys, once they got involved with girls or got married, he wanted to control them because they wouldn't be living with him. [He felt] if you don't do exactly what I tell you, then I don't want anything to do with you."

Cricket was well aware of the physical abuse in Lloyd's house. "It's sad. I came from a very close family, as most people do. For people down here who knew the situation, you go, 'God, how did these boys turn out so good for the abuses they had to endure when they were kids?' I used to come home and tell my parents Randy had a black eye. They couldn't fathom it either. His mother would come to the track with a black eye. It was always, 'She ran into a cabinet.' The principal knew about it. The teachers knew about it. Back then, nobody did anything. If what they went through happened in this day and age, he'd be in jail."

Cricket ran into Lloyd at the tack room at Delta Downs one evening. "He looks at me and says, 'You don't have to worry, I'm not going to hit you,'" Cricket remembers. She responded, "I know you're not going to hit me."

Nothing happened that night, but the rift between Lloyd and Randy's family remains more than three decades later. "My son they saw when he was born, and maybe only one other time in their lives," Cricket states. "He cut his wife out. Randy would call her to tell her happy birthday or happy Mother's Day, and she'd hang up on him." Of course, staying on the line might have incurred the wrath of her husband.

Not that Randy and Cricket didn't experience marital problems too. About a year after Randy was nearly burned alive in the sweatbox accident, they briefly divorced. A year later, they reunited, living together for a couple of years before getting remarried in Saratoga Springs, New York.

"I love my wife to death," Randy emphasizes. "I'll tell you what, me and her are really tight. She's a special woman. To live with a jockey, you have to be special. It's tough, but she handled it. I couldn't have a better friend. I love her. She's the best thing that ever happened to me. She really is."

Cricket can document how Randy overcame obstacles during his riding career and afterwards. "I don't even know how he gets out of bed, to be honest with you," she says. "I can't explain it. Determination and love for the game. He loves it. That's his life. He lived it and breathed it."

But once, briefly, he breathed something else, and it nearly wrecked his marriage, his career, and his life. He began using cocaine. "I was winning all kinds of races, and I started messing with the wrong crowd. I was nineteen years old and I thought I had the world by the tail. I was too cocky. I thought I was a hotshot. Then I got busted. It was the best thing that ever happened." He had been doing cocaine for three weeks. "I did some coke in a friend's car and the cops grabbed me. I cried like a little baby. I was scared I was going to lose my riding career. I was really frightened. They brought me in, in handcuffs. They had me in cuffs behind my back. They put me in jail. It was a mess, man."

Cricket was stunned when her brother woke her up with the news that her husband was in jail for cocaine. "I just never would have thought it," she says. "He'd gone out with his brother and my brother. We were living in Bossier City. He was riding at Louisiana Downs. They woke me up and told me he was in jail. I was like, 'What? He wouldn't have done this.' It was disappointing. I know that growing up is experiencing things, but he was always so into riding horses. I never anticipated him making that left-hand turn."

Randy made a vow to himself that evening, before he was released on bail the next morning (no charges were filed because of a lack of evidence): "I said I would never get involved in this again. I wasn't hooked on it yet. It probably would've gotten worse, and I'm glad I did get caught. It was going to mess up my career, which it does to everybody's. It just made me a better man."

Yet he knew he had hurt the one person he loved the most. "My wife, it was tough on her," he realizes. "She was really upset about it. She was shocked when I did it. I says, 'I ain't going to do it no more. We're going to have kids.' And she got pregnant. Had a baby five years later. That's my son. Everything works for a reason. That's how I look at it."

Randy made good on his promise, both to himself and to his wife. And on the day he was released from jail, he won three races at Louisiana Downs.

Asked what she was proudest of about Randy, Cricket says, "Just being the person he is. He's a wonderful husband and father. I think his determination is amazing. I'll tell you what, even right now, I would match him against anybody."

4

Art Imitating Life

Rocket's Magic was the best quarter horse Randy rode in his entire career. He was good enough to win his first five starts and then post the fastest qualifying time for the richest race in America at the time, the $1 million All-American Futurity for two-year-olds at Ruidoso Downs in New Mexico in 1975.

Evans Abshire, a poultry dealer in New Iberia, had purchased a quarter horse mare in foal for eighteen hundred dollars, and the colt she delivered was Rocket's Magic. Abshire gave Rocket's Magic and two other yearlings to Lloyd Romero to train. When Lloyd was seriously injured in a car accident, Randy's older brother Gerald trained the horse in lieu of their father.

"The first time I ever rode him, I breezed him, and I said, 'Gerald, when this horse runs he's going to break the track record,'" Randy recounts. "He said, 'Randy, you're nuts.'" Randy was prophetic. In his first start, under the lights with no whip at Delta Downs, Rocket's Magic did indeed break the track record. "He was a running s.o.b.," Randy says. "He was so damn fast. He was something else. With quarter horses, you usually win by a neck, a nose, a head. He beat them by a length or two lengths or three lengths. He was an extraordinary animal."

Executives at Columbia Pictures thought so too. They had a film crew on hand when Randy, still in high school, rode Rocket's Magic to victory in a futurity at Florida Downs in Tampa Bay in track-record time. Their enthusiasm did not diminish when Rocket's Magic won his elimination for the $1 million All-American Futurity, posting the fastest elimination time in the process. That made the colt an unblemished six for six.

In preparing for the million-dollar final, however, Rocket's Magic came up sore. "They breezed him way too fast," Randy explains. "He broke the track record breezing for another rider. I was in school. He was a little sore afterwards. My brother tried to patch him up."

In the most important race of his life, Rocket's Magic had a poor start. "He was looking around and he broke a step slow," Randy says. It is nearly impossible for any horse to recover from a slow start in a race of just 440 yards, a quarter of a mile. Rocket's Magic finished third to Bugs Alive in 75.

Columbia Pictures decided to do the movie anyway. Maybe the movie guys were taken with the Romero family's Cajun accents or the fact that they had paid so little for such a valuable horse. Maybe it was that the film crew had been following the horse for a month. Or that they could take artistic license and make a happier ending.

Called *Casey's Shadow,* the movie starred Walter Matthau and Alexis Smith and was produced by Ray Stark. Director Martin Ritt's other films include *Norma Rae, The Great White Hope, The Molly Maguires,* and *Sounder.* Both Ritt, who owned Thoroughbreds, and Matthau were longstanding racing fans and bettors.

A promotion of the film presents Lloyd Bourdelle, played by Walter Matthau, as a struggling and impoverished horse trainer whose son brings home an old pregnant mare instead of buying the quarter horse he was sent to purchase. The mare, who is believed to have superb bloodlines, gives birth to a colt that proves to be a strong racehorse. Just as the horse is to be entered in a million-dollar race, it injures its front leg. Over the objections of his son and the veterinarian, Bourdelle enters the horse in the race and wins the purse.

In real life, Rocket's Magic finished third under Randy in the million-dollar race. There were three sons in the movie instead of five. In the movie, their mother had bolted, and the house was a mess with beer cans floating in the bathtub. In reality, Randy's mother kept their house spotless. In the movie, Randy's girlfriend was another jockey, not the daughter of a trainer as Cricket was.

References to the movie in stories about Randy say it was "loosely based" on his family. "Some of it was true and some of it wasn't," Lloyd Romero claims. "They spent sixty days with us. They took our story and they were amazed by the Cajun accent. They interviewed all the trainers and me and the boys."

Randy has a different take. No one connected to the film spoke to Randy before he was portrayed on screen. The only one of his brothers who was interviewed was Gerald. Lloyd took care of everything else. "Daddy did it all," Randy stresses. "They interviewed my daddy and I had nothing to do with it. My dad was involved in the script. Nobody talked to me about it. Some parts of the movie weren't true. They didn't do a good job. In a way, it wasn't the real deal. My daddy never charged them. They didn't give us anything, not a penny."

When the movie was released, Randy and his new wife, Cricket, along with friends and family went to the Robert E. Lee Theater in New Orleans to watch *Casey's Shadow* having no idea that the events would be fictionalized. "I didn't," Randy declares. "I swear I didn't." The theater was packed. "There were a lot of racetrackers that went. We laughed like hell. It was a great feeling. It really was. When it was all said and done . . . We were poor, but not that poor. But I enjoyed it."

He and his party almost enjoyed it too much. "We almost got thrown out," Cricket recalls. "Randy hadn't seen any of it, and it was really funny. We were laughing. Horses were different. People were different. They changed the last names so they didn't have to pay anybody for the rights [even though the on-screen family lived in Erath]. A lot of the scenes were filmed at Evangeline Downs, and we knew a lot of people. You'd see someone in the movie and you'd recognize him."

Randy's mother saw the movie as well. "She watched it," Randy says. "She's a very religious lady. She didn't say much."

5

Better and Better

Randy spent the late 1970s honing his craft and winning riding titles at Evangeline Downs, Jefferson Downs, Delta Downs, and Louisiana Downs before moving on to Louisiana's premier meet at the Fair Grounds in New Orleans, where he captured four riding titles in a span of six years, setting a still-standing track record for victories in a single meet with 181 in 1983-84.

From his limited first year of riding Thoroughbreds in 1973, when he won nine races and earned $16,484, Randy increased his number of winners every year through 1980, when he won on 283 of his 1,502 mounts, and his earnings every year through 1982, when his horses made more than $3.85 million, allowing Randy to earn more than $385,000. Jockeys make 10 percent of a horse's earnings from the purse, which is distributed to either the top four finishers—60, 20, 12, and 5 percent, respectively—or to the top five finishers—50, 25, 12, 8, and 5 percent. If the jockey's horse does not earn any purse money, he receives a minimum fee.

Randy did well despite the repeated injuries, and he barely avoided another serious one. For once in his career, Randy escaped relatively unscathed. Another jockey was less fortunate.

One night at Jefferson Downs, where a levee separated the track from Lake Pontchartrain, the lights went out during a race. "The card had started and I broke on the lead," Randy describes. "And all of a sudden the lights went out. I said, 'My God!' I thought it was the end of the world. I could hear people and horses screaming and making noises. I fell. I covered up my head. And a horse stepped on my leg, the back of my leg, and made a big hoof print. They found my horse swimming in Lake Pontchartrain with the saddle still on her. The horse came back okay. There were three riders that got hurt. They rushed us to the hospital. One boy got hurt real bad, a kid named Ralph Dupas. He lost an eye and his hearing."

Randy went back to riding. By then, his immense talent and unerring work ethic had become obvious to trainers, and he began riding better horses. That, in turn, made him work even harder. "Randy, his work ethic was his biggest asset," his older brother and trainer Gerald explains. "Randy would always go back and check on horses at the barn. That's unheard of."

Randy's work ethic did not diminish after he became successful. "He would win five one day and he'd be out there the next morning, getting on as many horses as he could," says trainer Frankie Brothers. "It's hard to do both. That was just Randy."

One of Randy's jockey agents, Larry "Doc" Danner, whose clients have included Hall of Famer Pat Day, Larry Snyder, Corey Lanerie, and Shaun Bridgmohan, wonders if Randy pushed himself too far. "He damaged his career because he rode all the time in the morning. He'd want to work all the horses to figure out which one he wanted to ride. There's nothing to getting on two or three a day, or ten in a week, but to ride ten a day in the morning? That's like riding twenty a day. He'd be there at 5 A.M. when the track opened and he was there when the track was closed. He was so hard on himself to become a great rider, and he did. He was a great rider."

Randy knew no other way to work. He had been working long, full days since he was five years old. If he could work that hard doing farm chores, how could he not work just as hard at something he loved? "I was so dedicated to riding," Randy says. "I wanted to be a jockey. I wanted to be the best rider I could be."

And he wanted to win. He wanted to ride champions. In time, he would want to test himself against the best jockeys in the country. To do all that, he needed to make a name for himself in Louisiana first. And the horses that helped him start that journey hold a special place in his heart.

One of his favorites was Oil Patch Pappa, who was trained by his older brother Gerald's father-in-law, Eldridge Hebert, Jr. "He was a sweetheart, big and strong, a chestnut, a beautiful horse," Randy says. "And he could really run." Only top horses and top riders compete at the highest level of horse racing: stakes. With Thoroughbreds, the best stakes races are graded either 1, 2, or 3, with 1 being the highest, although not all stakes are graded. Oil Patch Pappa gave Randy his first Thoroughbred stakes victory, taking the $10,000 added Lafayette Futurity at Evangeline Downs on September 6, 1976. Nine weeks later, Oil Patch Pappa gave Randy his second: the $5,000 Lakefront Futurity at Jefferson Downs. Randy was eighteen years old. He would win 340 more stakes races at thirty-two different tracks.

Racing at Evangeline Downs while he was still in high school gave Randy time to spend with his mother. "I told her that I wanted to be the best that ever lived," Randy relates. "She was happy for me. She was all for me. Momma was always a sweetheart, always laughing. I really feel sorry for my mother not being able to see her grandkids." Lloyd would not let her. "She's so scared of him," Randy says. "If I call, she'll put him on the line." Although his poor relationship with his father has prevented him from maintaining a relationship with his mother, Randy cherishes the time they did spend together when he was growing up. "My momma would pick me up at school. She'd drive me to the races. She watched me ride all night. Then drive me back. Sometimes, we'd get out of the races at ten or eleven or twelve at night."

She watched Randy's emergence as a dominating rider at Evangeline. He won three consecutive riding titles from 1976 through 1978 with 107, 135, and 141 victories, respectively. The 141 winners tied Eddie Delahoussaye's state record of 141 victories in a single meet in 1978. "She was so proud," Randy says.

She still is. "He was a success," Joyce Romero affirms. "He loved to ride, and he was a natural."

A Louisiana training legend, Junius Delahoussaye (a cousin of Hall of Fame jockey Eddie Delahoussaye), was duly impressed. Randy, in fact, won stakes races at Evangeline Downs, Jefferson Downs, and Delta Downs in 1978 on A Toast to Junius, who was trained by Junius himself and was named Louisiana Champion Two-Year-Old Colt after posting ten victories and one second in eleven starts that year.

But after Randy won the Louisiana Breeders' Futurity on A Toast to Junius at Delta Downs on October 29, 1978, he was confronted by his father. "Four of us jockeys took a jet from New Orleans to ride in the Futurity," Randy recounts. "I won the race for Junius Delahoussaye and my father drives up and hollers at me to get in his car. I said, 'What do you want?' He said, 'I'll tell you at the barn.' I got in. He had his girlfriend in the car. I said, 'I got to go meet the other jocks,' but he took off. He started driving to the barn and had to go over a speed bump. He was still going thirty miles an hour and I jumped out of the car and nearly broke my damn neck. I went to meet the other jocks. I called security on him, but they didn't show up." Randy never discovered the reason behind his father's behavior.

Junius Delahoussaye eventually provided Randy with many live mounts, but when Randy began riding at Evangeline Downs, Delahoussaye had not been sure that Randy would succeed. "At first, I didn't think he'd make it," Delahoussaye told Glenn Quebedeaux of the *Lafayette Morning Advocate* in a story in May 1980. "He'd been riding those Quarter Horses for so long he didn't know how to handle the Thoroughbreds. When he learned, though, I could tell he was going to be a good one.

"The thing that impresses me about him is he's honest and he rides like you tell him to ride. . . . When you tell Randy how to ride the horse, that's what he does. Some jockeys ride the way they want to ride and the heck with what you say; they come back with all kinds of excuses. At my age [he was seventy-two], I've heard enough of that.

"Randy's as good as any I've seen down here and that includes Eddie Delahoussaye. They both rode for me, and I know they're as good as anybody riding today."

Quebedeaux also interviewed Evangeline Downs information director Bob Henderson for the story. "I'll tell you, I've been here for seven years now and Randy's the best I've seen," Henderson said. "No one rider dominated the standings year in and year out like he did. He's a competitor."

Eddie Delahoussaye witnessed Romero's progress from his early days at Evangeline Downs. "He was an apprentice when I was riding at Evangeline Downs," Eddie Delahoussaye remembers. "He was very aggressive. He showed he had a lot of talent, but it took him some time to pick up his head [pay attention]. He got into a lot of spills. He was going through holes and trying to make it instead of biding his time and going around horses. He was just green. It's part of being an apprentice. Then, all of a sudden, he started learning. Thank God he got all through that. You could see the talent."

That was only one of Randy's attributes. "I've never seen a more courageous rider in all my life," Eddie Delahoussaye continues. "He's done things on horses that I wouldn't have done. He rode horses that other guys wouldn't. That's what made him a great rider. He was a hell of a rider."

6

Moving Up

Randy's increasing domination of Louisiana racing convinced agent Bud Aime to sign him in November 1979. Aime had represented Eddie Delahoussaye, who had led the nation in victories (384) the year before on the way to a Hall of Fame career, but Delahoussaye relocated to California in 1979 and Aime stayed behind because he was battling cancer. Aime, who also represented David Whited in Louisiana in 1979, saw incredible potential in Randy.

By the spring of 1979, Randy had won three consecutive riding titles at Evangeline Downs, two at Delta Downs, and one at Jefferson Downs. He had finished fourth twice at the Fair Grounds in 1977-78

Randy and his father-in-law, Clyde McKean Sr., far right, receive prizes from Delta Downs president Lee Berwick for being the leading jockey and leading trainer, respectively. In the background, just to the left of McKean, is Randy's mother in-law, Shirley.

and 1978-79 and finished thirteenth nationally in victories with 257 in 1978. He hoped Aime would take him to the next level, and to do so, he split 1979, leaving after the first half of the Evangeline Downs' meet to race at Louisiana Downs.

On September 28, 1979, well before his twenty-second birthday, he won his one thousandth career race. Slice O' Pie was his third winner of the day at Louisiana Downs. The horse had made seventy-five previous starts, but Randy had never been on him until that afternoon when he broke a twenty-four-race losing streak by seven lengths in a five-thousand-dollar claimer. Randy had won the previous race on Sweet N Pretty by 10½ lengths. The three-year-old filly would carry Randy to two stakes victories later that year.

But Randy was thinking more and more of trying tougher competition. "I want to make it big, and I can't make it big just riding at Evangeline," Randy told Bob Forrest in Forrest's August 10, 1979, column in the *Shreveport Journal.* "I want to be one of the top riders in the nation, and one day I'll get there."

At the time, Randy was sixth in the jockey standings at Louisiana Downs behind Larry Snyder, David Whited, Ronald Ardoin, Alonzo Guajardo, and Tony Rini. Randy would have been closer to the leaders had he not missed the first eight days of the meeting due to a broken shoulder he suffered June 10 at Evangeline, an injury he worsened by trying to come back too soon. "I wanted to be leading rider here," Randy told Forrest. "I was anxious to ride, and most of my horses were fit."

Randy's accident at Evangeline Downs would not have occurred had he not decided to add a last-second mount. He had just ridden Fly Johnny Fly to a two-length, wire-to-wire victory in the $15,875 Texas Breeders Sales Stakes, his third consecutive victory in that stakes, following Chateau Mark in 1977 and Ideal Mame in 1978. The Texas Breeders Sales Stakes was the ninth of ten races that Sunday. "I came back to the jockeys' room and there was an open horse in the tenth race, a long shot, and they wanted me to ride him," Randy explains. "He was 20-1. I was leaving to go to Shreveport for the opening of the Louisiana Downs meet. My car was packed and I was ready to roll."

Randy took the mount on Agfolate anyway. Forty yards past the wire, after finishing next to last, Agfolate stumbled, tossing Randy to the track. He suffered a hairline fracture of his shoulder. Doctors inserted a pin, and Randy rode with the pin sticking out of his shoulder. "The doctor told me I shouldn't be rushing things, and my wife thought I was crazy," Randy told Dave Koerner of the *Louisville Courier-Journal.* "But it looks like if you stay away too long, people forget who you are."

He missed the first three weeks of the Louisiana Downs' summer meeting. When he returned to action, he began winning races in bunches: three on August 15; four on August 19; four again in mid-September. On Sunday, October 21, Randy won the inaugural running of the $162,800 Louisiana Downs Handicap, the richest Thoroughbred race ever in Louisiana, on Incredible Ease, by a nose over the odds-on favorite Prince Majestic, ridden by Don Brumfield, another Hall of Fame jockey. It was Randy's first victory in a $100,000 stakes. *Shreveport Journal* writer Bob Forrest credited Randy with a "well-judged ride," as Incredible Ease finally wore down Prince Majestic to give Randy his third winner that day.

Aime, who represented Bill Hartack and John Sellers, as well as, briefly, two other Hall of Fame jockeys, Braulio Baeza and John Rotz, was also impressed with Randy's ride. "He hooked up with Don Brumfield on Prince Majestic at the top of the stretch," Aime told Claude Williams in his January 18, 1980, story in the *Daily Racing Form.* "He realized for the first time he could ride with people like Don Brumfield. Don't get me wrong; he still has a lot to learn. But he's willing and he's eager and that means a lot. I've had some good ones, but Randy has a good future." Having represented other top jockeys, Aime knew that Randy was only beginning to become a top rider. "He is beginning to really use his head on a horse," Aime told Williams. "He started riding where speed is the most important thing. As he gets around riders from other parts of the country, he finds out that it's not all stick and holler. He has always been a good gate boy, but now he's learning to relax his horse and rate him. He's studying his horse now, and studying what's in the race with him. I want Randy to get as much experience as he can against riders from other parts of the country. That's the way to learn. Ride against the best every chance you get."

Randy, for his part, had gained perspective on how much he still had to improve to become one of the country's elite riders. "I rode a lot of winners at Evangeline and Jefferson, but I didn't start to ride really top horses until I hooked up with Bud Aime last year at Louisiana Downs," Randy told Williams in that same story. "Bud is a great agent. He knows almost every horse on the grounds and he seems to have a knack of knowing when a horse is sitting on a win. He knows the condition book backwards and forwards and he goes after the live mount."

Randy tacked on another four-win day in the fall, including a nose triumph by All Bob's Fault in the feature that afternoon. Incredible Ease gave Randy his ninth Louisiana Downs stakes victory of 1979 by capturing the $25,000 Barksdale Handicap on November 24. Randy won his first Louisiana Downs riding title with a track record 133 victories in 1979. He had beaten 1978-79 riding titleholder Ronnie Ardoin by twenty-six despite having missed the first three weeks of the meet. That was considerably less lost time than Larry Snyder, who was ahead by five wins in the jockey standings when he suffered a broken collarbone, which sidelined him for nearly two months. A year later, their roles would be reversed.

Randy finished 1979 with 257 victories, including nineteen stakes, and more than $1.8 million in purses, both career highs. Randy realized Aime's role in his burgeoning success. "Until I hooked up with Bud Aime, I didn't get many mounts with really top outfits," Randy told Williams. "He just has the connections."

The day after Williams' story, A Letter to Harry gave Randy his first stakes winner of 1980, taking the $33,375 Louisiana Handicap by two lengths as the heavy 2-5 favorite at the Fair Grounds, one of Randy's five winners that afternoon. "He's dominating the riders here because he is an excellent rider," Bud Aime told the *Times-Picayune*.

Randy was on the way to his first Fair Grounds title. A two-length victory by Five Star General, a California shipper trained by Hall of Famer Bobby Frankel, in the $40,000 Spring Fiesta Cup was Randy's 122nd of the meet, thirty-eight better than Ardoin in second. But as spring approached, Kentucky beckoned. It was time to find out how good this twenty-two-year-old rider was. Keeneland would provide the answer.

7

Winning Everywhere

There is only one opportunity to make a first impression. Full of ambition and armed with increasing skills and one of the best jockey agents in the country in Bud Aime, Randy announced his presence in Kentucky by winning the first race on the opening day of the spring meet at Keeneland, a unique setting in American racing. Six miles west of Lexington, Keeneland is home to one of the most important yearling sales in the country and is operated by the Keeneland Association. This for-profit company with a not-for-profit mission reinvests earnings in purses, capital improvements, industry innovations, and charities. Keeneland opened in 1935 and annually runs a short meet each spring and fall. In 1980, Randy walked into Keeneland a stranger and emerged as one of the most dominant riders in the track's history, evidenced by six riding titles and a record for victories in the spring meet that still stands today.

He won the 1980 opener when he rallied Kerrydale County in deep stretch, then captured the fourth, a maiden race (for horses who have yet to win a race) for three-year-old fillies, on My Little Castle, a splendid start for the fifteen-day meet.

Randy was on his way to a sensational meet, and Maryjean Wall, who would win two Eclipse Awards writing for the *Lexington Herald-Leader*, did not wait long to write about the Louisiana youngster. "The last time jockey agent Bud Aime pulled a Cajun rider out of his sleeve, he turned Eddie Delahoussaye loose on Kentucky," her story on Randy began. "The young Louisiana jockey was unknown outside his home state when Aime brought him to Keeneland in the spring of 1965. But Delahoussaye shot straight to stardom, dominating the rider standings here for several years and becoming the leading rider in the nation.

"Aime, not one to miss, turned loose another rajin' Cajun Saturday when he sent out Randy Romero to ride two winners on Keeneland's opening program."

Wall pointed out that Aime had prompted Romero's move to Keeneland. "Bud told me if I wanted to be a top rider I'd have to travel a lot," Randy explained in Wall's story. Obviously, Aime's decision could not have been more timely.

On Saturday, April 19, 1980, Flos Florum gave Randy not only his first stakes win at Keeneland, but also his first of 123 graded stakes victories when she drew off to win the first of two divisions of the $50,000 Grade 2 Ashland Stakes for three-year-old fillies. Winning her stakes debut in her fourth lifetime start, Flos Florum defeated heavily favored Cerada Ridge, giving Randy his third winner of the afternoon.

Randy finished his first Keeneland meet as the leading rider with twenty victories. He also had twenty seconds and nineteen thirds from ninety-three mounts. His win percentage (21.5) and in-the-money percentage (63.4) were astronomical considering that this was his first excursion out of the state of Louisiana. He had won riding titles at Evangeline Downs, Jefferson Downs, Delta Downs, Louisiana Downs, and now, Keeneland.

On closing day, Randy capped his first Keeneland meet by rallying 52-1 long shot Jolie Dutch to take the $40,000 Bewitch Stakes. She paid $106.80 for a $2 win ticket.

Less than a month later, Randy would be riding another long shot—in the Kentucky Derby. His odds would be more than twice as high as those for Jolie Dutch.

On the Keeneland backstretch one morning, trainer Bert Sonnier, a fellow Cajun and Randy's cousin, approached Randy and Aime with a proposition. Would Randy care to work his three-year-old Execution's Reason, who might start in the Kentucky Derby?

Execution's Reason had won four races as a two-year-old, including the Arlington-Washington Futurity and the Arch Ward Stakes, but had not won at three. With Eddie Delahoussaye aboard, Execution's Reason had finished second to Plugged Nickel—who would be the 5-2 second favorite in the Kentucky Derby—in the Hutcheson Stakes at Gulfstream Park and eighth in the Arkansas Derby under James McKnight. Sonnier wanted a new rider for Execution's Reason in the upcoming Stepping Stone Stakes, the final prep for the Kentucky Derby on opening day at Churchill Downs in Louisville. If Execution's Reason ran well in the Stepping Stone, he would run in the Derby. Was Randy interested?

"Mr. Sonnier is a down-home guy from Church Point," Randy told Bob Roesler, the sports editor of the *New Orleans Times-Picayune*. "Well, he asked me if I wanted to ride this horse, Execution's Reason. He asked me to come over and work him one morning. I said, 'Sure, yes sir.'"

Roesler was impressed by Randy's demeanor at the age of twenty-two (not twenty-three as reported in many stories; Randy had listed his age a year older to get his license). "Romero has handled fame and fortune well," Roesler wrote. "He is a polite, soft-spoken man in a business that can be cut-throat, profane and tough. His conversation is sprinkled with a lot of yes-sirs and thank-yous."

The $20,000 Stepping Stone would determine whether Execution's Reason would give Randy his first mount in the world's most famous horserace. The 2-5 overwhelming favorite in the Stepping Stone was Jaklin Klugman, a misnamed gray colt originally thought to be a filly, owned by actor Jack Klugman and John Dominguez.

Klugman's many credits in film and television include his unforgettable portrayal of the sportswriter slob Oscar Madison in the series *The Odd Couple*. Oscar shared an apartment with neatness freak Felix Unger, played perfectly by Tony Randall. In reality, Klugman had a lot in common with Oscar, especially when it came to sports and specifically about horse racing. In one episode, Oscar wins a greyhound named Golden Earrings in a poker game and begs Felix to race him as a partner to pay a debt. Oscar tugs at Felix's heart by telling him that his dream as a sportswriter who covered horse racing was to own and race a Thoroughbred. He never could afford to do that, and Golden Earrings was as close as he was ever going to come. Felix gives in.

With Jaklin Klugman, Klugman had a real shot at winning the Kentucky Derby. "I had dinner with him the night before the Derby," Randy says. "He was a nice man and funny as hell." Before the Stepping Stone, Jaklin Klugman had won the California Derby, his third victory in just five starts. Under Darrel McHargue, Jaklin Klugman won the Stepping Stone by four lengths over Execution's Reason, who edged Withholding by a nose. The second was good enough for Sonnier. Randy and Execution's Reason were headed for the $339,300 106th running of the Grade 1 Kentucky Derby on May 3, 1980.

"I thought he ran a very good race in the Stepping Stone," Randy told Roesler. "I think he's going to do real well. He's got the speed. Can he go that distance? Well, isn't it the same for the others? Can they go a mile and a quarter, too?"

Randy had a point, one the bettors would completely ignore. They would send Execution's Reason off at 111.80 to 1, by far the longest odds in the thirteen-horse field. The 2-1 favorite would be Rockhill Native. Plugged Nickel would be 5-2, Rumbo 4-1, Jaklin Klugman 7-1, and Genuine Risk, attempting to become only the second filly to ever win the Kentucky Derby, 13-1.

On the day before the Derby, sportswriter Glenn Quebedeaux interviewed Randy's mother. "Randy always did talk about riding in the Kentucky Derby ever since he began riding," she said. She told Quebedeaux that she would watch the Derby in her living room with her husband and her son John.

Breaking from the outside 13 post, Execution's Reason did show speed, disputing the early lead with Plugged Nickel and Rockhill Native through a modest opening quarter-mile in :24. Rockhill Native would clear his two rivals, and Execution's Reason would fade back to finish eleventh, seventeen lengths behind the historic winner, Genuine Risk, and ahead of two other long shots, Gold Stage and Hazard Duke.

"It was an honor to me just to ride in the Derby," Randy told Dave Koerner of the *Louisville Courier-Journal* in a May 9 story. "When I was real small, I sat in front of the TV and told my brothers and my friends, 'Look at that. Some day I'll be riding in the Kentucky Derby.' And it came true." Nearly thirty years after his first Kentucky Derby, Randy says, "It was wild. It made chills come down my spine. I can never forget that. He led in the race. He was a beautiful chestnut. He was a long shot, but I was just happy to ride him."

By riding him, Randy became the first jockey to ever compete in the All-American Futurity for quarter horses and the Kentucky Derby for Thoroughbreds. Terry Lipham would be the second. He rode in the All-American Futurity ten times, winning on Hot Idea in 1977, and then finished tenth in the 1983 Kentucky Derby on Paris Prince.

Despite his loss in the Derby, Randy was doing very well at Churchill Downs. Noting that Randy, "a newcomer on the Kentucky circuit this spring," was battling for the lead in the rider standings,

Graham Ross of the *Daily Racing Form* wrote in a May 21 story: "Although Aime deserves a lot of the credit for getting him started in Kentucky, the youngster's continued success here is the result of his own ability. He is a modest, polite young man, but those years of match races at the bush tracks left a mark on his style. . . . He has a fluid stick-handling motion that allows him to switch the whip almost at will several times in the stretch without losing a beat, and it is that hard-charging attitude that has made him become a favorite with the local fans."

Randy was leading Churchill Downs in victories through May 23 with twenty-eight, three ahead of Don Brumfield. Julio Espinoza had just ten at the time but would win his third consecutive spring meet riding title with forty-four after Randy decided to forgo the final month of the Churchill Downs meet to return to Louisiana Downs. "That's what my agent wanted me to do," Randy explains.

He felt he left Keeneland and Churchill Downs a better rider than when he arrived that spring. "I learned a lot while riding there," Randy said in a June 19 story in the *Daily Racing Form.* "I'm always trying to learn. You never know too much. You can always pick up a lot of things by watching good riders. It's beautiful country, the people are nice, and the money is good."

Through June 8, Randy was fourth in the country with 139 wins, trailing only Angel Cordero, Jr. (165), Cash Asmussen (154), and Chris McCarron (150). But four days after winning the $27,050 King's Court Stakes on Turbulence, July 13, Randy was back in the hospital. In the fifth race on July 17, Randy was trying to get home favored Daisetta. When he swung his filly off the rail to the outside to make his move, she clipped the heels of the horse in front of her, Honky Tonk Special, ridden by Richard Halajian. Both jockeys were thrown to the track. The other rider was not injured, but Randy lay motionless. When an ambulance crew slid a plywood board underneath him, he moved slightly. Randy was taken to Schumpert Hospital and in the emergency room was told he had broken his right collarbone and would be out at least six weeks. "I went back that Monday and had it X-rayed again and they said it wasn't as bad as they thought," Randy told sportswriter Keith Hartstein. "It turned out to be a hairline fracture. In the emergency room, they thought it was a complete break." Though he missed the final two weeks of July, he still ranked tenth nationally in victories with the fourth best winning percentage of riders who were in the top twenty-five in earnings. What would his numbers have been if he had not been hurt?

Randy began working out at a local spa to soak his shoulder in a whirlpool and exercise to stay in shape. He wound up missing a total of four weeks due to his injury yet returned to Louisiana Downs in time to make a late surge and repeat as leading rider, breaking his own record for stakes victories at that track with eleven.

In an interview with Bill McIntyre of the *Shreveport Times,* Randy conjectured about his injuries: "You've got to be careful. Sometimes I wasn't. I should have been watching what I was doing, should have been more cautious." Regardless, his older brother, trainer Gerald Romero, had seen his kid brother mature. "He's learned a lot the last couple of years," Gerald told McIntyre. "He's a good rider, but not a great rider yet. He's learned to have patience. And he can switch a stick real fast, as good as any left-hander or right-hander. He has as good a seat as I've ever seen, but he still got a lot to learn." Randy acknowledged that. "I used to be a speed rider. I've learned to sit back and relax."

He continued to learn by watching other riders. He told McIntyre that he watched Cordero, Brumfield, Laffit Pincay, Jr., and his local nemesis Larry Snyder, who had already won more than four thousand races. Soon, however, Randy would be watching someone new. Cricket was pregnant.

8

Ups and Downs

Having won his second consecutive riding title at Louisiana Downs in 1980, Randy headed for New Orleans in late November, hoping to repeat his first title at the Fair Grounds. He was leading the Fair Grounds rider standings when he went down before the sixth race on February 5. His horse, Prince Bicker, flipped in the starting gate. Randy was taken to the Fair Grounds infirmary, then rushed to Baptist Hospital for X-rays, which revealed he had fractured his left ankle. Prince Bicker was uninjured and finished second under substitute rider Ronnie Ebanks, Randy's protégé.

"I was the leading rider and a horse flipped in the gate and broke my ankle because my leg got caught," Randy says. "My left ankle. They put screws in there. I was out two months."

When he came back, he immediately realized that although his ankle had healed, the screw was starting to come out: "The screw needed to come out. But I had committed to ride that day. They wanted to put me under." Doing that would have prohibited him from riding that afternoon. His solution was chilling. "They took it out while I was conscious," he relates. "No pain medication. Wow, I was screaming."

He won three races that day. And he kept on winning, repeating as the Fair Grounds leading rider for the 1980-81 meet with 104 victories. He would also do phenomenally well that summer at Louisiana Downs, breaking his own record by winning fifteen stakes. The riding title, however, went to Larry Snyder. Randy had a three-win lead on Snyder with five days left in the meet, but Snyder rode twelve winners to Randy's one to finish the meet.

That was okay with Randy because he had experienced the joy of becoming a father. Cricket delivered their son, Randy II, on June 16, 1981. "The greatest thing in the world, a little boy, which is just what I wanted," Randy says. "I changed his diapers and fed him. I loved being a dad." Becoming a parent helped Randy, then just twenty-three years old himself, mature. "Absolutely," Randy says. "It was like turning a switch on. Night and day. It kept me out of trouble."

But it made little impact, if any, on his work ethic. He had more responsibility than ever. Randy rode a day/night doubleheader at two different tracks, a personal salute to Labor Day on September 7. Later in his career, Randy would do doubleheaders by riding at Belmont Park on Long Island in the afternoon and then at the Meadowlands in East Rutherford, New Jersey, in the evening.

In 1981, Randy began Labor Day weekend by journeying to Belmont Park on Friday, September 4, finishing third on Turbulence in a $100,000 Fall Highweight Handicap, Randy's first start in New York. He returned to Louisiana Downs and won the $25,000 Beau Brummel Stakes on Shiskabob on turf on Saturday and the $50,000 Pelican Stakes on Restless Navajo on Sunday. On Monday afternoon, he rode in the first three races at Louisiana Downs, finishing second in two of them, before hotfooting it to Evangeline Downs on a private jet for what would be the richest running of the Lafayette Futurity. Five years earlier, Oil Patch Pappa had captured the Lafayette Futurity to give Randy his first stakes victory. Randy had won it again in 1979 on Bold and Active for Junius Delahoussaye.

In explaining the reason for his doubleheader, Randy told Bruce Brown of the *Daily Advertiser*, "I'm leading the jockey standings up there, and I wanted to get in as many rides as I could before flying down. The guy right behind me [Snyder] is close, and he picked up some of my mounts on the card up there after I left."

A record Labor Day crowd of 6,310 packed Evangeline Downs on the track's final day of the meet to see if Randy could three-peat in the $90,000 Lafayette Futurity on speedy Cherokee Circle. He won by a length and a half, and Randy headed for Lexington, Kentucky.

Although he did not win a stakes race at the ensuing Keeneland fall meet, he did win the riding title with twenty-five victories, including five on the afternoon of October 27, a feat only accomplished four times previously by Steve Brooks on April 16, 1955; Manny Ycaza on April 10, 1963; Kenny Knapp on October 21, 1966; and Eddie Delahoussaye on April 24, 1978. Randy rode seven horses that day, capturing the first race with Rangus ($9.00), the second on Rose Banquet ($4.00) to complete a Randy Daily

Double paying $17.20, the fifth on Bold Maraja ($8.40), the sixth on Sweet Revenge ($2.80), and the eighth with Amherst Wayside. Randy finished fifth in the fourth race and seventh in the seventh on his two other two mounts that day.

In a story about Randy's five-win day in the *Lexington Herald-Leader,* Maryjean Wall called Randy "one of the hardest working jockeys, getting on horses from the time the track opens at 6 A.M. until the last race." At that point in the meet, Randy had won seven maiden races. Only one had gone off the favorite.

In November 1981, Randy went out of town to capture a pair of Grade 3 stakes, the $40,000 Chrysanthemum Handicap on Cannon Boy at Laurel Park and the Kentucky Jockey Club Stakes at Churchill Downs with El Baba, who was in the midst of a seven-race win streak. Randy had worked El Baba earlier in his two-year-old season, but the colt was ridden in races by Don Brumfield. Brumfield broke his shoulder before the Kentucky Jockey Cup and Randy replaced him for that one race, winning the stakes by 3½ lengths at 6-5. "I really liked him, but my agent had me committed to another two-year-old," Randy states. That two-year-old never broke his maiden.

After the colt finished eleventh under Brumfield in the 1982 Kentucky Derby at 3-1, Randy got another opportunity to ride El Baba in two allowance races at Arlington Park, finishing second at 1-5 and first at 2-5. El Baba finished his career with twelve wins, four seconds, and a third from twenty starts and earnings of $569,575.

Back at the Fair Grounds, Randy was well on his way to a third consecutive riding title when he went down again. He was atop the riding standings with seventeen winners in the first ten days of the winter meet when a horse he was riding in the second race on a Thursday afternoon, Smokey Lane, broke a leg in the stretch and catapulted Randy to the track. He escaped with an injured, but not broken shoulder and missed a month.

By then, Randy had a new agent, Larry "Doc" Danner. Randy went through jockey agents as if they were Kleenex during his career, unaware, of course, that he would become one himself when he retired. While he was riding, he used more than twenty agents. "I liked to give everyone a chance," Randy jokes. "If they couldn't keep up, I got another one."

When he started out at Evangeline Downs, his first agent was Darlene Traham. "She really worked hard for me," Randy says. "She did a good job." But it wasn't enough. Frank Rock and Tommy Sibille preceded Bud Aime, whom Randy would have loved to have kept, but Aime's battle with cancer forced him out of the business. Randy turned to Danner for three years, before using Aime's son, Fred. Both would come back for a second run with Randy, who would go through more than a dozen additional agents, including Harry "The Hat" Hacek in California and the late Lenny Goodman, who presided over Steve Cauthen's remarkable early career before Cauthen decided to ride in Europe.

"I always thought Randy was a pretty boy, but he's got more heart and guts than I do," Danner says. "His dream and his goal in life was always riding. That is what he was born to do. And he always wanted to be a winner."

But where? Randy returned from his shoulder injury and resumed riding at the Fair Grounds late in 1981 before bolting to Oaklawn Park in Hot Springs, Arkansas. "It's awfully hard to leave a place where you've done so well, but I love it here," Randy said in a January 31, 1982, story in the *Arkansas Gazette*. "I've thought about coming here for quite a while."

It was Danner, however, who convinced him to make the move. Although Danner, who represented Randy in the early 1980s and in 1993, spoke with reverence about replacing Bud Aime—"I try hard, but I'm no Bud Aime," he said in the *Gazette* story—he knew it was best for Randy's career to take him out of his home state. "Randy's gotten to the point now where he can't improve himself in Louisiana. And there's so much pressure on him. People expect him to win every race. When he gets on a losing streak, all his brothers and uncles start telling him he's doing this wrong and that wrong, and he tries to listen to everybody and gets all confused. Up here, there's no pressure at all."

The *Gazette* story noted Randy's work ethic, calling him "one of the backstretch's hardest working jockeys." Just as it had at Keeneland, his hard work would convince trainers to give him a shot. And that is what he wanted. He wanted to see how far his talent would take him and learn if he was good enough to try California or New York, home to the two toughest and deepest jockey colonies in North America.

In the span of six days in March, Randy won his first two stakes at Oaklawn Park. Bob Wisener, the sports editor of the *Hot Springs Sentinel-Record,* called Randy "a newcomer to Oaklawn Park but learning fast" after watching him take Plaza Star, a 16-1 long shot, gate to wire to capture the $50,000 Essex Handicap on March 6 before a crowd of 49,012 who had braved forty-degree temperatures and a stiff north wind. Though he was riding Plaza Star for the first time in a race, he had worked the horse the morning before for trainer Ron Ochs. Plaza Star rated kindly under Randy in the Essex and held off Vodka Collins by a length and a quarter. That moved Randy into fourth place in the jockey standings with fourteen winners. The leaders were Larry Snyder, who was seeking his eighth Oaklawn title, and Pat Day. "It's taken a while for people to get to know us," Randy told Wisener.

Six days later, March 12, Randy guided Jasmine Jule to an upset three-length victory over eleven rival three-year-old fillies in the $50,000 Magnolia Stakes at odds of 6-1. Jasmine Jule, trained by Tim Walker, had won her maiden just nine days earlier in her second lifetime start. In the Magnolia, she defeated the 3-5 favored entry of Ambassador of Luck, who had won her four previous sprint starts, and unbeaten Snow Plow. Randy was not having a particularly successful afternoon before the stakes, finishing out of the money on five previous mounts.

Randy decided to venture back to Kentucky to ride the spring meet at Keeneland and at least part of the summer meet at Churchill Downs. At Keeneland, Randy rode his first great horse. His name was Wavering Monarch. "He was a running s.o.b., probably the best horse after the filly [Personal Ensign] I ever rode," Randy says.

Trained by George "Rusty" Arnold and bred and owned by John Greenhouse and his sons' Glencrest Farm, Wavering Monarch was a huge son of Majestic Light, out of the Buckpasser mare Uncommitted. Arnold deemed him too big, too aggressive, and too immature to start as a two-year-old. As a three-year-old, Wavering Monarch would be asked to do the near impossible. He would walk into the starting gate for the 1982 Kentucky Derby making his fourth lifetime start a mere twenty-nine days after his career debut. That daunting demand did not deter Randy's typical optimism. "I thought he had a big chance, I really did," Randy asserts.

Only two riders would ever sit on Wavering Monarch in a race: Randy and the Louisiana legend who preceded him, Eddie Delahoussaye. Randy rode Wavering Monarch in his nine starts as a three-year-old. Delahoussaye would ride him in his four starts at four, all in California after Wavering Monarch was switched to Hall of Famer Laz Barrera's barn.

Wavering Monarch made a spectacular debut, winning a maiden race by 7½ lengths at Keeneland on April 2, 1982. Word had leaked out about his enormous talent. He went off the even-money favorite. "I thought he was a freak," Randy recalls. "I hadn't worked him, but they told me he could run."

Twelve days later, in an allowance race at Keeneland, Wavering Monarch was sent off the 3-5 favorite and romped by ten lengths. "Oh, my God," Randy exclaims. "I thought he was a super horse." He would have to be to win his next race, the $150,000 Grade 1 Blue Grass Stakes, on April 22. By then, Randy was the leading rider at Keeneland, attempting to capture his second consecutive spring riding title. But Randy could not get Wavering Monarch home first in the Blue Grass, though the inexperienced colt ran well to finish third. Wavering Monarch finished six lengths behind the runaway winner, Linkage, but just half a length behind second-place finisher Gato del Sol, who was ridden by Delahoussaye.

Though they knew they were asking an incredible amount out of their lightly seasoned colt—and, perhaps, knew deep-down that they should not—Wavering Monarch's connections decided to go ahead and run him in the Derby, though they initially indicated he would run in the Prelude, a different stakes race on Derby Day. "I didn't know how much the horse could take as much as we rushed him, but what are you going to do?" Randy asks. "Who doesn't want to run in the Derby?"

Maybe Randy wanted to ride in the Derby too much. He and Fred Aime, who had taken over Randy's book from Doc Danner, found themselves at the center of a brouhaha when trainer Ronnie Warren announced that Randy had committed to ride his horse Rock, Frank" Steady, who had finished fourth under Randy in the Derby Trial, in the Kentucky Derby. A headline in the *Lexington Herald-Leader* on April 30, the day before the Derby, proclaimed: "Romero's ride sparks controversy." In the story by James Griffin, Warrren said, "I'm riding Randy Romero. He came by our barn hustling a Derby mount. That cost Mr. Michael $5,000 [owner Russ Michael had paid the $5,000 starting fee]. The only reason we entered Rock Steady in the first place was because Romero was gonna be the rider." Randy disagreed, telling Griffin, "I always was riding Wavering Monarch. He was my first call from the start."

When the Derby field was published, Larry Melancon was listed on Rock Steady and Randy on Wavering Monarch. Warren still was not happy and told Griffin, "He [Randy] gave us the call and that's who he's gonna ride. I'm going to the stewards in the morning."

On Derby morning, May 1, a headline in the *Louisville Courier-Journal* blared: "Wherefore art thou Romero, spurned owner wondering." Mike Sullivan wrote the story, and in it, when asked about the controversy, Randy replied, "My first call was on Wavering Monarch at all times. I don't have nothing to do with that. My agent does. Have you talked to my agent?" Randy should have stopped there. He did not, explaining to Sullivan that he and Aime had in fact gone by the Warren barn, where they had been asked to ride Rock Steady. He claimed that they had agreed Randy would ride the horse only if Wavering Monarch did not run in the Derby. "But I'd rather you not even use what I've said. I don't want to make anybody mad. I want to stay neutral in these things."

Rock Steady's owner, Russ Michael, was not neutral, and he let Randy and Aime have it in the story. "He's still on the horse as far as I'm concerned. That's why I entered the horse, on the say-so that he was going to ride it. . . . It takes the fun out of it if you have to fight and argue. I don't believe in being a crybaby, but the point is that this boy hustled us for the mount. . . . I'd rather scratch him than just pay some rider $5,000 to go around the track. He [Randy] fits this horse. Do you know how important a jockey is in winning a race? One hundred percent. This is a wide-open Derby. With Romero, we have an actual chance to win this race."

Warren was next to weigh in: "It isn't only that Romero committed to us, it's that we committed to him. This is as dirty and sorry a thing as a jockey and agent could do. Fred Aime was a friend of mine. . . . I won't forget this."

Painting a smiley-face on this was not an easy proposition, but Aime tried in the story, repeating Randy's early assertion that they had only committed to ride Rock Steady if Wavering Monarch failed to enter. "We all thought Wavering Monarch would go in another race Derby Day. When they entered him only 10 minutes before the draw, that didn't leave Mr. Warren time to make other arrangements."

There was an irony here in that both Wavering Monarch and Rock Steady were lucky to be in the twenty-horse Derby field. If more than twenty horses were entered in the Derby, career earnings were used to determine who would start. Wavering Monarch ($36,947) and Rock Steady ($20,311) ranked twenty-second and twenty-third but lucked out when three horses ahead of them, the filly Snow Plow, Mid-Yell, and Cut Away, did not enter the race. Neither did Rock Steady. He scratched the day of the race.

Sent off at 38-1, Wavering Monarch struggled home twelfth in the field of nineteen, just a length behind El Baba. In an incredible performance, the late-running Gato del Sol overcame a wide trip on both turns to take the Derby by 2½ lengths.

The disappointment dissipated when Wavering Monarch bounced back as good as ever in his next start eleven days later, helping Randy launch an unbelievable run that late spring and summer. In June and July alone in 1982, Randy won fourteen stakes at eight different racetracks, allowing fans all over the country to see just how good this twenty-four-year-old rider was going to be.

He won his second riding title at Keeneland that spring and could have won his first title at Churchill Downs had he not decided to abandon his lead in the jockey standings to ride at Arlington Park in Chicago that summer. Randy was dominating the Churchill Downs meet. On a consecutive Monday, Tuesday, and Wednesday in mid-May, he posted three, one, and four wins. The four-bagger included victories for Hall of Fame trainers Jack Van Berg and Billy Mott and prompted Graham Ross to write in a May 15 story in the *Daily Racing Form:* "Randy Romero, leading rider at Keeneland this spring, and currently atop the standings at the Twin Spires oval, packs his tack this weekend and will head north to begin a Chicago-based summer campaign this coming Monday at Arlington Park. But he made sure, during the last week of his spring in Kentucky, that the local fans would remember him when he returns to Keeneland in the fall. . . .

"With such a hot hand here, and a new home in Shreveport, La., that would allow him to commute to Louisiana Downs each day, why would he head for Arlington Park, where he will rent an apartment for the summer and try to crack a circuit that has never been his base of operations before?"

Randy told Ross, "Yes, I've usually left Churchill Downs about this time and gone home to Louisiana Downs, but a lot of the people I've been riding for are going to Chicago, and will be back at

Keeneland in the fall before going to New York. I've always wanted to try the New York circuit, so I decided that I'd better try it now and do my traveling while I'm young. . . . Shreveport is home and I can always go back if things don't work out. Louisiana has been good to me, and Kentucky has, too, but it's always worth it to try and better yourself."

Before leaving for Chicago, Randy was one of many people saddened by the sudden death of trainer Del Carroll, whom Randy had ridden for all spring. Carroll was killed in a training accident at Keeneland while he was galloping Sportin' Life. The accident happened before dawn, and details were sketchy at best.

Randy said to Ross, "He rode me when he didn't know me from Adam and Eve. He just trusted Bud Aime's word. He was an exceptional horseman, a former eight-goal polo player. He was really gifted, a very special man, but for some reason or another, he never wore a helmet when he was working a horse." Randy described Sportin' Life as "a real nervous horse, kind of hyper, but he wasn't real bad or mean. We [Del and Randy] were just beginning to get really close. His little girl and my little boy played a lot together and his wife, Claudia, and my wife got along really well."

It haunts Randy to this day because he believes the accident could have been avoided. The day before, Randy told Carroll's assistant that Sportin' Life's saddle was falling apart. "I put it on the side to get fixed," Randy says. Whether or not it was fixed will never be known, but Randy has always known what he told Ross, "Racing is going to miss him. It really hurt me. The whole thing is such a shame."

Randy would ride for Del Carroll II, who was instrumental in uniting Randy later in his career with yet another agent, Lenny Goodman.

Despite mourning Carroll, Randy wasted little time making an impression in Chicago. By mid-June, he had ridden thirty-one winners, just four less than leading rider Pat Day. Randy won the $50,000 Shecky Greene Handicap on Straight Flow, the $40,000 Real Delight Stakes on Touch of Glamour, and the $75,000 Equipoise on Summer Advocate, part of an incredible run of fifteen stakes victories in sixty-four days at seven different racetracks.

In a June 14, 1982, story in the *Daily Racing Form*, Don Grisham asked Randy if he had changed his riding style in the last few years. Randy replied, "No, but I am learning a lot. Even when you're winning races, you need to be learning. Riding with very good jocks helps me. My experience at match races taught me to be a good gate boy. I learned to switch sticks at an early age. But there are so many other things to work on, such as relaxing your horses in a race, to judge pace, and learn to finesse your mount out of close quarters without snatching up on him. When to move is important, so I'm always working on that."

Randy returned from Arlington to Churchill Downs for a day to ride Wavering Monarch, who shook off his loss in the Kentucky Derby to take the $35,125 Jefferson Cup at Churchill Downs by 7½ lengths on June 12. He then won the $113,000 Omaha Gold Cup at Ak-Sar-Ben (that's Nebraska spelled backwards) by 6½ to set up an important confrontation in the $200,000 Grade 1 Haskell at Monmouth Park on July 31 against Linkage and Preakness Stakes winner Aloma's Ruler, who would be ridden by Bill Shoemaker and Angel Cordero, Jr., respectively. The kid from Louisiana was taking on two of the greatest jockeys in racing history.

At stake, too, was the leadership of the three-year-old division. Gato del Sol had won the Kentucky Derby, skipped the Preakness, and run an extremely distant second to Conquistador Cielo in the Belmont Stakes. Gato del Sol would skip the Haskell and point to the Travers at Saratoga. So would Conquistador Cielo. Linkage had skipped the Kentucky Derby, lost the Preakness to Aloma's Ruler by half a length, and run a badly beaten fourth in the Belmont Stakes.

In the Haskell, Linkage would go off the 3-2 favorite, Aloma's Ruler at 2-1, and Wavering Monarch at 5-2. Randy, as always, was confident, but this time he had a second opinion to reinforce his own: "I didn't get a chance to breeze him before the race and Don Brumfield worked him. He said, 'Randy, the horse worked real well. I think he can win the race for you.' I said, 'Thank you, Donnie.'" Randy, though, had trouble in the first turn with Linkage, ridden by Bill Shoemaker. "I was in tight," he relates. "I hollered at Shoe because he was coming over pretty quick on me in the first turn. I yelled, 'Whoa, Shoe!' And he gave me room to get position. He gave me room." That was all Wavering Monarch needed. At the top of the stretch, Linkage wilted and the Haskell became a two-horse race with Aloma's Ruler and Cordero trying to hold onto the lead. They could not. Wavering Monarch wore him down to win by half a length. "He ran down Aloma's Ruler with Angel Cordero," Randy says twenty-seven years later, the pride still evident in his voice. "It was one of the most exciting races I ever rode. I'm a young kid, and I beat Shoe and Cordero."

Wavering Monarch, Aloma's Ruler, and long shot Lejoli, who was a distant third in the Haskell, all pointed to the Travers and a showdown with Gato del Sol and Conquistador Cielo. Wavering Monarch, though, did not make it. Three days before the Travers, Wavering Monarch threw a shoe during a workout and bruised his foot. In a field of five in the Travers—matching three separate winners of the Triple Crown—long shot Runaway Groom beat them all, adding to Saratoga's legacy as "the Graveyard of Champions."

Wavering Monarch returned to action in a difficult spot, challenging older horses for the first time in the Grade 1 Woodward Stakes at Belmont Park. He finished a well-beaten sixth to Island Whirl. Then in the Super Derby at Louisiana Downs, he finished sixth again to Reinvested. Shipped to California, Wavering Monarch posted a win, a second, and two thirds in four stakes races under Delahoussaye, finishing his career with six wins, one second, and three thirds from thirteen starts and earnings of $466,773.

At Arlington Park, where he had arrived as a new rider just as he had at Keeneland, Randy won the riding title with an incredible 181 victories. Neil Milbert, in a story in the *Chicago Tribune*, wrote that Randy's "achievements at Arlington in less than three months are unprecedented." Milbert was right. Randy had beaten Ray Sibille's 1980 record of 137 victories by 44. He had averaged 1.5 winners a day at Arlington. What's most amazing about Randy's accomplishment is that when he arrived in Chicago, he was unfamiliar with at least half the riders and 90 percent of the horses at Arlington.

Randy was named the July Jockey of the Month in North America by Thoroughbred Racing Associations and the Turf Publicists of America (an award he also would win in January and February 1984). All Randy had done was win 51 races, including seven stakes, that month.

He had flown back to Louisiana Downs to ride horses in two $30,000-added divisions of the Old South Stakes on July 18. Both horses, Pretorienne and Lacey, won. Randy was greeted like a rock star when he walked Pretorienne back to the winner's circle after taking the first division. "The people cheered me," Randy said afterwards. "They are still my fans."

He was creating new fans in Chicago every day. "I had good

outfits behind me," Randy says. "I was a workaholic. Nobody gave me anything. I worked for it. I'd breeze five or six horses in the morning. I never took a day off. The only time I took was when I was hurt. I wanted to be the best. I wanted it really bad. That's why I worked so hard."

Where would his hard work take him after Arlington's meet ended in September?

9

California Dreamin'?

Randy had said repeatedly that he wanted to try New York. Instead, he, Cricket, and one-year-old Randy II headed west for California, a decision he regrets to this day. "I was ready to go to either place," he says. "I had a lot of winners under my belt. I was riding stakes all over the place and I wanted to make the surge. I went to California. That was a bad move on my part. I should have gone to New York. But Harry "the Hat" Hacek [a jockey agent in California] kept calling me and telling me to come out there. He came and met me in Kentucky and convinced me to go there."

Hacek had represented several jockeys, including Darrel McHargue, Chris McCarron, Eddie Delahoussaye, Eddie Maple, and Steve Cauthen after Cauthen split with Lenny Goodman and moved to California. Hacek was looking for a new rider after he and Sandy Hawley split at the end of the Hollywood Park meet earlier that year.

In Mike Marten's *Daily Racing Form* story of October 14, 1982, Hacek explained his interest in Randy: "Bobby Frankel had seen him race at Oaklawn Park. In fact, he won a race for Bobby there. Bobby was telling me about him, and he was so positive about Romero, it motivated me into getting the jock. Even before that, Gary Jones met Romero two springs ago at the sale in Lexington and he was telling me some nice things about him. And while Eddie Gregson was in Kentucky with Gato del Sol, he saw Romero ride and had nothing but good things to say about him." Hacek concluded, "I knew how tough it is out here, and after Hawley and I split I had reservations about trying to bring another rider out here, but, him, I couldn't resist. Romero looks like he has the aggressiveness and the ability to make it here. He's coming in with the right attitude. He knows he will have to work hard, but that's nothing new for him."

Randy's work ethic wasn't a problem; Harry the Hat's was. "I was getting up at around five in the morning everyday," Randy says. "I'd get to the track around six. At the beginning, he was there with me all the time for the first three weeks. Then, after that, I couldn't find him. I didn't know where he was. I hadn't seen him in a couple of days. So I went and I asked a couple of guys, good friends of his, where he was at. And he was in an apartment, playing cards [in an all-night game]. So I knocked on the door. He opened the door and they're all playing, six or seven or eight guys. I said, 'Harry, you're not coming to work?' He said, 'Oh, yeah, yeah.' I said, 'No. You just sit down. I'll get another agent. I don't need you.' So I just left. I was mad.

"Getting Harry was the biggest mistake I ever made," Randy emphasizes. "I had fired Freddie Aime and hired Harry the Hat. I should have taken Freddie to California." Randy then signed with George "Blackheart" O'Brien, whose son was Eddie Delahoussaye's agent.

Randy arrived in California for the first time on October 15, 1982. He rode his first horse at Santa Anita the following day. The day after that, he rode his first California winner, Fifth Division, in the eighth race, October 17. "It was great; it was like winning my first race," Randy said afterwards. "It was exciting. I love to win." After his first six days, he had three wins, six seconds, and four thirds from thirty-nine mounts. Not a single one of the thirty-nine horses Randy rode was a favorite. In Louisiana, then at Keeneland, Churchill Downs, and Arlington Park, he was riding live horses most of the time. In California, he would have to earn that privilege.

The California jockey colony in the fall of 1982 was incredibly tough and included Bill Shoemaker, Laffit Pincay, Jr., Chris McCarron, Eddie Delahoussaye, Sandy Hawley, Ray Sibille, Darrel McHargue, and Patrick Valenzuela. "That's a tough place to break into," Eddie Delahoussaye explains. "A lot of them can't stand not being top rider. They don't want to be second on the pole. In California, that's the way it is. If you stayed in the top five, you were doing great. Cordero, [Jorge] Velasquez, they didn't want to stay and be second banana. They wanted to be on top." When they couldn't get there, they went back east. Randy would too.

Before he left, when Southern California racing shifted to Fairplex for a week, Randy, Cricket, and Randy II joined Bill Shoemaker, Ray Sibille, Eddie Delahoussaye, and their families for a week at Big Bear Lake. "We went in Shoe's Winnebago and stayed in two cabins," Randy says. "It was really a lot of fun. We had cookouts and we went skiing. We had time to relax. That's when I asked Shoemaker what makes a good rider and he said the one who makes the fewest mistakes." Randy would remain close with Delahoussaye. "He put me under his wing," Randy says. "He's a good man."

When Randy returned to Santa Anita, he was unhappy: "I was winning races on horses who then went on to stakes, and they'd use Pincay and Shoemaker and Delahoussaye. I couldn't handle it. I was young, and I thought I was better than that. I was used to winning a lot of stakes. It was discouraging. I should have stuck it out. I didn't." Despite having worked his way up to fifth in the jockey standings, ahead of Shoemaker and several other top riders, with thirty-one victories, he headed back to Kentucky. He still finished tenth for the Santa Anita meet despite skipping the final four weeks.

"I went back to Kentucky for the opening of Keeneland [April 8]," he told Maryjean Wall of the *Lexington Herald-Leader.* "It [California] was paradise, but it was hell. I'm young, and I like to ride a lot and win a lot. I was riding six or seven a day, but they weren't live mounts."

He was used to live mounts. He had arrived in California in the fall of 1982 second in the nation in victories, just seven behind Pat Day. Despite slower business at Santa Anita, Randy finished seventh nationally in victories with 295 from 1,584 mounts and fifteenth in earnings with a career best $3.85 million.

He had won a stakes at Santa Anita before leaving, the $60,000 Bolsa Chica Stakes on Dedicata, on February 22, 1983, for Jack Van Berg. Randy would not win another stakes for more than six months. He could handle that. He would be happy just to be alive.

10

On Fire

Randy and trainer Billy Mott flew from Keeneland in Lexington, Kentucky, to Chicago to race John Franks' Derby Wish in the 1985 Secretariat Stakes at Hawthorne Park. Derby Wish won the stakes, which had been shifted to Hawthorne after Arlington Park burned down.

That night, Randy and Mott shared a room at the Hilton near the track. "In the middle of the night, I heard this noise that woke me up," Mott recalls. "Randy was making all this noise. I woke him up and shook him and said, 'What's going on?' He said, 'I was dreaming I was on fire.' It was one of the saddest moments in my life."

Randy's dream was not just a nightmare. It was also a memory. He had literally been on fire, nearly been burned alive in a freak accident in a sweatbox at Oaklawn Park in Hot Springs, Arkansas, two years earlier. "Oh my God, what a terrible thing to have to live with, to be plagued by that, to go home at night and go to sleep, it must be a terrible thing," Mott says. Living through it was much worse.

Randy and Cricket decided in the fall of 1982 that California was not working out, so the following spring, Cricket and Randy II drove home to Kentucky with her brother. Randy flew back to ride seven horses on opening day at Keeneland, April 8, 1983, winning three races on a sloppy track, including the $25,000 Taylor Made Purse on Bracadale, who won gate to wire by 5¾ lengths. A story in the *Louisville Courier-Journal* the next day noted that the year before when Randy left Churchill Downs to go to Arlington, it took weeks for James McKnight and Mark Sellers to overcome his lead in the rider standings. They eventually tied for the riding title.

Randy was the early leader at the new Keeneland meet with five victories when he headed to Hot Springs on April 14 to ride Rackensack for trainer Shug McGaughey in the $100,000 Count Fleet Sprint Handicap. Randy did not make the race, and Shug's horse would not hit the board.

Randy did not have another mount that day at Oaklawn, nor did he need to lose any pounds to make weight, but he headed for the sweatbox anyway. "I was tired from flying and riding the day before," Randy says. "And I was all tight. I wanted to loosen up a little bit."

The white three-foot-by-three-foot metal sweatbox was entirely enclosed except for an opening at the top for the user's head to stick through. "It was an old sweatbox with light bulbs around it on the inside," Randy says. He grabbed an oil-based alcohol and rubbed it

The sweatbox where Randy was burned in 1983. Covered in oil and alcohol, he broke one of the hot light bulbs, instantly catching fire, and suffering significant burns to his back, chest, and arms.

on most of his body before he got in the box. "The alcohol will dry your skin out, and the oil keeps the skin moist," Randy explains. He left his face uncovered. "Thank God I didn't put some on my face." He sat down inside the sweatbox. As he reached his left arm back to brush sweat off his right shoulder, he accidentally hit one of the light bulbs, shattering it. The exploding light bulb ignited the alcohol on Randy's body. "It blew up. An explosion. It blew me out of there. I was on fire. I could see it on my back. I'm crawling to get out of there. I'm on all fours. I'm trying to roll, but I couldn't roll. It was hurting me so damn bad. There was glass all over the place. I'm hollering and screaming. It took, like, forever for somebody to come. Hours. But it was only minutes. Or seconds. Somebody came and put out the fire with his hands and a towel. I'm on all fours and I'm screaming. I said, 'God almighty, why me?'"

Jockey Don Pettinger was taking a shower in the next room when he heard Randy's screams. "I heard some screams and they got louder and louder," Pettinger said in an April 16 story in the *New Orleans Times-Picayune*. "I was the first one there. He had some fire on his shoulders and back. I slapped the fire out and then pulled him into the shower in the other room." Randy continued to roll on the floor in utter agony. "He was in a lot of pain, and, I imagine, probably shock."

Charles Swain, the clerk of scales in the jockeys' room, also rushed in. "We heard him screaming," Swain told Maryjean Wall in her story the next day in the *Lexington Herald-Leader*. "We ran into the sauna and he was on fire."

Randy suffered second- and third-degree burns over 60 percent of his body. The worst burns were on his legs, across his back, over and under his right shoulder, and on the upper right part of his chest.

Hall of Fame jockey Jorge Velasquez, who was at Oaklawn to ride a horse in the Count Fleet Sprint Handicap, saw Randy on a stretcher. "I'll never forget when they had him on the stretcher how he was screaming," Velasquez recalls. "It was horrible. I felt so bad for him."

Randy was rushed to Ouachita Hospital in Hot Springs. "So they take me to the hospital and they left me in the damn hallway for half an hour," Randy describes. "I'm dying. I'm in the hallway for half an hour before they ever got to me. It was pitiful."

Randy needed immediate transfer to another hospital. "I knew my brother Gerald was in Shreveport [racing at Louisiana Downs],

so I said, 'Take me to Shreveport. My brother's over there. Let my
brother take care of me.' Then I blacked out. They flew me there.
After Hot Springs, I don't remember anything. I don't remember
going to Shreveport."

Jockeys Sam Maple and Kerwin Clark, a boyhood friend of
Randy's, arranged the flight to the burn center at Louisiana State
University Medical Center at Shreveport and hired a nurse to
accompany him.

Cricket and Randy II were staying at the airport hotel in
Lexington, Kentucky, near Keeneland, on April 14. "I had gone to
pick up our car; it had been in the shop," Cricket remembers. "And
the lady who was watching little Randy at the time, she came out and
met me in front of the hotel. She said, 'There was an accident.' But
the races hadn't even started yet. I was confused. I had just talked
to him. She said, 'He got burned.' I said, 'What do you mean?'"
Cricket called the Hot Springs hospital and spoke to Randy. "He
said, 'Cricket, you might have to come down. It might be bad.' But
I felt better having talked to him."

Quickly, she learned that Randy was being flown to the LSU Burn
Center in Shreveport. Brownell Combs, the president of Spendthrift
Farm, arranged for Cricket and Randy II to fly to Shreveport on the
farm's private jet. "News travels fast on the racetrack," Cricket says.
"Randy was very popular and very hot at the time. I don't know who
initiated getting the jet."

When she reached the Shreveport hospital, she could not believe
what she saw: "He looked like a raw piece of meet, completely singed.
He didn't know what world he was in. It was bad. He looked like he
weighed two hundred pounds. That's how swollen his body was."

Doctors quickly assessed Randy's condition and decided to
transfer him immediately by air ambulance with a nurse aboard to
John Sealy Hospital in Galveston, Texas. Cricket went with them.
Her parents had rushed to the hospital to take care of Randy II.

John Sealy Hospital, part of the University of Texas Medical
Branch burn unit, is considered to be one of the best in the
country. Opened on January 10, 1890, the hospital was founded by
the widow and brother of John Sealy, a wealthy Texan, following his
death. A second John Sealy Hospital was built in 1954 to replace
the 1890 building. The current hospital was completed in 1978.
The late Dr. Sally Abston, the director of the burn unit, would be

Randy's attending physician. "She was my surgeon, too. She saved my life; she really did," Randy says.

Randy's agent, Fred Aime, was at Keeneland when he got the call about Randy. "They called me and told me that Randy was in a fire in the hotbox. They said it wasn't very bad, like a sunburn." Then his phone rang again. And again. "The more phone calls I kept getting, the worse it was starting to sound. The next thing I heard, they were in the hospital and they were getting ready to transfer him to the Galveston burn center. Each report was getting worse. His skin was blistering off. I got to the airport and flew to Houston and drove to Galveston. When I got there, it was pretty bad. They had gauze all over him. He was almost mummified. He had one arm up in a sling. One underarm was worse [than the other]. There were IVs hooked up to him. He was on medication. He was almost delirious with all the pain he was going through."

When Cricket arrived in Galveston, she was asked to sign papers okaying the skin grafts her husband would desperately need. "They said he might not come out of surgery," she acknowledges. "I hesitated. I knew I had to sign it, but when they say that, you second-guess yourself. I was twenty-two." Her twenty-five-year-old husband was fighting for his life.

Here is what Randy was facing. In a story about the U.S. Army Institute of Surgical Research's Burn Center at Fort Sam Houston, Texas, Donna Mills of the American Forces Press Service wrote:

> Regardless of their cause, burns inflict tremendous damage to the body. Infection threatens exposed tissue. Skin can't retain fluids, sometimes threatening to shut down the kidneys. Body temperatures plummet, causing patients to shiver from cold, even when under heat lamps. Lungs often are damaged by fire, smoke and chemicals.
>
> "This is probably the worst kind of injury a person can endure," said Army Staff Sgt. Dave Waymon, a licensed vocational nurse at the center for almost five years. "The treatment is long, extensive and painful to the patient."
>
> And while the pain of the injury can be unbearable, the treatment can sometimes feel worse. Staff members at the center say the hardest part of the job isn't working 12-or-more-hour shifts in wards heated to 85 to 100 degrees. Nor is it having to scrub up and don a mask, gown, gloves and boots every time they come near a patient. It's not

treating patients so deformed that they're unbearable to look at.

It's knowing that everything they do for a patient, however therapeutic, inflicts even more pain. Dressing changes, dead tissue removal, antibiotic cream applications and skin grafts—all necessary to fight infection and speed up healing—can be unbearable. Spray from a shower nozzle can feel like bullets against charred flash. Physical therapy exercises, critical to keeping a patient's muscles from tightening as they heal, can by torturous.

"When a new patient is admitted to the center, one of the first steps is to remove any dead skin or hair from the wound that can harbor bacteria and lead to infection," Waymon explained. That requires a thorough scrub-down that some burn patients say they don't remember [because they are heavily medicated]—and that those who do remember wish they could forget.

According to the Galveston Shriners Burn Hospital and the University of Texas Medical Branch Blocker Burn Unit, every year 1.2 million Americans sustain a burn injury requiring medical attention. About fifty thousand of those require hospitalization, and up to ten thousand people die every year from burns and burn-related injuries or infections, although improvements in the past three decades have improved the survival rate of major burn injuries.

Burns are categorized in four degrees. The least serious are first-degree burns, which come from momentary exposure and cause superficial damage which heals within a week. Sunburn is a typical example. Second-degree burns involve both the inner layer of skin as well as the skin surface. The hallmark of such a burn is a weeping, blistering, painful wound that will likely heal within two to six weeks. Third-degree burns damage even the deepest layer of skin and may require skin replacement. Fourth-degree burns may require amputation. Determining the extent of a burn injury can be misleading because tissue destruction is progressive over the first forty-eight hours. Infections are the most common and most serious complications of such an injury and are responsible for 50 to 60 percent of deaths in burn patients. A major burn injury is defined as greater than 25 percent body surface area. Randy's was 60 percent.

The severity with which the body responds to burns is greater than any trauma or infection. Pain management can not be undervalued; pain is the most immediate concern of burn patients. Suffering, a combination of physical discomfort and mental torment, increases the body's post-burn stress reactions, making the body more susceptible to infection, illness, the wasting away of fat and muscle, and prolonged recovery times. The key to pain management—and a faster recovery—is closure of the burn wound. In the interim, reduction of pain and suffering by sedatives, narcotics, and psychological support improves comfort and quality of life.

But Randy was not like most burn patients who have healthy organs. Randy had lost his spleen—which recycles and destroys old red-blood cells, supplies the body with blood in emergencies, and traps invasive organisms—and had punctured his liver, kidney, and lungs, stacking the odds of survival even higher against him. Doctors told Randy and his family that he had a 40 percent chance of surviving and no chance of ever riding again.

His brother Gerald called their father to tell him about Randy. Not only did Lloyd Romero not come to visit Randy in the hospital, he forbade Randy's mother and grandmother from seeing him. "My daddy wouldn't let my mom or my grandmother come and see me in the hospital," Randy says, a trace of sadness in his voice so many years later. "Could you imagine your son getting burnt, life-threatening burns, and you not being there?" trainer Sturges Ducoing, Randy's close friend, asks. "Forget anything else in your life. It doesn't mean anything. This is your child. I'd be at his side. You couldn't drag me out. They'd have to put a bed in there so I could sleep."

In Galveston, doctors tried to save Randy's life despite the complications caused by his earlier injuries suffered on the racetrack. "The big thing was that he didn't have his spleen," Cricket says. Yet in another regard, being a jockey helped him survive. "They said the only reason he lived was because he was in great physical shape. That was a big part of why he made it."

But first he had to convince himself that he wanted to survive. "They say burn injuries are three times worse than a heart attack," Randy's brother Gerald remarks. Treating them can be even more painful than the initial injury. Doctors did two skin grafts at the hospital on April 15 and May 3. A third one would be done months later. The first two operations grafted skin from his legs, groin, and buttocks onto his back and under his right arm. "They tried to use other people's skin, but it didn't take," Randy explains. "They also tried pig skin. That didn't take either." Fred Aime watched nurses staple grafted skin onto Randy's back. "It almost looked like a netting instead of a skin," Fred states. "Every time they did a skin graft, it was like he was burned again."

Randy was asked to drink two pints of milk an hour. He was not eating and quickly his weight dropped from 114 to 98. "I didn't want to eat," he states.

He felt as though he was dying when he had to take daily baths in a large tub filled with diluted chlorine solution and warm water. Randy would be strapped onto a stretcher, which was lifted up and lowered by a pulley into the water. Two male nurses would hold him down. "They strapped me in there and I can't move. And they drop me in a big pool. They've got Clorox and warm water in there and they start cutting the bandages. I could smell the burn. Burned skin. Burned hair. It stinks. I look in the water. I can see the blood. And I start screaming. They take the rags [bandages] off me, and with the rags, the damn skin would go with it. And the Clorox and the warm winter burned the hell out of me."

Aime says, "He was doped up on morphine, but as soon as he hit the water, he was as sober a judge." That was before his nurses would scrub his body to get the dead skin off to prevent infections. "They take a brush and start scrubbing me," Randy describes. "I was screaming bloody murder. I couldn't handle it. They gave me more morphine. Oh, they couldn't give me enough. So they gave me a psychiatrist. I said, 'I don't need a psychiatrist. I am hurting. Give me some more pain medication. I don't care how much pain medicine. Kill the pain of the burn.'" Doctors even tried hypnosis. That didn't help. "It can knock you out and you'd still be screaming. It was the saddest thing." Aime says of the baths, "It's unbelievable. You hear people screaming like it was medieval torture. To see him like that, only God was in control of what was going to happen."

Randy was medicated on morphine or delirious much of the time. It was hard to distinguish between the two. The constant was the baths. "He would beg me not to go to the baths," Cricket says. "They asked me if I would go in with him, which I did. They thought he might be more relaxed with me in there." He was. "I just wanted someone with me," Randy says. "[But] they couldn't stay in there because I was hollering and screaming too much." Cricket and Aime alternated accompanying Randy to the baths. "Fred was real good with me," Cricket says. "We'd take turns."

Gerald tried watching his brother receive his daily bath and could not handle it. "I couldn't stay," Gerald admits. "It doesn't matter how much medicine you give somebody; it doesn't kill the pain. He was hallucinating, but he still couldn't handle the pain."

Nor could any of the other burn patients when they took their baths. "People don't realize, someone makes a dying holler when they take the skin off," Gerald relates. "They had to scrub the skin off. I couldn't handle that. It's an eerie thing. You wouldn't wish that on your worst enemy."

"Everybody in the clinic was dying," Randy says. "After about three or four days, I told my wife I couldn't handle it. I told my wife I wanted to die. I was in so much pain. I was suffering. And she brought our son into the room and said, 'This is what you have to live for.' I started crying. I had to get up and bite the bullet and move on and that's what I did. I thought of my grandpa a lot. I sure did."

In one of his more lucid moments, Randy decided he wanted to be the first patient into the baths every morning. "So he wouldn't worry about it the rest of the day," Aime explains. "They'd prep him up at 3 or 4 A.M. to go into the tub room. That opened at 5. Then they filled him up with morphine. They had a schedule of patients coming in up on the wall. Randy's name was first. It had his weight listed, 114. The first day he went in there, he thought it was the jockey standings. He said, 'Freddie, we're really having a good meet, aren't we?' I said, 'Yeah, Randy. We're going good.' He said, 'I don't recognize the names. Who are the other jockeys?'"

Racing was a point of reference Randy always understood. "He would be laying there, literally, and go, 'Shhh, I'm in the gate,'" Cricket describes. "He would ride and ride until he got to the finish line. He was confused a lot. He was on so much morphine. He put everything in terms of racing."

Aime remembers walking into his room one day and seeing Randy looking at a window. "I walked in and he said, 'Be quiet. I'm watching the replay of the race.' I'd say, 'Good, Randy.' He seemed happy doing it, so I wasn't going to say anything."

As he began to make progress in his treatment, Randy got to know other patients. "One guy, I played checkers with him," Randy says. "He was working on a telephone pole and he nearly got electrocuted. He got his shoes blown off. Coins in his pocket made holes in his leg and blew off his penis. He said, 'I blew off my pecker and they put in a new one that was bigger than mine.' Another guy was in a submarine when it blew up. He was burned from head to toe. He wore a mask to go to the Clorox baths. No eyes, no ears. His skin was white, white, white. I've seen some sad things. I said, 'I could have been like them. But I wasn't.'"

That was small comfort, but Randy took any that he could find. "They give you morphine; they can't give you enough morphine. A burn is the worst pain I ever had in my life. It was steady, steady. It never would stop." But Randy wouldn't stop either. Randy won. "I got stronger," he says. "I was just trying to get strong, and finally, they got me off all this medication. I prayed. Thank God it was not my time to go. God wasn't ready for me. I started walking the halls at night to build up my strength and energy. Then I started doing exercises. I was still young and I was physically and mentally healthy. I stayed there about six weeks. I got better."

He would tell Pat Trotter of the *Thoroughbred Record* in an August 9, 1983, story, "I've never suffered so badly. I haven't always been lucky riding and I've had some pretty bad spills. I've probably broken every major bone in my body, but nothing compares to the pain of burns. This was just like someone cutting off my leg."

Even today, he still has nightmares. "Every now and then," he says. "I also have dreams all the time about being in a race, and I wake up soaking wet."

Randy had hoped to spend the first Saturday of May at Churchill Downs, riding Chicago-based Play Fellow in the 1983 Kentucky Derby. Since he was still in the hospital, Jean Cruguet inherited the mount for trainer Harvey Vanier, and Play Fellow finished sixth in the field of twenty to Sunny's Halo, who gave Eddie Delahoussaye his second consecutive Run for the Roses following Gato del Sol's triumph in 1982. When he finally returned to the jockeys' room after scores of interviews and presentations, Delahoussaye remembered he had forgotten something. "I was nervous on television. I couldn't think straight," Delahoussaye told John Schulian of the *Baton Rouge Morning Advocate*. "Damn, I should have said something. I just should have let Randy know I was thinking about him."

Randy was allowed to go home in late May. After getting settled in, he allowed Bob Fortus of the *New Orleans Times-Picayune* to visit him in Pearl River, Louisiana, where Randy, Cricket, and Randy II were staying with Randy's in-laws, to do a story about his recovery. The story, which ran on June 17, 1983, was accompanied by a large picture taken by Lionel Cottier of Randy's backyard, where Randy II had his own merry-go-round horse to ride. In the photo, little Randy, wearing a helmet, is hugging his dad around the neck. Randy, stooped down so his boy could reach him, is smiling, but both his arms are unnaturally high and bended at the elbows in a locked position. Randy would have to keep one arm upraised for another two months.

Fortus wrote, "It was weeks after the accident, Romero said, when he first understood the severity of his injuries: 'I couldn't believe I was burned that bad. I've broken my knee, my ankle, ribs, my cheekbone, my jaw. You can put them all together, and it couldn't match this here. . . .'

"He fights the tendency to feel depressed about himself. He said. 'Sometimes, you can just sit down and cry, but you have to keep your head up.'

"Working hard to return to the saddle helps keep up his spirits. He still walks stiffly, and his weight—after weeks of home cooking—is at 130, about 16 above his riding weight. The extra pounds make his face somewhat puffy, but an exercise program that is becoming more rigorous every week should prevent him from ballooning any more."

Randy told Fortus he would not be riding again anytime soon: "It'll be the first of the year when I start." But Randy added the caveat, "If I get my arm better than it is, I might ride sooner." He did.

First, he had to get in shape. Gerald helped him. "I have to thank my brother a lot," Randy told Gary West in his story in the March/April 1989 issue of *Spur Magazine*. "He talked to me and made me do my exercises. I was going to a spa every day and working out on machines, lifting weights, doing pushups and swimming."

Three and a half months after the accident, Randy returned to the racetrack. Gerald helped him there too. "Randy wasn't in a good frame of mind," Gerald says. "He was getting depressed. It was something he wanted to do to get his life back in order. He really pressed the situation. I thought it was early, but in the same breath, to keep his sanity, it was a good thing for him to ride."

First, Randy rode a horse or two in the morning at Louisiana Downs in early July. His target was a maiden race at Louisiana Downs on July 28. The horse he would ride would be Pepperrera, a two-year-old trained by Gerald who had made quite an impression in his debut, finishing third in a stakes race. Ninety-nine percent of Thoroughbreds begin their careers in easier maiden races. After his first start, Pepperrera bucked his shins and was given time off. Randy would ride him in his return, weighing 130 pounds, including a pressure suit.

"I had to wear this cloth that goes over the skin and a pressure suit to keep the skin from growing," Randy says. "I rode with that damn thing. It made it 20 percent hotter. It was a nightmare."

Pepperrera went off the 2-5 favorite. "He probably should have been 4-1, but everyone was pulling for me," Randy told Bob Fortus in his *Times-Picayune* story the next day. Pepperrera broke well, and Randy let him settle in third or fourth. When he asked his horse to run, Pepperrera delivered, passing the front runners to win by one length. It was Randy's 1,952nd career victory, and it seemed liked every television station in the state had come to document Randy's return.

Randy told Fortus that the race seemed to take place in slow motion, like a dream: "Everything fit in position. I didn't make any mistakes. It was automatic, just like old times."

Not entirely. Randy was much more tired than his horse. "When he came back to the winner's circle, he could barely pull the horse up," Cricket says. Randy thought it was worth it. "It was awesome because the doctors said I would never ride again. I proved them wrong. I might have started back a little too quick, but I had to prove to myself I could still ride. It's in my blood. It's all I know, and I love it. It was a relief in my mind." Gerald was relieved too: "We were all pretty excited that he came home safe."

Randy began riding regularly at Louisiana Downs and accumulated twenty-four victories before stopping in late September to have another skin graft on his right arm. When he came back from that, he was physically, mentally, and emotionally ready to resume his career. When the Fair Grounds winter meet opened in late November, Randy rode seventeen winners in the first nine days, including back-to-back four-baggers on an early December Saturday and Sunday. In the eighth race at the Fair Grounds, December 14, 1983, Randy guided long shot Bastogne to victory, his two thousandth career triumph.

"At Shreveport, he wasn't exactly 100 percent," Fred Aime told Fortus. "He was still having trouble with his potassium level. It was taking him a long time for him to heal internally. . . . I can just tell by his eagerness to work and his attitude—he's back to his old self. Just working with him in the mornings, I can tell he's back together again."

Though Randy had virtually lost his 1983 season, he would begin to make up for it in 1984. Then he broke his leg.

11

The King of Louisiana Makes Connections

Truthfully, Randy had already become the king of jockeys in Louisiana before 1984 began. He was the leading rider in the state eight times and remains the only rider ever to win titles at the state's five racetracks, Delta Downs, Evangeline Downs, Fair Grounds, Jefferson Downs, and Louisiana Downs. It is a tough record to match. Jefferson Downs, which opened in 1959, closed on November 22, 1992.

In early 1984, Randy was winning races at the Fair Grounds like no other jockey before him. Following his sensational start to the one-hundred-day meet at the end of 1983, he continued to win races in bunches. After a seven-day suspension interrupted his momentum, he compensated with an afternoon jockeys can only dream about. On February 8, 1984, Randy became just the third rider ever to win six races at the New Orleans track in a single afternoon. Riding in all eleven races, he captured the third on London Charm, the fifth on Reservist, the sixth with Saber Shin, the seventh on Callaborator, the tenth on Eternally Yours, and the eleventh with Bob Mac B. Previously, only J.P. Bowles (March 11, 1965) and E.J. "Elvis" Perrodin (November 18, 1979) had ever won six in one day at the Fair Grounds.

Randy was not only leading the Fair Grounds riding colony, he was also leading the nation. And he showed no signs of slowing down. First, he eclipsed Eddie Delahoussaye's Fair Grounds record for victories in a single meet, 141, also the state record for victories in one meet, which Randy had tied in 1978 at Evangeline Downs. Randy recorded his 142nd win of the Fair Grounds meet in the fourth race, February 28, 1984, when the three-year-old colt Zuppardo's Love won a maiden race by 3½ lengths.

Marty Mulé of the *New Orleans Times-Picayune* captured the moment beautifully in his story the next day, writing, "The winner's circle in this case symbolized more than victory. It symbolized the human spirit." Randy's spirit was soaring. That very day, he was leading the country with ninety-five victories, forty-three ahead of Chris McCarron, who was leading the nation in earnings.

Before the one-year anniversary of his burning accident at Oaklawn Park, Randy set a Fair Grounds one-meet record that still stands: 181 victories, an average of nearly two wins a day for the ninety-three days he rode. More importantly, he had begun to ride frequently for trainers Billy Mott, Frankie Brothers, and Shug McGaughey. Randy would ride for hundreds of trainers in his career, including legendary Woody Stephens, whose five consecutive Belmont Stakes victories remain one of the most amazing feats in racing history; Jack Van Berg, racing's second all-time leading trainer in victories (6,389); and D. Wayne Lukas, who is racing's all-time leader in earnings ($251 million) and fifth in victories (4,506). All are Hall of Famers. But the trainers who would be pivotal in Randy's successful venture into New York in 1986 were Mott, McGaughey, and Brothers.

Mott, who is the third all-time leading trainer in earnings and tenth in victories, was just beginning to establish a national presence. He would become the youngest trainer ever inducted into the National Museum of Racing Hall of Fame and train two-time Horse of the Year Cigar to a record-tying sixteen consecutive victories. McGaughey, who ranks eleventh all-time in career earnings, would give Randy a steady stream of stakes-caliber horses, including Personal Ensign, and follow Mott into the Hall of Fame. Both McGaughey and Mott considered themselves fortunate to hook up with Randy in the early through mid-1980s.

"When I started training, he was one of the top riders, he and Pat Day," McGaughey says. "I was trying to build my stable up. He would go to New Orleans [the Fair Grounds], pass through Hot Springs [Oaklawn Park], and go on to Chicago [Arlington] and Kentucky [Keeneland and Churchill Downs]. That was kind of what I was doing. Those two guys [Randy and Day] weren't the easiest to get."

Mott recalls, "It seemed as though back then we all hung out together. At that point we were all basically starting out. I hadn't been to New York. We knew Randy from Oaklawn Park, Fair Grounds, Kentucky, and Arlington Park. He was riding horses [we trained] for [owner] John Franks."

Mott got to know Randy well: "I think he's a very kind person, very likable. Most everybody loves Randy. He is one of the true racetrack characters, what I call a 'racetracker.' There are people that have to come to the racetrack, and then you've got racetrackers. Certain people are lifers. He's one of them. He started at the bottom and got to the top and went to the bottom again, and he still came back. He bounced back. He was always able to bounce back. I don't remember Randy having any fear. He just started riding back. Obviously, he had to get fit again [after an injury]. He was always so interested in getting back in competition. I don't know if the fear factor was ever there."

The talent and the horsemanship certainly were. "The thing about Randy is that he had two things going for him that I really think mattered a lot," Mott continues. "I think horses just liked him and ran for him. He had a good feel for them. He wasn't particularly what you'd call a real strong rider like an Angel Cordero finishing. He wasn't one of the pretty riders. But horses just ran for him.

"The other thing, and maybe it's the most important thing, was that he thought he could win every time he went out there. It didn't matter what type of race. When he left the paddock, he thought he could win. That goes a long way, that confidence, that belief that he could win. It's good positive energy because you're giving that a horse a chance to do his best. You're not giving the horse negative symbols that he can't win."

On January 14, 1984, Randy rode for the first time Mott's Kentucky Derby hopeful, Taylor's Special, in a $25,000 handicap that would be the colt's three-year-old debut. He won by a head. Randy rode him to two more victories sandwiched around a second-place finish.

Exactly two months later, Randy rode Mott's mare Heatherten for the first time, and she won an allowance race in her 1984 debut by 5¼ lengths as the heavy favorite at 3-5. "She is a nice mare, not only because she has a lot of ability, but she knows how to best use it," Randy told Don Grisham of the *Daily Racing Form*. "She can go to the front or can be rated just off the lead."

Heatherten was owned by John Franks, and Randy became good friends with him and his wife. "I was riding everywhere for him first call," Randy says. "He's the guy that got me to the next level." One day Randy returned the favor. A bloodstock agent offered Randy ten thousand dollars if, after working a horse who was a maiden, he told Franks he liked the horse and was worth one hundred thousand dollars. "I flew from Shreveport to Baton Rouge to work him, and I didn't like the way the horse worked. He was sore. He had some problems. He was a maiden. He's still a maiden. I told Mr. Franks not to buy the horse. That's just the person I am."

The sixty-two-year-old Brothers, a native of New Orleans, ranks thirty-fourth in all-time career earnings and forty-second in career victories. Just as Randy dominated Louisiana racing in the late 1970s through the mid-1980s, Brothers put together two astounding runs, finishing as the leading trainer at Louisiana Downs for nine consecutive years and first or second at the Fair Grounds for nine years. He also won training titles at Keeneland and Churchill Downs in Kentucky. Brothers became not only close friends with Randy, but also one of his biggest supporters. "He was an immensely talented guy from day one to the end," Brothers says. "He had more try and want and love for the game than anybody I've ever seen. He had a natural talent on a horse. He wasn't the prettiest rider, but horses ran for him, and he had a passion for the game. It's incredible the things he's overcome to ride, starting back at Delta Downs when he looked dead on the track and woke up. He's an amazing guy."

Randy would win the $100,000 Grade 3 Fair Grounds Classic on Police Inspector and the $15,000 Dolly Val Handicap on Madame Secretary at Balmoral Park in Chicago for Brothers in 1985. Then, nearly, five years later, after riding Brothers' two-year-old colt Hansel to a 3½-length maiden debut victory at Arlington Park, Randy convinced Brothers to send the colt to New York to compete in the Grade 3 Tremont Stakes. "He broke his maiden," Brothers relates, "and Randy encouraged me to take him to New York. He loved them all, and they all were going to win the Derby. That was the enthusiasm he had." Randy was right about Hansel, and he rode him to a three-length victory in the Tremont. The following spring, Hansel would capture two-thirds of the 1991 Triple Crown. Randy would have ridden him had he not been injured. "Randy got hurt and missed some of the stakes," Brothers explains. That did not impact their business relationship or their friendship, one Brothers treasures. "He'd give you his heart if you asked him to. He could walk into my barn today and he'd be greeted with open arms. That's just the type of person he is."

Asked about Randy's accident in the sweatbox when he nearly burned to death, Brothers answers, "That was a horror story. There's not many people who could stand that rehab. It just shows how tough an s.o.b. he was. He just fought through it."

Randy had plenty of practice. As he was finishing his record-breaking meet at the Fair Grounds, he decided, after winning two races on a Friday afternoon at the Fair Grounds on March 23, to ride Miss Hippy Dip at Delta Downs under the lights that night in the trials for the rich Jean Laffite Futurity. At the time, Randy was leading the country in victories with 131.

Bernie Flint, a trainer and a pilot, offered to fly Miss Hippy Dip's owner and trainer, Clement Hebert and his son Doris, as well as Randy to Delta Downs. But when the weather turned ugly, Flint did not want to take off. "I tried to talk him [Randy] out of it every which way I could," Bernie Flint says. "I tried talking his agent, Fred Aime." Randy, though, was adamant, stubborn, and utterly unwavering. He said, "I've got to ride this filly. She broke the track record [in her previous start]. You have to get me there." Years later, Randy reflects, "God was trying to tell me something."

The weather turned worse during the flight. "The weather was awful," Flint says. "It was probably the worst weather I've ever flown in. Thunderstorms were at 35,000, 40,000 feet, tremendous black pillars of thunderstorms with anvils hanging over them." Randy agrees: "It was a terrible ride. It was raining and it's thundering and we finally got there. We almost didn't make it in time to ride the race." Unfortunately, they did.

"We're in the paddock, and the filly is crazy," Randy recalls. "She was washed out [sweating profusely]. She was so nervous in the paddock. She was a nervous wreck." When the race began, Randy was too. He was on the 2-5 favorite, but his filly did not want to go around the only turn in the race. "She wanted to bear out to the outside fence. I tried everything I could to get her to turn. After a while, I was scared. There's a ditch on the other side. I thought the best thing to do was jump off, and I did and I broke my femur. My left leg was behind my back. I said, 'I broke my femur bone!'"

Randy's brother Kenny and Bernie Flint raced onto the track." I was in shock at the time," Randy says. "It wasn't hurting me yet. I said, 'I'm the leading rider in the country, and I broke my femur. My brother said, 'Randy, you broke your leg bad.' I said, 'I know I did.'"

Delta Downs was not well prepared for such an injury. "They taped my leg and they got a two-by-four and wrapped it up with an ace bandage, and they put me in an ambulance and took me to the jockeys' room," Randy explains. "I says, 'I need a doctor.' I started hollering and screaming. Tears started pouring. I said, 'I need a doctor to give me some pain medicine.' They said, 'There's no doctor.' So I said, 'Get me a veterinarian. Get me somebody.'" Eventually, Randy was taken to West Calcasieu Cameron Hospital in Sulphur, the closest hospital to Delta Downs. "It was about a thirty-minute drive. I'm screaming and hollering like an s.o.b. Then I passed out."

At the hospital, Randy was finally given pain medicine. Doctors then inserted a rod in his left leg to stabilize the femur. The accident would leave Randy's injured leg five-eighths of an inch shorter than the other. A subsequent elbow injury would do the same to one of Randy's arms.

The timing of the broken femur could not have been worse. The very next day, Randy was scheduled to ride Mott's Heatherten in a $50,000 stakes at Oaklawn Park. The day after, he was to ride Mott's Taylor's Special in the $200,000 Louisiana Derby. Both horses won with Sam Maple, whose brother Eddie was a top jockey in New York, subbing for Randy. Randy would get the mount back on both horses and resume his increasingly successful career. Eventually.

He began exercising horses in mid-May at Arlington Park. But his thigh continued to ache. Doctors discovered that a wire wrapped around the steel rod had unraveled and was digging into his flesh. So Randy had another surgery to fix that. Then he suffered a groin pull when a horse he was exercising threw him.

Randy finally began riding again on June 20 and won nine of forty-one starts despite suffering increasing pain in his knee. A trip to southern Illinois to ride a horse for trainer Ray Lawrence in a stakes race at Fairmount Park put Randy over the top. "In the airport on the way out, I couldn't walk," he told Eddie Donnally in a November 1984 story in *Derby Magazine*. "I had to get a buggy to walk myself out of the place."

Randy flew to New Orleans to see another doctor about his throbbing knee. The doctor discovered the source of Randy's pain. "They put a damn rod in my femur, and they never X-rayed the knee," Randy says. "They never took an X-ray of the knee. I had torn cartilage in my damn knee. I had to stop riding again for surgery on my knee."

Following the surgery to repair the cartilage—with the rod still in his femur—he was expected to miss six weeks. He came back after four, resuming riding at Louisiana Downs on August 22. On his first day back, Randy rode in two races, finishing fifth and third. "I felt a little tired. A little fatigued," Randy told Mark Gordon of the *Daily Racing Form*. "I'm going to ride a little more as time goes along. Two or three a day is all I want now."

Regardless, he won thirty-seven races from his first 199 mounts. Then he took his career to another level, the highest in racing. He made headlines out of town as Heatherten gave Randy not only his first Grade 1 stakes victory, but his second as well. They would also be his first two stakes victories in New York. At Belmont Park on September 30, 1984—just a day after he was dumped by Shiskabob when the horse broke his leg in a race at Louisiana Downs—Randy won the Grade 1 Ruffian Handicap on Heatherten, who outran her 11-to-1 odds to defeat Miss Oceana by a length and a quarter. In her prior start under Sam Maple, Heatherten had finished sixth, 11¼ lengths behind Miss Oceana, in the $100,000 Maskette Stakes at Belmont.

Randy returned to New Orleans and on opening day at the Fair Grounds on Thanksgiving Day, November 22, captured the $40,000 Thanksgiving Handicap on Temerity Prince by a nose over Timeless Native, the 1-2 favorite. Temerity Prince was Randy's third consecutive winner and fourth of the day.

On November 23, Randy won two more races at the Fair Grounds. Randy's valet, Dallas Stewart, remembers that Randy arrived in the jockeys' room carrying a copy of the magazine *GQ*. "Dude, what are you doing reading that?" Dallas asked Randy. Randy replied, "I'm going to New York tomorrow. I've got to know how to dress."

The following day, Randy traveled to New York and reunited with Heatherten. They had finished third to the brilliant mare Princess Rooney in the Grade 1 Spinster Stakes at Keeneland, but back in New York, Heatherten dominated the Ladies Handicap at Aqueduct, winning by 6¾ lengths.

Back at the Fair Grounds the next day, Randy won two more races, including the $25,000 Old Hickory Stakes on The Royal Freeze, who was trained by Billy Mott.

Heatherten, with Randy in the saddle, would give the jockey his first Grade 1 stakes victory as well as two other Grade 1 wins, beginning Randy's very successful association with Hall of Fame trainer Bill Mott. (Photograph by Barbara D. Livingston)

Randy ended 1984 with a flourish, winning five races at the Fair Grounds on December 31. He won the second race on Joe's Trouble ($9.00), then swept the final four races, the eighth on long shot First Clair Flute ($39.30) for trainer Donald Stemmans; the ninth on another long shot, Frankie Brothers' Heir to the Legacy ($25.20); the $25,000 Diplomat Way Handicap on Aspro ($6.60); and the finale on yet another outsider, Silver Swap ($27.30). Joe's Trouble, Aspro, and Silver Swap were all trained by Cracker Walker.

But Randy could not share his success with the love of his life. On August 14, 1984, Randy and Cricket had divorced. On the day the divorce became official, Randy sent Cricket a dozen roses and called her to tell her he would make it up to her. Randy's injuries had taken an emotional toll on their marriage. "It was just a bad time," Cricket says. "After he got burned, he was just like a different person. He was on a lot of medication. We just kind of grew apart. I know that we were probably against the odds of making it because we were young and there were ups and downs."

Randy was devastated. "It really crushed me when she left," he confesses. "I was on a lot of medication to try to kill the pain, and instead of spending time with my family, I was in the gym trying to get back into shape after the injuries. I wasn't showing her any love. I could understand why she left." That did not mean he was able to handle it. Randy grew so depressed that he checked himself into a hospital for two weeks. "I liked to have gone nuts," he told Susan Finley in her March/April 1989 story in *Spur Magazine.* "I mean it all hit me at one time. So much had happened between us and we couldn't handle it any more. I couldn't take anything. I couldn't take more pain."

Although three-year-old Randy II remained with Cricket, Randy maintained his relationship with his son. And within a year, Cricket and Randy were again living together. Eventually, they would remarry. "It's the best thing I ever did," Randy says. "I've loved Cricket all my life." The feeling is mutual. "We're very close," Cricket confirms. "It doesn't mean we always agree. But we never put demands on the other. I never said, 'You can't do this; you can't do that.'" Randy might not have listened anyway. He spent his whole life not accepting what people told him he could not do.

Relatively healthy for the first time in nearly two years in 1985, Randy began winning races in bushels, especially for Mott. Randy won twelve stakes for Mott that year. Heatherten accounted for three, including the $125,000 Grade 1 Hempstead Handicap at Belmont Park. Derby Wish, who triumphed in the $150,000 Grade 2 Secretariat Stakes and the $100,000 Grade 3 Hawthorne Derby; Taylor's Special; and Sefa's Beauty each won two.

Sefa's Beauty, owned by Farid Sefa, gave Randy his first of an incredible thirty-two stakes wins at thirteen different racetracks in 1985, romping to an eight-length victory in the $47,950 Furl Sail Handicap at the Fair Grounds on January 19. "She should have beat this field," Randy told New Orleans sportswriter Waddell Summers. When someone asked Randy when he knew he had it won, another jockey in the race piped up, "He had it won when the overnight sheets came out."

She had to work a bit harder to add the $32,100 Mardi Gras Handicap exactly one month later. Spotting her rival fillies and mares six to sixteen pounds, she overcame tight quarters on the first turn to win by a length and a half as the 3-to-5 favorite over 70-to-1 Kazankina. "We got squeezed on the first turn, but I got her straightened out," Randy said afterwards. "Then she ran her race. When I asked her to run, she ran."

On March 27, Randy filed a $3 million personal injury lawsuit against Oaklawn Park and the Burdick Corporation of Milton, Wisconsin, the manufacturer of the sweatbox, for the explosion that had nearly killed him two years earlier. More than a year and a half later, on November, 23, 1986, Randy reached a delayed settlement with the two parties out of court for a reported $1.92 million. Oaklawn and Burdick agreed to make $60,000 annual payments to Randy for thirty-two years beginning on his fortieth birthday, with a stipulation that if he died, his survivors were guaranteed $1.285 million.

He made money a lot quicker on the racetrack, and he ended March as the nation's leading rider with 118 victories, 29 ahead of Jose Santos.

At Keeneland, Foxy Ladino and Proudest Hour gave Randy a great send-off on the opening day of the fifteen-day spring meet at Keeneland, April 6. Foxy Ladino won the first race, and Proudest Hour captured the $54,050 Lafayette Stakes for three-year-olds by a nose. The 4-1 second choice despite losing his previous three races by a combined 54¾ lengths, Proudest Hour survived a wicked speed duel with Felter on the Quay and then withstood a claim of foul by the loser's jockey, Keith Allen, to give Randy his second winner of the day on a windy, chilly afternoon.

Two weeks later, on his return to Keeneland, Randy set out to do a favor for one of his compatriots, Don Brumfield. "He took me under his wing when I first came to Kentucky," Randy says. "He was the leading rider there. He respected me and I respected him. We became very good friends." So on the way back to Lexington from New Orleans, where Randy had made a quick trip to sign documents for his attorney, he decided to bring Brumfield a hundred-dollar box of seafood. "There were crawfish and oysters and etouffee [a sauce served over rice]," he told Maryjean Wall of the *Lexington Herald-Leader.* Unfortunately for Brumfield, Randy forgot the box in the overhead bin of his plane. "I like to have died when I realized I left them on the plane," Randy said.

If that was not bad enough, that same day Randy won the $100,000 Grade 2 Ashland Stakes for three-year-old fillies on Koluctoo's Jill for New York-based trainer Bruce Levine by defeating the 1-2 favorite, Fran's Valentine, who was ridden by Brumfield, a last-second replacement for Pat Valenzuela. "I told him about leaving the food on the plane, and he said, 'No, you forgot me,'" Randy says. "I said, 'No, I didn't. I just left it on the plane.' We laughed about it."

Randy cleverly rated Koluctoo's Jill on the front end in a race devoid of other early speed. She had plenty left to defeat Lucy Manette by a length and a quarter. "I got 'em," Randy says. "After I got the half-mile backed down just like I wanted, I went to the five-eighths and I still had it backed up like I wanted."

Randy went on to win the Keeneland spring meet with seventeen victories, his fourth riding title at one of America's most prestigious racetracks.

At Churchill Downs on May 8, 1985, Randy again made history, winning on all six of his mounts that afternoon. At the time, only three other jockeys had won six at Churchill Downs on a single day: Jimmie Lee on June 5, 1907, Steve Brooks on May 15, 1948, and Pat Day on November 15, 1984. One of Randy's victories was on Loblolly Stable's Cullendale in the featured $10,500 Vagrant Purse for Shug McGaughey. Randy had to improvise to win on the 1-2 favorite. "I told Randy to lay just off the lead," McGaughey relates. "He got left at the gate, and Randy had to ride his own race." Randy did, winning by half a length over Cabrini's Dream.

Through the end of May, Randy was still first in the country in victories. "I want to win a championship, and I want to win it badly," Randy told Don Grisham of the *Daily Racing Form* in his June 3, 1985, story. "Last year, when I broke my leg at Delta, I was 60 winners in front, nationally, over the next rider."

Randy returned to Arlington Park, capturing his second riding title there with 159 victories. On Thursdays, when Arlington Park was dark, he returned to Louisiana Downs as he battled Chris Antley for the national riding title. On September 14, after winning on one mount and finishing second twice and third once at Louisiana Downs, Randy told Mark Gordon of the *Daily Racing Form,* "I've had a great time being back. I got here Wednesday night. My mama cooked dinner for me—shrimp gumbo. Then I had a good day here."

At that point in 1985, Randy's 311 victories—already a career high—were 13 behind Antley, who had been riding at Philadelphia Park on afternoons and at the Meadowlands on evenings. "I've been in front all year except for the last few weeks," Romero told Gordon. "As long as he doesn't get more than 15 wins or so ahead, I can handle that."

And in a remarkable October 23 story by *Lexington Herald-Leader*'s Maryjean Wall, under the headline, "Romero overcame pain that made him want to die," Wall mentioned that Randy had tried to encourage children at the same Texas hospital where he was treated for his burns and that he readily talked to other burn victims who sought him out: "People ask me for advice, how I felt about it, what kind of feelings I have. They just want to see if they were depressed as much as I was. There's a lot of depression in it. I talk to them on the phone. I give them confidence. You know, you've got to be confident. You can't be a quitter. A lot of people, they give up. You can't give up. If you want to live, it's a struggle till it's over. . . . I tell them, 'You're lucky to be alive, and I wouldn't worry about the scars. It's just a thing that had to happen in life.'"

When Arlington closed, Randy went to Keeneland. Antley, who continued to ride day and night, opened a substantial lead of forty victories in the national rider standings, so Randy opted to finally have surgery to remove the rod from his injured leg. He missed four weeks, then finished 1985 at the Fair Grounds.

He contemplated riding in New York, hoping to catch on with New York jockey agent Lenny Goodman, who had orchestrated

Steve Cauthen's incredible apprenticeship in 1977 and also represented Hall of Famers Braulio Baeza and John Rotz. "I was having problems with Freddie [Aime], who wanted to work with Pat Day," Randy relates. "I called [trainer] Del Carroll II and he knew Lenny Goodman. Bud Aime had told me before he died that if I ever go to New York, get Lenny Goodman. I talked to Lenny Goodman and told him that. He liked that, and he said he'd heard good things about me. He said he'd take me, but not until the winter. So I went to Florida and he was my agent."

Randy had nothing but good things to say about Aime. "Fred Aime is a great guy," Randy said in a story by Mark Gordon in the *Daily Racing Form.* "He's not only a great agent, he's a good friend of mine. I respect him a whole bunch. We had good times together. When I was in the hospital all that time, he stayed by my bedside. Freddie's doing the thing that he wants to better himself in life and I don't blame him in any way. I hope things will work out for the best. He's stood by me 100 percent."

In Art Grace's January 2, 1986, horse racing column in the *Miami News,* Goodman explained, "He [Randy] called me from New Orleans a few months ago and asked me if I'd take his book. Why wouldn't I? The kid's a terrific rider."

Before he reached Florida, where he had never ridden Thoroughbreds before, Randy won the $50,000 Warminster Handicap at Philadelphia Park on Spectacular Sky, December 28, 1985, and the $25,000 Diplomat Way Stakes at the Fair Grounds the following afternoon.

Randy finished 1985 with a career-high 412 victories, second in the nation to Chris Antley, whose 469 victories came from 2,335 mounts, which remains the highest number of mounts by a leading rider in racing history. Randy had a career-high 1,828 mounts in 1985 and a career-high number of seconds (327) and thirds (229). His earnings of more than $5.3 million ranked fourteenth nationally. Randy would top that in each of the next four years.

But his first ride at Calder Race Course in Miami on New Year's Day did not go as well. He won a three-horse photo by a neck on Hot Metal but was disqualified for interfering with third-place finisher Mount Oliver and placed third. Randy then finished third on A Chara in a later race but did not hit the board on Dictina in the $200,000 La Prevoyante Invitational Handicap.

Calder closed on January 7, and Florida racing shifted to Gulfstream Park, where Randy got off to a good start despite another spill. Esteemed *Daily Racing Form* columnist Joe Hirsch wrote about it in his column: "On his second day at Gulfstream, in a rain shower, his horse propped near the clubhouse turn and Randy went sailing over his head, landing on a shoulder. The offending horse stepped on his arm, and after he said, 'Ouch,' he finished his riding assignments for the day and rode two winners."

In another story, Randy explained why he was riding in Florida before trying New York. "Lenny thought it would be better to get some business here in the East first to get a foundation. You know, looking back, I probably should have left to come here earlier in my life. I love it here. But I wasn't ready. Now, my life is changed. It was finally time to move on."

It took time for him to win his first stakes race at Gulfstream. And when he did, the *Fort Lauderdale Sun-Sentinel* did not exactly go nuts over it. Randy's flawless ride allowed Skip Trial to win the $300,000 Grade 1 Gulfstream Park Handicap on February 22, 1986, by a smidgen of a nose. That was also Randy's fourth Grade 1 stakes win, the first three coming on Heatherten. The headline over Dave Joseph's story about the race led the *Sun-Sentinel*'s sports section the next day: "'Other horse' wins Gulfstream—with other jockey." Skip Trial, owned by Mrs. Ben Cohen, trained by Hall of Famer Sonny Hine, and usually ridden by Jean-Luc Samyn, was dubbed the 'other horse' because he had fewer credentials than the two favorites in the field of just five: Crème Fraiche, the 1985 Belmont Stakes winner who had captured the 1986 Grade 1 Donn Handicap in his previous start, and Proud Truth, who had won the 1985 Breeders' Cup Classic. But Skip Trial was no slouch. He had finished in the money in fourteen of twenty starts and would go off at 5-2.

Randy, even though he ranked second in the Gulfstream Park jockey standings, was dubbed the 'other jockey' filling in for Samyn, who had been hit with a ten-day suspension for a race four days earlier at Gulfstream when Samyn's horse in the seventh race, Wayar, interfered with another horse. Ironically that horse, Prospector Al, was ridden by Randy. Samyn appealed the suspension, but it was upheld by the Florida Division of Pari-Mutuel Wagering. Then Samyn's attorney asked for a stay of the suspension so he could ride Skip Trial in the Gulfstream Park Handicap. That prompted another hearing, one that produced the same result: Samyn was suspended.

Randy, who had been named Skip Trial's substitute jockey thanks to the good work of his agent, Lenny Goodman, made the most of the opportunity despite breaking from the outside post on a track that favored the inside. Four of the first five races that day were won by horses from the one post. Important Business made the lead on the inside and Randy positioned Skip Trial right alongside. "The rail was the thing and Important Business annoyed us by rushing inside, so we did the next best thing," trainer Sonny Hine told Joseph. Behind them, Proud Truth, ridden by Jorge Velasqeuz, and Crème Fraiche, ridden by Eddie Maple, sat a close third and fourth with long shot Mo Exception last.

When Skip Trial finally began to clear Important Business, Proud Truth, who was carrying four pounds more than Skip Trial as the highweight in the field, moved up three-wide. In early stretch, Skip Trial and Proud Truth drew clear of Important Business, then battled each other the rest of the way. "About the eighth pole, and just past it, Skip Trial was a head in front," Joseph wrote. "But as they approached the sixteenth pole, Velasquez and Proud Truth began to pull even. Some 70 yards away from the wire, it appeared Proud Truth would pull away as he moved dead even with Skip Trial."

Actually, Proud Truth stuck his nose in front of Skip Trial. That is when Randy deftly switched hands with his whip and hit Skip Trial left-handed. "Proud Truth got in front of me, and I switched sticks about four strides before the wire," Randy explains. "I hit him left-handed. When I did, he gave me another surge." Randy had made the difference. "I think I made him win that day," he says. A lot of horsemen were impressed by the performance of Skip Trial's 'other' rider. "I picked up a lot of people's heads and showed them that I had a lot of talent," Randy concludes.

He would more than prove the point, capturing the riding title at Gulfstream Park with 41 victories. He would show everybody—literally. In less than eight months, from December 28, 1985, through August 19, 1986, Randy won twelve stakes at twelve different racetracks around the country: Philadelphia Park in Pennsylvania, the Fair Grounds in New Orleans, Gulfstream Park and Hialeah Park in Florida, Oaklawn Park in Arkansas, Garden State Park in southern New Jersey, Sportsman's Park in Chicago, Belmont Park on Long Island, Detroit Race Course, Saratoga Race Course in upstate New

York, and Hawthorne and Arlington Park in Chicago. Incredibly, Randy did not win a single additional stakes in that time frame, almost as if he were doling them out to maximize his exposure.

Back in the fall of '85, when Mott and McGaughey were racing horses at Churchill Downs, Randy was riding for both of them. Mott and McGaughey lived in nearby townhouses in a complex in Louisville. "We were all over in Bill's house eating dinner," McGaughey recalls. "We [Randy and I] kind of walked out together. Randy said, 'I'm thinking about going to New York in the spring. Will you help me when I go up there?' I said, 'Yeah, I'll help you.'"

Boy, did he. McGaughey, who had begun training for the powerful Ogden Phipps racing stable in November 1985, gave Randy the mount on a pair of two-year-olds in 1986, a colt named Polish Navy and a filly named Personal Ensign, as well as her unraced three-year-old full brother, Personal Flag, whom Randy would ride to three graded stakes victories in 1987 and '88. Polish Navy would win his first four starts, including two Grade 1 stakes in the fall of 1986, the Cowdin and the Champagne. Personal Ensign would make racing history.

12

New York, New York

Was a young man from rural Louisiana ready for New York? On the racetrack? Yes. Otherwise? Not quite.

Trainer Sturges Ducoing, who had moved to New York in 1985, did his best to ease Randy's transition in the spring of 1986. "I've known Randy forever," Ducoing says. "He's got a terrific work ethic. He's there every morning. All he wants to do is ride horses. Period. End of story. I knew him from when he was riding at Evangeline Downs when he first started riding. One of the guys that was one of my grooms was one of Randy's first agents, Ronald Reeder. So I knew Randy forever.

"So I got this little apartment, a nice place in Valley Stream [on Long Island] and I'm giving him directions. He's driving. He gets up there about 10:30, eleven o'clock one morning when we're racing at Aqueduct. So I got a horse in that day. So I said, 'Okay, put your car in the garage. We'll close it.' I told him to stay there, because Randy was scared of the big city. He didn't want to go anywhere. I said, 'I'm going to go run this horse and then I'll be back. When I get back, we'll unload the car. We'll do everything we got to do. Here's the TV.'

"So I go to the track. I come back to the house about four o'clock in the afternoon. Well, when my foot hits the first step, the door opened. He said, 'Neg [a Cajun term of endearment], where you been? 'I'm starving. We got to go eat.' I said, 'I went to run the horse, Randy. Let's go eat.'

"Now I'm thinking. I said, 'Randy, why didn't you just eat some of the stuff I had?' I'm by myself, so I got like maybe a little strawberry jam and a can of tuna fish and, I don't know, maybe some cereal and some milk and ham and bread. I didn't have a whole lot. I said, 'Man, why didn't you just eat something that I had here?' He said, 'Neg, I ate all that,'" Sturges says, laughing loud and hard. "He cleared out the whole place." Still laughing, Sturges continues, "He ate everything. Now, he says, 'Come on, let's go eat.' Well, we go eat. He's got a good appetite. He says, 'Come on, we got to go to the grocery.' I said, 'Well, yeah. You ate everything in the house.' Well, I'll tell you. Him and I went to the grocery and we left with a whole basket of groceries."

Randy stayed with Ducoing for a week, then found his own place, but Randy never really got the hang of New York City or Long Island.

"Everybody has a Randy Romero story," trainer Billy Mott says. "Some would be embarrassing to him, but it's good-natured. Somebody was telling me one time—I believe he [Randy] was in downtown Manhattan—he called somebody up for directions. He said, 'I'm lost; I don't know where I'm going.' They said, 'Randy, look up at the street sign at the corner and tell me what intersection you're at.' He said, 'Hmmm. I'm right at the intersection of Walk and Don't Walk.'"

In a story in the March/April 1989 issue of *Spur Magazine,* Randy told Susan Finley, "The lifestyle in New York is very tough for a country person. To be honest, I don't know if I could have stuck it out if I didn't have my kid in my life.

"I never had a childhood. It was always work, work, work. And now I'm like a kid when I'm with him. I play ball, do things with him—things I never enjoyed when I was a kid because I never had the time. I was in a man's position from the time I was eight years old. I said to myself when I was growing up that I never wanted my kid to have to work as hard as I did. I'm trying to give him the best, but I want him to appreciate it, and I want him to work for it, also."

New York City may have intimidated Randy. The remarkably talented New York jockey colony—which included Hall of Famers Angel Cordero, Jr., Jerry Bailey, Jorge Velasquez, Mike Smith, Jacinto Vasquez, and Jose Santos—did not. "Hell, no," Randy says. "I had been the leading rider at a lot of places. I had won a stakes at Aqueduct with Heatherten. I thought I could really ride. I put myself third [in New York] behind Cordero and Bailey. On a given day, they were the two I didn't want to hook up with, but I was never scared of them."

Yet a moment later, Randy adds, "I won all these races, but I didn't know how to ride until I came to New York. When you ride with better riders, you learn. I learned how to pace. I learned how to save horses, how to cut the corner. I learned how to ride the grass. The rider I watched a lot was Jerry Bailey on grass. He was awesome."

Randy, though, more than held his own. "It was a very, very strong jockey colony, but Randy was a good rider," Velasquez says. "He fit in good right away. He's a class act."

By this time in his career, Randy spent extensive time handicapping every day. He would spend one hour each night noting speed horses and any relevant statistics, then mark any late changes the next day and handicap the races he was in again on race days, many times while sitting in the sauna or in the jockeys' room. He would focus on other riders' tendencies: who lets horses off the fence, who goes wide, who uses horses early, whose horse bears in or out, who does not cover up his horse on grass to get his horse off the bit. "The more you do it [handicap], the better you get," Randy says. "There are no geniuses in this game."

Randy quickly discovered the awesome possibilities he would be presented when Shug McGaughey kept his word about helping him in the Big Apple. In the summer of 1986, New York newcomer Randy Romero would ride two of the most exciting two-year-old prospects in the country, a colt and a filly. McGaughey, who had a wonderful apprenticeship under Hall of Fame trainer Frank Whiteley—whose top horses included Damascus, Ruffian, and three-time Horse of the Year Forego before starting his own stable—was an emerging star when he began training horses for Loblolly Stable, owned by John Ed Anthony, in 1984. McGaughey's success with Loblolly's top horse, Vanlandingham, drew the attention of the legendary Phipps family and Claiborne Farm president Seth Hancock. The Phippses, Ogden Phipps and his son Dinny, had entrusted their stable to just a handful of trainers over the years, including legendary Sunny Jim Fitzsimmons, who conditioned their horses for thirty-eight years. He was followed by Bill Winfrey, Eddie Neloy, Roger Laurin, John Russell, and Angel Penna. Fitzsimmons, Winfrey, Neloy, and Penna are all in the Hall of Fame. The Phipps Stable had been a powerhouse in American racing for some six decades. But in 1984, the stable had won just four races with earnings of a little over one hundred thousand dollars. In the summer of 1985, the Phipps Stable and Penna split, leaving an incredible opening for a new trainer. Hancock suggested McGaughey.

Dinny Phipps interviewed McGaughey at his Long Island home

on the morning of the 1985 Grade 1 Jockey Club Gold Cup at
Belmont Park. McGaughey would saddle Vanlandingham in that
stakes and Dinny, the Jockey Club chairman, would be presenting
the winning trophy. McGaughey aced his conversation with Phipps,
then won the Jockey Club Gold Cup with Vanlandingham. Phipps
presented McGaughey the trophy. Four days later, Dinny told
McGaughey the job was his. It was November 1985.

Despite missing part of the Aqueduct 1985-86 winter meet while
riding at Gulfstream, Randy finished third in the rider standings
with 85 wins from 216 starts, an incredible winning percentage of
nearly 40.

The following spring, McGaughey would be presented with
the Phipps' regally bred two-year-olds. Randy would get to ride the
two best, Polish Navy and Personal Ensign. By September 28, 1986,
the day of Personal Ensign's winning debut in a maiden race, Polish
Navy was three-for-three, including a victory in a $150,000 stakes.
That made Randy's assessment of Personal Ensign even more
remarkable. After her maiden win, the first time he had ridden her,
Randy told Shug, "She's better than the colt."

13

Once in a Lifetime

When Shug McGaughey signed on to become the Phipps Stable's trainer in November 1985, he knew he would be training well-bred two-year-olds. In the early spring of 1986, he traveled to Slew's Nest, the farm in Ocala, Florida, where the Phipps sent their babies for early training, to review his first crop of Phipps' two-year-olds. McGaughey was impressed with a two-year-old by Private Account—not the filly out of the mare Grecian Banner who would be named Personal Ensign, nor the Danzig colt who would be named Polish Navy. "There was a full brother to Private Account there, by Damascus out of Numbered Account," he says. "I was more enthralled with him. He ended up getting hurt before he ever came to me."

His take on Polish Navy and Personal Ensign? "Polish Navy's mother [Navsup, who went winless in eleven starts and earned just four thousand dollars] never had been anything, and I didn't know who Grecian Banner was," McGaughey says.

Nevertheless, when Polish Navy made his debut at Belmont Park on June 12, 1986, under Randy, the word was out that he could run. He won his first start by five lengths at odds of 6-5, paying a paltry $4.60 for a $2 win ticket. Polish Navy did not race again until August 30, when he won an allowance race at Belmont Park by 4¼ lengths as the 1-2 favorite.

In between Polish Navy's victories, Randy won the Grade 1 Coaching Club American Oaks on Valley Victory at Belmont Park; the Grade 2 Michigan Mile and Eighth on Ends Well at Detroit Race Course; the Grade 2 Ballerina Stakes at Saratoga on Gene's Lady, Randy's first Saratoga stakes win; the Grade 2 Budweiser Hawthorne Gold Cup in Chicago on Ends Well; and the Grade 1 Arlington Classic on Sumptuous. Randy flew to Hollywood Park to ride Herat for the first time in the $500,000 Hollywood Gold Cup on July 20 for Hall of Fame trainer Jack Van Berg. Herat finished fourth by eight lengths at 19-1 in the field of six. The following day at Hollywood Park, Randy rode a two-year-old first-time starter for Van Berg. The horse's name was Alysheba, and he finished fifth in his maiden debut at 2-1. Randy never got the chance to ride him again, but he would have loved to have had the opportunity. The following year, Alysheba went on to be Three-Year-Old Champion after winning the Kentucky Derby and Preakness, and the year after that, he was Handicap Champion and Horse of the Year. He earned it by winning the final four starts of his career, all Grade 1 stakes and all by less than a length: the Iselin at Monmouth Park, the Woodward at Belmont Park, the Meadowlands Cup at the Meadowlands, and the Breeders' Cup Classic at Churchill Downs. Hall of Fame jockey Chris McCarron rode Alysheba in his final seventeen starts.

Back in New York, Randy continued to roll. On September 20, he posted a same-day stakes double at two different tracks, capturing the Leixable Stakes at Belmont Park on Fama in the afternoon and the Grade 3 Cliff Hanger Handicap on Explosive Darling at the Meadowlands that night.

A week later at Belmont, in the $150,000 Cowdin, Polish Navy defeated Java Gold by a length as the 4-5 favorite. In the $250,000 Grade 1 Champagne, Polish Navy edged Demons Begone by a nose with Bet Twice another length and three-quarters behind in third. Polish Navy was four-for-four and headed for the $1 million Breeders' Cup Juvenile at Santa Anita as the leading two-year-old colt in the East. All of his four starts had been at Belmont, where Randy would win the fall meet with fifty-four victories. That was the ninth racetrack where Randy had finished as leading rider.

At Santa Anita in the Breeders' Cup Juvenile, Polish Navy finished seventh, 11¼ lengths behind Capote, who would be named Two-Year-Old Champion Colt.

Randy, who was honored with a Randy Romero Day at the Fair Grounds in mid-December, finished 1986 with 224 victories, twenty-fifth in the country, down from his career best of 415 victories the year before. His number of mounts, though, had also dipped from 1,828 to 1,401, while his earnings increased from $5.3 million in 1985 to a career high of just over $8 million in 1986, sixth highest in the country.

As a three-year-old in 1987, Polish Navy won an allowance race, finished a distant third in the Grade 2 Dwyer Stakes, captured the Jim Dandy Stakes under Pat Day (his only start without Randy), finished third behind Java Gold and Cryptoclearance in the $1 million Travers Stakes on a sloppy track, and won the $500,000 Grade 1 Woodward Stakes. In his final start, the $750,000 Marlboro Cup, Polish Navy led almost the entire way before weakening late to finish third behind Java Gold and Nostalgia's Star. Polish Navy had posted seven victories, one second, and three thirds from just twelve races and earned more than one million dollars.

Personal Ensign was one of seven two-year-olds shipped from Ocala to Keeneland in Lexington, Kentucky, in April 1986. She was a big, gangly dark bay with a white snip splitting her nostrils and another small white mark at the top of her head. "I remember when she shipped in," her groom, Terry Cooney, says. "She didn't have a name then. She was the Grecian Banner filly. When they ship in, their halters are wrapped in strips of flannel. I was taking them all off. She wouldn't let me touch her. Wouldn't have anything to do with me."

It was nothing personal. "You were not going to pet her," points out Lena Eriksson, one of Personal Ensign's exercise riders who also accompanied Personal Ensign on a pony during the post parade before her races.

Jean Dolan, the filly's first exercise rider, was immediately impressed with her. McGaughey was not. "She hadn't shown me a whole lot. I was skeptical. She'd go a half mile in fifty seconds or fifty-one seconds. Hell, anybody can do that. But she [Dolan] kept telling me, 'This filly is something else.'"

McGaughey upgraded his opinion after Personal Ensign, whose summer debut at Belmont Park was delayed because of a skin disease, worked a half-mile on the deep Oklahoma Training Track at Saratoga. "Oklahoma was a different track than it is now," he says. "It was about two seconds slower at least [than the main track at Saratoga]. And she worked a half in forty-nine seconds here one morning." That would convert to a half-mile in forty-seven seconds or faster, a remarkable workout for an unraced two-year-old filly. "Every year you're really basically looking to get a good horse out of the crop of two-year-olds you're getting," McGaughey explains. "I maybe get more excited running a first-time two-year-old that I think can run than anything else in the business."

Randy at Saratoga in 1986. (Photograph by Barbara D. Livingston)

And he thought she could run. So did a lot of people. She would be sent off as an overwhelming 4-5 favorite when she made her debut under Randy in the sixth race at Belmont Park on September 28, 1986, against six rival maidens. In fact, Personal Ensign would go off under even money in twelve of her thirteen starts. She went off at 6-5 in the other, the only time she was not favored in a race.

Personal Ensign broke slowly, but she would do that in many of her races. "She was a little high-strung," Randy says. "I'd talk to her in the post parade to settle her down." McGaughey's decision to use Randy on the filly paid immediate dividends: he did not panic after her poor start in her debut. "She broke real bad," Randy recalls. "I just rode it the way the race came up. I let her get settled and she started running. The good ones overcome a lot."

Not as quickly as she did. Personal Ensign circled the entire field with stunning ease, rallying from last to first before the first half-mile of the seven furlong (seven-eighths of a mile) race. And then she simply drew off, winning by 12¼ lengths in 1:22⅖, which would be three-fifths of a second faster than the winning time for the Grade 1 Matron Stakes for two-year-old fillies at Belmont Park an hour later.

"You don't see horses do that very often," Randy says. "That was awesome. I never hit her with the stick. I think Shug knew she was good, but I didn't know if he thought she was that good. When I told Shug, 'She's better than the colt [Polish Navy],' Shug said, 'You're kidding me.' I told him, 'She's a freak. I never rode anything like her. She is the real deal.'"

McGaughey has spent most of his Hall of Fame career not rushing his horses, not asking them to do too much too soon. He made an exception with Personal Ensign, asking her to jump up from a maiden race to a Grade 1 stakes, the $274,000 Frizette Stakes at one mile at Belmont on Columbus Day, October 13, just fifteen days after her first start. In a field of six, front-running Collins, ridden by George Martens, and Personal Ensign, ridden by Randy, put on a show, running head-to-head for the final half-mile, Collins on the inside and Personal Ensign right alongside. Martens hit his filly right-handed once then switched hands and hit her twelve times left-handed. Randy used his whip eleven times right-handed and Personal Ensign inched clear, winning by a head. "She really had to run," Randy says.

But rather than taking a lot out of the filly, the Frizette emboldened her. "When Randy had to ask her to run a little bit, she learned about running because she had never been asked to run," McGaughey relates. "She didn't get anything from her maiden race [because she won so easily]. She came out of the Frizette a different horse. She knew what was going on. She showed me something right after the Frizette that I had never seen in a horse I had. She'd go a minute like it was nothing. I've worked other horses faster, but it was the ease that she was doing it in. She was working with a 130- to 135-pound exercise rider. I never saw a horse change that quick."

Thirteen days after the Frizette, there was another change. In training for the $1 million Breeders' Cup Juvenile Filly at Santa Anita on November 1, Personal Ensign worked five furlongs under exercise rider Jean Dolan on a cold Sunday morning at Belmont Park. Personal Ensign was scheduled to fly to California the next day. She worked in a minute flat and galloped out six furlongs in 1:12, an excellent time. She cooled out for twenty-five minutes and was taken to her stall. McGaughey's longtime assistant Buzz Tenney, an excellent horseman himself, checked on her. She could not walk out of her stall. She would not drink water. She was lame.

X-rays revealed that Personal Ensign had fractured her left rear pastern. She had likely broken it during her workout, but endorphins had kicked in and masked the pain initially. Now she was hurting and would require surgery. McGaughey was relieved to find that her life was not in danger, but he assumed her career was over. However, she had fractured the bone side-to-side rather than front-to-back, which made it easier to fix. Informed that there was a chance she could race again, McGaughey said, "We'll have to wait and see." Later he said, "It was hard to believe."

Randy heard the unfortunate news when he stopped by the barn. "They told me she couldn't walk. I said, 'Oh damn!' What can you do? I said, 'Not the best one we've got.' I thought she was gone. I never thought she'd come back." Years later, McGaughey says, "We all thought that was the end of it, that she'd join the Phipps' broodmare band." Instead, she resumed her career. Left unanswered was this: could she possibly be as good as she had been?

Randy missed her comeback in an allowance race at Belmont Park on September 6, 1987, because he had committed to ride Dance of Life for Hall of Fame trainer Mack Miller in the Arlington Million the same day. McGaughey did not have a problem with that, telling Randy he would have the mount back. "This is only an allowance race,"

McGaughey told Randy. "Win, lose, or draw you've got her back."

Ironically, Dance of Life scratched from the Million. Randy found out when he arrived in Chicago. "I called Shug and told him I could make it back, but he said, 'Bailey will ride her; you'll get her back.'" With Jerry Bailey subbing for Randy, Personal Ensign won her comeback by 3¾ lengths. True to McGaughey's word, Randy would ride the undefeated filly in all her remaining starts, beginning with another allowance victory at Belmont Park by 7¾ lengths eighteen days later.

She was back, but how good was she? McGaughey upped the ante, racing Personal Ensign in the Grade 2 Rare Perfume Stakes at Belmont, which she won by 4¾ lengths on October 10. She was not the favorite, but it took a five-horse entry (usually an entry is two horses; rarely is it three or more) sent off at 4-5 to earn that distinction. Just eight days later, Personal Ensign captured the Grade 1 Beldame Stakes by 2¼ lengths, making her six-for-six lifetime.

Like so many other horsemen, Randy marveled at the training job McGaughey had done bringing their special filly back. "He's patient and very smart," Randy says. "Shug is a perfectionist. It's a good thing, but he's hard on himself. He really is."

Other trainers might have sent Personal Ensign to the 1987 $1 million Breeders' Cup Distaff at Hollywood Park, where a victory would assure her the three-year-old filly championship. But the Breeders' Cup was unusually late that year, on November 21, more than a month after the Beldame. "We had gotten her back," McGaughey says. "We had accomplished what we wanted to do. We said, 'Next year, we'll get a full campaign for her.'"

Randy, however, did not have to wait a year to ride in the Breeders' Cup Distaff, finessing his way onto a top contender trained by D. Wayne Lukas. Randy had ridden fillies successfully for Lukas before, winning with a first-time starter at Saratoga Race Course earlier that year, August 13. Her name was Winning Colors. Randy did not get to ride the filly who would win the 1988 Kentucky Derby again, but he would ride against her.

Randy, though, won a championship on another Lukas-trained filly, Sacahuista, after he snatched two stakes victories from her on disqualifications. In both races, Randy's mounts had been moved up from second to first. In the Grade 3 Cotillion Handicap at Philadelphia Park on September 12, Randy rode Silent Turn for Hall of Fame trainer Angel Penna, Sr., and finished second by a neck to Sacahuista, who was ridden by Craig Perret. But Randy claimed foul on the winner. "She bumped me on the turn, and they took her number down, and they put me up first," Randy explains. Just fifteen days later, it happened again in a Grade 1 stakes at Belmont Park, the Ruffian Handicap. Randy rode Coup de Fusil for trainer Jan Nerud, the son of Hall of Fame trainer John Nerud, and finished second by a head to Sacahuista, ridden this time by Richard Migliore. But Sacahuista had lugged in on Coup de Fusil. The stewards launched an inquiry and Randy claimed foul. Again, Sacahuista was disqualified and Randy's mount placed first.

Wasting little time in maximizing his good fortune, Randy approached Lukas about getting a new rider for Sacahuista: himself. Randy believed Sacahuista's problem was not changing leads going around a turn. "The next morning after the Ruffian, I go to Wayne and said I'd like to ride Sacahuista," Randy says. "I said, 'Let me ride her. I can make her change leads.' He said, 'Go ahead.'" Lukas named Randy on Sacahuista for the prestigious Grade 1 Spinster Stakes at Keeneland. Sacahuista won by three lengths. Then she won the Breeders' Cup Distaff handily by 2¼ lengths and was named Champion Three-Year-Old Filly.

Randy's name, however, will forever be linked to the other three-year-old filly he rode that year. At the age of four in 1988, Personal Ensign breezed through consecutive victories in the Grade 1 Shuvee Handicap by a length and three-quarters and the Grade 1 Hempstead by seven lengths. Both those stakes were at Belmont Park, the only track Personal Ensign had ever raced on. Any thought that she could not win on another track was forever put to rest when she journeyed to Monmouth Park in New Jersey to win the Grade 2 Molly Pitcher Handicap by eight lengths.

On the way there, Randy had a conversation with Ogden Phipps, the patriarch of the Phipps family and father of Dinny Phipps, the former CEO of the New York Racing Association and the chairman of the Jockey Club. "I had flown with him to ride in the Molly Pitcher at Monmouth in his chopper," Randy says. "I asked him, 'What's the best filly you ever had?' And he started rattling off some other fillies and mares. Then I asked him, 'What's the best horse you ever had?' And he named Buckpasser and a couple others. And I looked at Mr. Phipps in his eyes and I said, 'Mr. Phipps, this is the best horse you ever had right here.'"

At Saratoga, on a sloppy track, Personal Ensign challenged two males in the Grade 1 Whitney Handicap: Gulch and King's Swan. She won by a length and a half, upping her record to ten-for-ten.

There had not been an undefeated major American Thoroughbred since Colin completed a fifteen-for-fifteen career by winning the Tidal Stakes at Sheepshead Bay Racetrack in New York on June 20, 1908. That was eighty years earlier. Others had come close to perfection: Man o' War (twenty-for-twenty-one with one second), Native Dancer (twenty-one-for-twenty-two with one second), and Ruffian, who was ten-for-ten before her fatal breakdown against 1975 Kentucky Derby winner Foolish Pleasure in a match race at Belmont Park. Once in a great while, a Thoroughbred completes a perfect career by dominating local competition without being tested at racing's major venues.

When the Phippses announced that Personal Ensign would be retired at the end of her four-year-old season to become a broodmare, McGaughey mapped out her fall campaign. There would be three more starts: two Grade 1 stakes at Belmont Park— the Maskette and the Beldame—and then the $1 million Grade 1 Breeders' Cup Distaff at Churchill Downs.

For the one-mile Maskette, McGaughey was surprised and deeply concerned to learn that Lukas had entered his front-running Kentucky Derby-winning filly Winning Colors in the race under her regular rider Gary Stevens. McGaughey decided to enter Cadillacing as a rabbit, a speed horse to compromise Winning Colors' chances, but changed his mind. McGaughey had named Angel Cordero, Jr., to ride Cadillacing, who had won the Grade 1 Ballerina Stakes at Saratoga. "It was the third race [the Maskette was the eighth], and Cordero was going to ride the rabbit, and he came to me and said that Lukas was livid that he was going to ride the rabbit, and this and that," McGaughey says. "And I said, 'Okay, we'll just scratch the rabbit.' Then during the race, Winning Colors is six lengths in front going down the backside, and I'm going, 'What an idiot I am. I don't know if we'll be able to beat her.'"

Though she was carrying five pounds more than Winning Colors, Personal Ensign ran her down late, beating her by three-quarters of a length. "I thought she [Winning Colors] was a winner going down the stretch," Stevens says. "When the other mare came to her, she really dug in and really tried hard. I'm a little upset she ran that good and didn't win, but the other mare is a superstar."

Personal Ensign defeats Kentucky Derby winner Winning Colors in the 1988 Maskette Stakes at Belmont Park. (Photograph by Barbara D. Livingston)

An undefeated one. When Personal Ensign added a 5½-length victory in the Beldame at odds of 1-10, she was twelve-for-twelve and chasing history.

Twenty days later, in the Breeders' Cup at Churchill Downs, she would make her final start. Suddenly, it seemed like the whole world knew about the undefeated filly's bid for immortality. And the pressure built daily for two men: Randy and McGaughey. The pressure on McGaughey ended when he gave Randy a leg up on Personal Ensign in the paddock that afternoon. McGaughey's job was completed. There was nothing more he could do. It was all up to the filly and the jockey riding her. Randy's job that day had just begun.

Randy could have ridden Banker's Lady, a filly trained by Phil Hauswald, in the $145,850 Grade 2 Long Look Handicap at the Meadowlands Friday night, the night before the Breeders' Cup. After speaking with McGaughey, Randy decided to fly into Louisville, Kentucky, that night instead. Banker's Lady won the Long Look Handicap, but Randy did not regret his decision. "I just flew into Louisville, which was the best thing I could do, because, let me tell you, I was very restless," Randy says. "If I went into the Meadowlands and something bad happened . . . I didn't want to take any chances. I knew it [the Distaff] was the defining moment of my career. It was going to make me or break me in life."

Staying with Cricket and seven-year-old Randy II at the Galt House, a hotel in downtown Louisville, Randy slept little that night. He woke up at 5:30 and headed for barn 42 on the backstretch at Churchill Downs.

The morning of November 5, 1988, dawned unseasonably cold, wet, and dreary. Rain the previous night had left the track a quagmire. The track condition would be listed as sloppy for the first Breeders' Cup race, the Sprint, and then muddy the rest of the day. Intermittent rain would suddenly stop when the fillies and the mares in the Distaff walked to the paddock to be saddled.

Personal Ensign's appearance in the Distaff would be Randy's third Breeders' Cup ride that afternoon. He would win the $50,000 Abrogate Stakes on Littlebitofpleasure before the first Breeders' Cup race. Undefeated Mining, who was also trained by McGaughey, would go off the 2-5 favorite in the $1 million Sprint. Then Randy would ride Seattle Meteor, who had taken him to victory in the Grade 3 Astoria Stakes and Grade 1 Spinaway Stakes and would go off the third choice in the $1 million Juvenile Filly, before mounting Personal Ensign, who would be 1-2 in the Distaff.

McGaughey, too, was a busy man that afternoon, saddling five horses in four Breeders' Cup races. Besides Mining and Personal Ensign, he would send out Easy Goer in the $1 million Juvenile and both Seeking the Gold, with Pat Day aboard, and Personal Flag, who would be ridden by Cordero for the first time, in the $3 million Classic. Randy had lost the mounts on Seeking the Gold and Personal Flag several starts earlier. "It was a business decision," Randy says. "I understood." So did Day. He had been replaced by Cordero on Personal Flag. Seeking the Gold and Personal Flag would finish second and sixth in the Classic, respectively, behind Alysheba. Randy's afternoon had peaked a couple hours earlier.

On the way to McGaughey's barn on the backstretch, Randy walked past Lukas's barn. Lukas would saddle Gulch against Mining in the Sprint and Winning Colors against Personal Ensign in the Distaff. "I wished him good luck because Wayne took care of me. I won a lot of big races for him. He always took care of me, and I always took care of him. He was a good horse trainer. Then I said, 'I'm going to beat you in the first race, too.'" Randy pauses for a second and laughs. "I can't believe I said that to him."

Randy wanted to visit Personal Ensign, but it was not easy doing so. "There were a lot of people on the backside," Randy explains. "There were so many. It was crowded. I could hardly get to Personal Ensign. I just kind of glanced in there, and I pet her, and I got the hell out of there as quick as I could. Everybody was hollering at me and I said, 'I got to go. I got to go. I got to pick up my wife.' So the press didn't have a chance to talk with me. After the races, fine. I'll talk to them all day long. But before the race, I got things to do that I've got to accomplish. I didn't want any stress. I went back to the room, picked up Cricket and Randy, and went to the track. I got them their seats."

Cricket and Randy II would watch the race in the box seat of Lukas's son and assistant trainer, Jeff, and Jeff's wife, Linda. "I met Linda at the track two years earlier and we got to be good friends," Cricket says. "We were best friends. We actually picked out our outfits together that day. We'd go to work out together. We'd shop together. We'd eat dinner together. We'd do everything together."

As Cricket and Randy II took their seats, Randy set his mind on the races ahead of him. Randy did not think Mining, who had won all six of his starts, could lose. "I thought Mining was a cinch because I beat Gulch in a gallop [easily] in the Vosburgh [both horses' previous race]. I never hit Mining. I never used him up. Cordero [who was riding Gulch] was beating the hell out of his horse. But I got some left in the tank. I said, 'I'll kill him in the Breeders' Cup.'" Instead, Gulch, befitting from a masterful ride by Cordero, won the Sprint by three-quarters of a length. Mining finished tenth in the field of thirteen. "My horse never did run," Randy recalls. "He never tried, and he pulled up sore. I was really upset because I didn't think he could lose."

After the race, Randy was well served by his professionalism. He never thought Mining's loss was the start of a bad day. "No, I would never do that. It's another race. Turn the page. I never look back. That's how you have to do it. You can't dwell on the past. Focus on the present."

So Randy focused on his mount in the $1 million Juvenile Filly, Seattle Meteor, who would be the 7-2 second choice in the wagering. "She ran fifth and she had no excuses. She had a good trip." Lukas's Open Mind, part of a five-horse entry that went off at 3-5, captured the Juvenile Filly by 1¾ lengths, giving Lukas his second Breeders' Cup winner of the day. Open Mind was owned by Eugene Klein, the former owner of the San Diego Chargers in the National Football League who also owned 1986 Horse of the Year Lady's Secret and Winning Colors.

Before the Distaff, Randy stayed by himself in the jockeys' room, watching some of the television coverage of the Breeders' Cup. He tried to sleep. "I couldn't," he says. "I just waited." The minutes dragged. Finally, it was time for Randy to go to the paddock to ride Personal Ensign for the final time. McGaughey said, "Good luck," and gave Randy a leg up on Personal Ensign, who would go off the 1-2 favorite in the Distaff. Randy said, "Thank you, Shug."

Winning Colors, who was coupled with Classic Crown, had followed her brave second in the Maskette with a badly tiring fourth by fifteen lengths to long shot Hail a Cab as the 1-5 favorite in the Grade 1 Spinster Stakes. Regardless, she and her entry-mate would be the 4-1 second choice in the Distaff. She had won the Kentucky Derby just five months earlier on this same Churchill Downs track.

There was another strong contender in the Distaff, Goodbye Halo, who had won three consecutive Grade 1 stakes before finishing third in her most recent start, the Grade 2 Las Palmas Handicap. She would be the 5-1 third choice. None of the other six fillies and mares in the Distaff would have an impact.

Personal Ensign was giving both Winning Colors and Goodbye Halo four pounds, carrying 123 to their 119. Gary Stevens rode Winning Colors; Eddie Delahoussaye was on Goodbye Halo.

After the post parade, Personal Ensign and the other fillies and mares jogged around the track to warm up. "Shug had her ready," Randy says. "Shug did a very good job throughout her career."

Goodbye Halo had the two post, Personal Ensign the six, and Winning Colors the eight. The outside draw would allow speedy Winning Colors to get a clear run to the lead.

As the horses loaded into the starting gate, announcer Tom Durkin, who was calling the race on TV for NBC, said, "Personal Ensign has taken her place in the starting gate, and she will certainly take her place in history as one of the greatest fillies of all time as she seeks to retire here undefeated, the first major American horse to do so in eighty years." Randy could not help but hear Durkin. He thought, "'All the world's on my shoulders.' I wanted to crawl underneath the gate."

14

Winning On-Track and Off

By the time Personal Ensign stepped into the starting gate for the $1 million Breeders' Cup Distaff on November 5, 1988, Randy Romero had crossed the boundary from good to great, from hot young flash into one of the best riders in the country. New York had been his final challenge, one he conquered completely, finishing as the leading rider at the 1986 Belmont Park fall meeting with fifty-four victories despite not riding in New York full-time until that spring. He had become number one at Keeneland, Arlington Park, and Gulfstream Park in his first season at each track in even shorter time. Going into a new venue, where a jockey is unfamiliar with most of the other riders and almost all the horses who race there, is an imposing obstacle, one Randy continually overcame.

But even he needed a break. In mid-December 1986, he invited Chris Antley, whom he had battled for the 1985 national riding title, to take a three-day vacation with him in New Orleans to go hunting and fishing. "We were riding in New York together and he came fishing and hunting," Randy says. That was the plan at least. "We bought the wrong shells for the guns," Randy explains, laughing. So they fished on Randy's close friend Jimmy Lafont's houseboat in nearby Cutoff.

Beginning in the early 1980s, Randy annually took a week off in mid-December to return to New Orleans to visit family and friends, and to hunt and fish. "It was good therapy," he claims. "It gets all the stress out. You're always intense working. I always looked for December to come. It was my birthday and Christmas."

Over the years, Randy invited trainers Frankie Brothers, Billy Badgett, and Norm Casse to join him. Randy recalls, "We cooked out, got drunk, played Bourré [a Cajun card game that combines elements of bridge and poker] all night. I had a blast. We'd get up in the morning and go hunting and bring our ducks back. Go fishing. Bring the fish back. We'd catch crabs and boil them right there. We did everything on Jimmy's houseboat. We spoke French. It was good therapy and good, good people. We had fun."

That did not preclude his buddies from playing jokes on Randy, even if he was recovering from an injury. "In deep-sea fishing, you set the line and wait," Jimmy Lafont says. "He had his arm in a sling. I reeled up his line and attached two dead fish together. I started screaming, 'Strike!' Randy pulled the reel in for three hours. He reeled and reeled. Then he saw the dead fish. He said, 'I'm going to kill you.' The next day we did it again with a five-gallon bucket. He thought he had a big one. Two hours and twenty minutes. He was sweating, hot as the dickens. We said, 'Don't let this big one get away.' He said, 'Look at this fish!' But it was a bucket." Randy still laughs about it. "Jimmy's a funny s.o.b.," Randy says. "He's my best friend."

After his three days of fishing, Randy made a trip to New Orleans, where he was honored with a Randy Romero Day at the Fair Grounds track. Randy rode a couple of races and signed some five hundred photos for fans.

Then Randy headed for Florida in early January. He tied Julio Pezua for leading rider with fifty-six victories at beautiful Hialeah in Miami, the tenth different track where Randy earned leading rider, then won seven stakes at Gulfstream Park, including the Grade 1 $250,000 Gulfstream Park Handicap, again with Skip Trial, on March 30, 1987. In doing so, Skip Trial became just the second repeat-winner of the stakes in its forty-two-year history. Crafty Admiral had pulled it off in 1952 and 1953.

Skip Trial, who had won the 1986 Gulfstream Park Handicap by a nose over Proud Truth, defeated two more high-profile opponents in '87: 1986 Preakness Stakes winner Snow Chief, the 3-5 favorite under Alex Solis, and 1985 Belmont Stakes winner Crème Fraiche by 4½ lengths. Snow Chief set incredibly slow fractions on the lead, getting the first quarter of a mile in :24⅖ yet had no answer when Skip Trial made his move. "When I asked him to move, he just exploded," Randy says.

Five days before the Gulfstream Park Handicap, on March 25, Randy rode his three thousandth winner on Full Courage. "I knew I'd get it," Randy said afterwards. "It was just a matter of time." Later that afternoon, Randy won the $59,400 Shirley Jones Handicap on Life at the Top, allowing Randy to open a two-win lead in the

Gulfstream rider standings. But Randy, splitting the spring between Gulfstream and Aqueduct, did not win that title.

He also spent a memorable afternoon in Hot Springs, Arkansas. Before a mammoth crowd of 46,583 at Oaklawn Park on April 4, Randy won five consecutive races, capped by Bolshoi Boy's victory in the $131,600 Grade 2 Razorback Handicap. Randy had previously ridden Bolshoi Boy to victory in the Gulfstream Park Budweiser Breeders' Cup Stakes for trainer Howie Tesher. At Oaklawn, Randy finished second, third, and out of the money in his first three rides, then won the four races preceding the Razorback Handicap on Hosston ($13.60), Cal Lex ($6.00), Charging Falls ($3.40), and Hail a Cab ($9.60).

Bolshoi Boy kept Randy's win streak alive. Randy held Bolshoi Boy perfectly placed in third as Sun Master, the co-favorite with Bolshoi Boy, dueled head-to-head with 34-1 long shot Lyphard's Ridge. "I knew they were going pretty fast," Randy told Kim Brazzel of the *Arkansas Democrat-Gazette*. "I thought that as fast as they were going that they would come back a little. I decided to sit on my horse chilly and when I asked him to run, at about the three-sixteenths pole, he went on by them." Bolshoi Boy had to work to do so as Lyphard's Ridge fought gamely to the wire despite his earlier speed duel. Bolshoi Boy prevailed by three-quarters of a length and paid $4.20 to win.

Randy was shooting for six wins in the tenth race but finished third.

Randy won two more Gulfstream stakes on Skip Trial, the $50,000 Fort Lauderdale and the $50,000 Olympic Handicap. The day before the Fort Lauderdale, Randy was at Aqueduct, taking the $50,000 Best Turn Stakes on Java Gold, who would go on to take both the Grade 1 Whitney Handicap and the Grade 1 Travers with Pat Day. Randy also won the $250,000 Grade 2 Carter Handicap on the magnificent speedy filly Pine Tree Lane. Doubles Partner won two stakes under Randy: the $50,000 Pearl Necklace Stakes at Laurel Park in Maryland and the $50,000 Sweet Tooth Stakes at Belmont Park on July 11. On that same day at Belmont, Randy rode Dance of Life to capture the $150,000 Grade 2 Tidal Handicap.

Randy's sixty-one victories in the 1987 Belmont Park spring/summer meet gave him his second New York riding title in less than a year. He could have had sixty-two had his horse not been disqualified after winning the Grade 1 Man o' War Stakes. At the time, Pat Day had first call on two outstanding grass horses in

New York, Dance of Life, trained by Mack Miller, and Theatrical, trained by Billy Mott. Randy had second call on both. "Whichever Pat Day rode, I rode the other," Randy explains. "Pat Day could choose between the two. I was working both of them. Theatrical was working better, and he decides to ride Theatrical. I said, 'The only way I can beat him with Dance of Life is if I move before he does and box him in.'" And that's exactly what Randy did in the race. "I moved at the three-eighths pole before Pat moved. He saw me move and it surprised him. I won by three lengths."

Unfortunately for Randy, his move also surprised the stewards, who were concerned that Dance of Life might have interfered with Theatrical. After a ten-minute inquiry and objection, the stewards disqualified Dance of Life. "They took my number down," Randy says. "But I almost got away with it."

When New York racing shifted to historic, beautiful Saratoga Race Course later that summer, Randy was on the sidelines, serving a seven-day suspension for the Dance of Life disqualification at Belmont. That gave Randy and Cricket plenty of time to prepare for their second wedding. With Linda Lukas as the maid of honor, Randy and Cricket were remarried in Judge Larry LaBelle's Saratoga home on August 15. There were many horsemen in the crowd of 150. Randy's best man, Joe Riccelli, hosted the reception for Randy and Cricket. Riccelli operates Riccelli Enterprises and its fleet of four hundred trucks out of North Syracuse, New York. Though he owns Thoroughbreds, Riccelli met Randy when they were fishing. "Since then, we became best friends," Riccelli says. "Randy is the toughest kid I ever met in my life. I don't think I could face the challenges he faced."

Randy had help: Cricket. Randy gave her a mink coat and a Rolex as wedding presents. "I was so excited we got together again," Randy exclaims.

Later in August, in one of the most competitive runnings of the $1 million Grade 1 Travers Stakes in its 141-year history, Randy rode Polish Navy to a third-place finish behind Java Gold and Cryptoclearance on an extremely sloppy track. Kentucky Derby and Preakness Stakes winner Alysheba, Belmont Stakes winner Bet Twice, and Gulch finished out of the money in the mile-and-a-quarter Mid-Summer Derby.

Six days later, Randy rode Fourstardave, owned by Richard Bomze and trained by Leo O'Brien, to take the $60,000 Empire Stakes for two-year-old New York-breds by 2½ lengths. Though Randy never rode him again, Fourstardave won at least one race at Saratoga for the next seven years. Of all the records in racing, his may never be touched: a horse winning a race at Saratoga for eight consecutive years.

The next day, Randy won the Grade 1 $150,000 Hopeful Stakes for two-year-olds on Crusader Sword.

Racing moved to Belmont Park, where, while facing older horses for the first time, Polish Navy defeated Gulch by three-quarters of a length in the $595,000 Grade 1 Woodward Stakes on September 6. Crème Fraiche was third, just a neck behind Gulch, and Bet Twice finished sixth in the field of nine as Randy won the biggest purse of his career. Less than three months later, Randy topped that when he won the $1 million Grade 1 Breeders' Cup Distaff at Hollywood Park on Sacahuista, whom he previously had ridden to victory in the Grade 1 Spinster Stakes at Keeneland.

Randy's final stakes win in 1987 was a three-horse thriller at Hialeah on December 26, the $175,000 Grade 1 Widener Handicap. In a three-horse photo finish, Randy and Personal Flag edged Jade Hunter by a nose with Entitled To just a head behind in third and Crème Fraiche fourth. "I thought my horse had won, but I wasn't sure since I wasn't standing right on the finish line," Shug McGaughey, Personal Flag's trainer, said. Randy, who had arrived in south Florida the night before, on Christmas, said he was concerned sitting off the lead on the backstretch. "The speed didn't seem to be coming back, and I was worried." Personal Flag and Crème Fraiche, carrying four pounds less than Personal Flag, who was the 123-pound highweight, moved together on the far turn, but Crème Fraiche could not sustain his move. Personal Flag provided Randy with his thirtieth stakes victory in 1987, and for good measure Randy won the following race on Seeking the Gold, who made a spectacular debut for McGaughey, winning a maiden race by twelve lengths as the 4-5 favorite.

Though his 1,370 mounts in 1987 were thirty-one less than the year before, Randy won 242, eighteen more races than a year earlier. He just missed a second consecutive $8 million season in earnings at $7,937,455, eighth highest nationally. Randy had successfully transitioned from quantity to quality, and that would continue through 1988, when he captured thirty-nine stakes, eleven of them

Grade 1s. But he could not keep all his mounts, even as the horses won with Randy aboard for the first time.

Randy had been impressed with a young trainer, Pat Byrne, who opened his own stable after working for Howie Tesher. "I liked the kid and the way he handled business," Randy says. "When he was getting started, I breezed a lot of horses for him." Byrne was delighted to have Randy on board: "His work ethic was second to none. At Keeneland, he'd breeze thirteen or fourteen horses in the morning, go home, then ride eight or nine in the afternoon. It's unusual. When you're at the top of your game, you slack off. He never did. He just loved to get on horses. When Pat Day rode, you'd never see him in the morning."

One of the horses Randy breezed for Byrne was a filly named Terri Nivas, who was owned by the late Marvin "Pete" Savin, a prominent businessman and avid golfer in Hartford, Connecticut. Savin named the filly for his daughter Terri ("Nivas" is "Savin" spelled backwards). "Pete was a wonderful guy and a big bettor," Byrne recalls. Terri Nivas made her debut at Belmont Park on October 18, 1987, under Nick Santagata, finishing fifth by 13¼ lengths at 24-1 in a six-furlong sprint. Byrne shipped her to Florida for the winter, and she began training sharply for her second start, a maiden race at a mile and a sixteenth. "Randy's like, 'I've got this race won,'" Byrne recounts. "Vintage Randy. Pete makes a huge bet. She opened up 20-1 and wound up second or third choice [at 4-1 in the field of twelve]."

During the race, Randy had trouble getting the filly to settle down. "She was very rank and she was trying to run off with me," Randy says. "I stuck her behind horses. I finally got her off the bit [less anxious]." A novice could tell Randy had a lot of horse left. "Randy's on this filly with a ton of horse covered up," Byrne says. "He actually rode a super race. In the interim, it looks like she can win the race easily." But sitting behind horses, Randy had nowhere to go, until he saw an opening on the inside in deep stretch and shot Terri Nivas through. She finished in a tight photo with So Rarely.

"She wins by a nose, but it was so close," Byrne recalls. "Going down the elevator, I said, 'Boss [Pete], what do you think? It's awful close.'" About then, Byrne noticed Savin's face turning blue. "He was getting ready to have a heart attack, which he did. Pete was crazy, livid mad. He felt the filly should have won by three or four lengths."

But she had won the race. In the winner's circle, Randy asks Byrne, "Where's Pete?" Byrne told Randy he had gone to the hospital. The next morning, Randy stopped by Byrne's barn and called Savin at the hospital. "Pete fired him," Byrne says.

It didn't matter. Terri Nivas only raced three more times, finishing fourth, second, and third. Byrne went on to train two two-year-old champions in 1997, the colt Favorite Trick, who was also named Horse of the Year after completing an unblemished eight-for-eight campaign by winning the Breeders' Cup Juvenile by 5½ lengths, and the filly Countess Diana, who won the Breeders' Cup Juvenile Filly by 8½ lengths, her fifth victory in six starts that year.

More than twenty years later, Randy still sounds a bit incredulous about losing the mount on Terri Nivas, saying, "He wanted a different rider." But most of Randy's clients did not, especially in 1988.

On Friday, March 4, Randy thought he was going to have a good weekend at Gulfstream Park. He swept both divisions of the Fort Lauderdale Stakes, first on Lordalik for Hall of Fame trainer Bobby Frankel and then on Kings River for Billy Mott. They would be the first two of his eleven stakes victories that month.

The next day he became the first jockey ever to win four stakes in a single day. Two of the four were improbable for many reasons. After winning the second division of the Davona Dale Stakes on Cadillacing for McGaughey, Randy boarded another of McGaughey's horses, unbeaten Seeking the Gold, in his stakes debut in the $58,500 Swale Stakes. Seeking the Gold had easily won a maiden debut and two allowance races—all at odds-on—and was so spectacular doing it that he went off the 3-5 favorite in the Swale against six other three-year-olds. However, Seeking the Gold almost failed to make it to the starting gate. Stepping onto the track, the colt noticed a cameraman on the track and wheeled and jumped on top of the inside rail. Randy jumped off. Then Seeking the Gold was helped off the rail and returned to the paddock.

"Shug was so upset," Randy says. "He took his jacket off and threw it to the ground. I said, 'Shug, he's going to be all right. He didn't panic.'" Most Thoroughbreds, especially young, inexperienced ones, would have panicked over the cameraman incident. But Randy was correct. Seeking the Gold was okay.

McGaughey re-saddled Seeking the Gold, and he won the Swale Stakes by a neck, getting seven furlongs in a blazing 1:21⅗, less than a second off the track record. That made him four-for-four lifetime and thrust him into the Kentucky Derby picture.

Randy's circuitous route to ride 32-1 long shot Brian's Time for Hall of Fame trainer John Veitch in the $547,176 Grade 1 Florida Derby, the next race, is remarkable. Randy rode Brian's Time only because he had lost the mount on another top three-year-old, Notebook, trained by D. Wayne Lukas. With Randy aboard, Notebook was nosed by Forty Niner, the 1987 Two-Year-Old Champion and the early favorite for the 1988 Kentucky Derby, in the Fountain of Youth Stakes. Lukas decided to bring in Laffit Pincay, Jr., from California to ride Notebook in the Florida Derby. That freed Randy for another horse.

When Brian's Time's regular rider, Jerry Bailey, decided to ride at Oaklawn Park that spring, Brian's Time needed another jockey for the Florida Derby. With Bailey out of town, Veitch reached out to Randy, who was more than happy to sign on aboard the horse, who had closed strongly to finish fourth in the shorter Fountain of Youth Stakes behind Notebook. Randy relates, "I jumped on him."

Brian's Time, a deep closer, joined the Kentucky Derby dialogue with a furious rally from next to last in the field of ten in the Florida Derby to overtake Forty Niner by a neck. Notebook was third, three lengths farther back. Ruhlman, the favorite in the race, finished eighth.

By winning the Swale for McGaughey and the Florida Derby for Veitch, Randy had two leading candidates for the Kentucky Derby, the one race he had been hoping to win since he was eight years old. Brian's Time's winning time of 1:49⅖ was decidedly slow, raising the question of which horse Randy would ride if both made it to Kentucky. Randy was politically correct about the issue. "I don't want to answer that because I don't compare colts," Randy told *Lexington Herald-Leader* columnist Billy Reed. "Both ran super. Both were very impressive. They're two nice horses."

Reed asked Veitch if he would stick with Randy, who had never ridden Brian's Time before. "I would think the question should be whether Romero will stick with me, considering the way Seeking the Gold ran," Veitch responded.

Today, Randy marvels at the elements that got him up on Brian's Time that day: "It goes to show you about these things. They take riders off, but sometimes it works out the other way and you can come back and beat them. That's what I love."

The Florida Derby was not Randy's final winner that afternoon. Native Mommy took the second division of the Buckram Oak Handicap, Randy's fourth stakes win in a single day.

Randy, who could have ridden Gulch or Risen Star (who would go on to win the Preakness and Belmont Stakes), wound up riding Seeking the Gold in the 1988 Kentucky Derby for McGaughey instead of Brian's Time, whom Randy had ridden to a second-place finish in the Jim Beam Stakes. Before Randy could decide between the two mounts, Veitch made his own decision. He felt he should get another jockey who could commit to riding Brian's Time in the Derby. Angel Cordero, Jr., was happy to oblige. "I'd love to have Randy, but it's just a thing that I can't take a chance with," Veitch told Billy Reed. "Cordero will be a very good replacement."

Seeking the Gold, who had finished second by three-quarters of a length as the 3-5 favorite in the Gotham Stakes—his first defeat—finished second by a length and a half to Private Terms in the Wood Memorial. In the Derby, Seeking the Gold finished seventh by 5¼ lengths to Winning Colors, who defeated Forty Niner by a neck. It matched Randy's best finish in the Run for the Roses. Two years earlier, Fobby Forbes, whom Randy had previously ridden to victory in the $200,000 Garden State Stakes, was also seventh.

Brian's Time finished sixth in the 1988 Derby under Cordero, three-quarters of a length ahead of Seeking the Gold. It was the only race in his career that Seeking the Gold failed to finish first or second. He would end his career with eight wins and six seconds in fifteen lifetime starts and more than $2.3 million in earnings.

After the Derby, Randy was replaced on Seeking the Gold by Pat Day, who rode the colt in all but one of his final eight starts. "Shug wanted to make a change," Randy says. "It was fine with me. He told me about it. It's a business. You do your job and it's fine."

Regardless, Randy continued his momentum in the spring and summer. On consecutive June afternoons at Belmont Park, Randy won the Grade 1 $200,000 Hempstead Handicap on Personal Ensign and the Grade 2 $100,000 Nassau County Handicap on her full brother, Personal Flag. At Saratoga, Randy added three more Grade 1 stakes: the $250,000 Whitney Handicap with Personal Ensign, the $100,000 Bernard Baruch Handicap on My Big Boy, and the $200,000 Spinaway with Seattle Meteor. In winning the Bernard Baruch for McGaughey, My Big Boy scored by half a length over heavily favored

Steinlen, who had just won the Arlington Million. "I saved ground on all the turns so I could make that one run with him," Randy told Matt Graves, the sports editor of the *Albany Times-Union*.

At Belmont Park, Randy won four more Grade 1 stakes: the $100,000 Gazelle Handicap on Classic Crown, the $100,000 Maskette and the $300,000 Beldame Stakes on Personal Ensign, and the $200,000 Vosburgh Stakes on Mining. He also won the $100,000 Grade 2 Queen Elizabeth Stakes on Love You by Heart at Keeneland.

There was not a hotter jockey in the world than Randy heading into the 1988 Breeders' Cup at Churchill Downs. But that had not helped Mining or Seattle Meteor.

15

A Game of Inches

How can two thousand-pound Thoroughbreds race a mile and an eighth and cross the finish line so close together that a photo is required to determine which of them finished first? How can they race 5,940 feet and finish a fraction of an inch apart? Hundreds of thousands of dollars in purse money, millions more in future breeding potential, millions of dollars wagered, awards, fame, and recognition are all riding on inches. Margin of error? There is none.

On a cold, overcast afternoon at 3:18 P.M. on November 5, 1988, the stalls of the starting gate at Churchill Downs clanged open, unleashing nine fillies and mares fighting to win the $1 million Breeders' Cup Distaff on a muddy track. One of the nine was chasing history. Personal Ensign, ridden by Randy, was trying to become the first undefeated major American Thoroughbred in eighty years.

Randy knew that Winning Colors, the gate-to-wire winner of the Kentucky Derby five months earlier at Churchill Downs, was a dangerous opponent. "I knew that I couldn't let her get out of my sights," Randy explains.

It didn't take Randy long to realize that Personal Ensign was having trouble on the gooey track surface. "She broke okay, but she was slipping," Randy describes. That was not the only problem. On the first turn, the horse immediately inside of Personal Ensign, Sham Say, who was ridden by Jacinto Vasquez, starting drifting wide, forcing Personal Ensign even wider. "I hollered at him, 'Jacinto, man, get your butt over!'" Vasquez complied, but part of the damage had already been done. "I got her around the turn wider than I wanted to be."

To compensate for the loss of ground, Randy moved Personal Ensign to the inside. She continued to struggle with the footing while Winning Colors, who had bounced loose and clear on the lead

133

under jockey Gary Stevens, drew farther and farther away. Personal Ensign was in trouble. "I kept on urging her, and we weren't going anywhere. I got so damn worried," Randy admits. Randy smooched to her, making a kissing noise. That was not working either. "I wasn't whipping yet, but I was tapping her with my whip on her shoulder. Usually, she'd respond really quickly. Nothing. She kept on dropping back."

After half a mile, Personal Ensign was fifth, 8½ lengths behind Winning Colors. After three-quarters of a mile, she was still fifth, 8 lengths behind, with just three-eighths of a mile left. Personal Ensign's owner, Ogden Phipps, said to himself, "I've run her in the damn Breeders' Cup and broken her record of being unbeaten." Trainer Shug McGaughey, watching the race with his friend Rogers Beasley, said, "Not today. She's beaten."

Randy's wife, Cricket, was watching the race with her best friend, Linda Lukas, whose father-in-law, D. Wayne Lukas, trained Winning Colors. "On the backside going into the far turn, I thought she was beat," Cricket says. "I think everybody in the stands thought she was beat. I think everybody in the world probably thought she was beat that day. I was starting to get upset, and she was saying, 'Don't give up, because she's overcome a lot. Don't give up on her.' She knew how important if was, not only to us, but to the racing industry to have a horse that's undefeated. She was that good a friend."

Then Randy, driven perhaps by desperation, hit Personal Ensign left-handed. Personal Ensign responded the way most Thoroughbreds would, veering to her right. When she did so, she finally discovered what she had been desperate to find the entire race: firm footing. "I had to do something," Randy recounts. "I just couldn't stand there and do nothing. When I got to the five-sixteenths pole, I hit her left-handed to wake her up and get her off the inside. I lost ground to get her to the four-path [four paths from the rail], where the ground was harder. And she took off like a jet." Now all she had to do was catch the Kentucky Derby winner six lengths in front of her. "I never did give up on her," Randy continues. "I always believed she was a champion, and I rode her that way. But I was very scared. I'd be lying if I told you I wasn't."

Personal Ensign, as well as Goodbye Halo, began cutting into Winning Colors' margin. "My mare kept running and Gary's filly started stopping," Randy remembers. Announcer Tom Durkin yelled, "Here comes Personal Ensign unleashing a furious run!" Randy was hitting Personal Ensign right-handed. Stevens countered by using his left hand repeatedly on Winning Colors. With a hundred yards left, Personal Ensign edged past Goodbye Halo. And still Winning Colors looked safe. Twenty yards from the wire, Personal Ensign drew even with the front runner. Randy stopped using his whip. "There was no more whipping," Randy says. "She was giving me her best. Why would I do that to get her mad? I said I'm going to hand ride her the rest of the way. If we win, we win. If we lose, we lose. We tried our best." One last time, Personal Ensign surged. "And we got up," Randy says.

Right after the horses crossed the wire, Stevens yelled, "What do you think, Randy?" Randy replied, "It's close, but I think I got you." He did. The official margin was a nose. "And then, all of a sudden, in my mind—and I'm not going to lie, I'm telling you the God's truth—I thought, 'This has to be an act of God, this filly winning today.'"

Cricket was not sure the filly had won. "It was kind of dark that day. It was overcast. The weather was terrible. It looked like, from where we were standing, she won. Everybody was saying, 'You got it! You got it!' At that point, they came and escorted us down the back way to the winner's circle. But I don't think any of us actually realized just how close it was until we saw the replay."

Personal Ensign, on the outside, edges past Winning Colors in the 1988 Breeders' Cup Distaff to become the first undefeated major American Thoroughbred in eighty years. (Photograph by Rick Samuels)

McGaughey still marvels at Randy's ride that historic afternoon: "Randy never gave up on her. When it was time to ask her and she went evenly, he stayed with her. He didn't hit the panic button and use the whip [early]. He kept her in stride and that was probably the reason she won. She kind of grinded it out."

The race was remarkably similar to another historic stakes, the 1976 Marlboro Handicap, when speedy Honest Pleasure seemed home free and three-time Horse of the Year Forego, carrying eighteen pounds more, got up in the last stride on the far outside under Bill Shoemaker.

Walking Personal Ensign into the winner's circle, Randy signaled to the crowd, holding up his left arm with his index finger raised, signifying his horse was number one. When he dismounted, he hugged McGaughey and said, "Shug, we did it. I'm glad it's over." Then he hugged and kissed Cricket and Randy II. "Mr. Phipps thanked me," Randy recalls. "He was not a man of a lot of words, but you could see it in his eyes. He was the happiest man in the world." Then Randy gave him his whip for a souvenir.

But it is hard to imagine that anyone was happier than Randy. Certainly, no one was more relieved than he. "I was so glad it was over. I couldn't take the pressure no more. It was eating me up inside. Everybody thought so much of her, which I did too. I sure didn't want to get her beat."

McGaughey, who was congratulated by Lukas as soon as the race was over, shared Randy's relief: "Thank goodness, it was over."

Randy did post-race interviews and photo shoots. He thought of going back to the barn, but he did not have the right credentials to get there. "To be honest with you, I was so exhausted," he says. "It took all the energy out of me. I was so weak. I just wanted to go home and lay down."

Later, he, Cricket, and Randy II went to dinner with Randy's friends Joe Riccelli, Carroll Angelle, Kenny Dunne, and Randy's brother Gerald. Afterwards, Randy could not sleep that night. "I was too pumped up," he explains. He had every right to be.

A compelling argument can be made that Personal Ensign was the most important mare of the twentieth century. After completing her racing career undefeated, a feat no other horse had accomplished in the previous eighty years nor has been able to pull off in the ensuing two decades*, she produced one outstanding horse after another and was named the 1996 Kentucky Broodmare of the Year. All eight of her starters won, including Miner's Mark, Our Emblem, My Flag, and Traditionally. Collectively, her offspring earned more than $3.4 million. My Flag, Miner's Mark, and Traditionally accounted for the majority of that purse money with six Grade 1 stakes victories by themselves. My Flag won the 1995 Breeders' Cup Juvenile Filly and produced Storm Flag Flying, who also won the Breeders' Cup Juvenile Filly in 2002. Personal Ensign, My Flag, and Storm Flag Flying comprise three generations of Breeders' Cup winners, an incredible feat.

Yet Personal Ensign will be remembered more for her performance on the track that unforgettable afternoon at Churchill Downs when she ran down a Kentucky Derby winner in virtually the last strides of her brilliant career. She never would have made it that cold afternoon without the jockey who knew her so well, her rider who believed in her so much that he could stay cool and focused when panic threatened to intrude. "She ran the best race of her life and I rode the best race of my life," Randy declares.

He will forever have the gratitude of Shug McGaughey, who remains Randy's good friend. "I think he's a remarkable guy," McGaughey says. "I'm really proud of him. We went though something together that nobody went through in a hundred years."

*Author's Note: In 2009, Zenyatta surpassed Personal Ensign's record. By becoming the first mare to win the Breeders' Cup Classic, she improved her lifetime record to fourteen-for-fourteen. However, Zenyatta's connections decided to race her in 2010, risking her undefeated record.

16

The Magical Filly

Randy did not have long to enjoy Personal Ensign's dramatic Breeders' Cup victory. Two and a half weeks after she secured her place in racing history—and a day before he and Cricket left for Japan to ride My Big Boy in the Grade 1 $1 million-plus Japan Gold Cup in Tokyo—Randy injured his left leg again in a spill at Aqueduct. "My filly stumbled at the start of a stakes race, and I fell, and she stepped on my leg, behind my left femur," Randy describes. "I went to the hospital. They put six stitches in my leg."

Randy did not tell My Big Boy's trainer, Shug McGaughey, that he had stitches in his leg because he did not want to lose the mount, one that would take him overseas for the first time in his life. "I wanted to go," Randy says. "I wanted to ride. I liked the horse. He beat Steinlen, who won the Arlington Million. I thought he'd be competitive."

The horse was not the problem. Randy's injured leg was. "I couldn't bend my leg," Randy says. Randy instructed Cricket to take the stitches out with tweezers. "It hurt like an s.o.b." Cricket wrapped Randy's leg with an Ace bandage, allowing him to ride in the stakes. In a field of fourteen contesting the mile and a half Japan Gold Cup on November 25, My Big Boy finished fourth. "I thought he was going to win it," Randy says. "But he got a little tired."

Randy's leg bled a little through the bandage, but he had made the race. And he and Cricket had a great ten-day vacation in Japan. "They treated us like kings, hospitality second to none," Randy relates. "The United States can learn from them. There was a lot of publicity. It was a lot of fun. Everywhere we went, we had a car. There was a party almost every night. They never stopped feeding us. We went to Sumo wrestling."

Randy had finished 1988 with 174 victories from 1,229 starts—the first time in five years he was not in the top twenty-five nationally—but robust earnings of $7.96 million, eighth best in the country.

Then, on one August morning at Saratoga in 1989, for once in his accident-marred career, Randy got lucky. Incredibly lucky.

Randy started 1989 with nine stakes victories in just forty-nine days at Gulfstream Park. He thought he had a top Kentucky Derby prospect after winning the $75,000 Grade 3 Hutcheson Stakes on January 28 and the $100,000 Grade 2 Fountain of Youth Stakes, February 18, on Dixieland Brass. But Dixieland Brass suffered a career-ending injury when he bowed a tendon in the first turn of the Florida Derby. "He was hitting the ground fine in the warmups, but on the first turn, he bowed and I pulled him up. I thought he might have been a real good colt," Randy says. Randy's other graded stakes winner at Gulfstream was Love You by Heart in the $50,000 Grade 3 Suwanee River Handicap on February 4.

In the February 26 issue of Gulfstream Park's *Trackside*, Randy was profiled by Joe McLaughlin. The headline read: "Randy Romero: High Performance, Low Profile." In the article, McLaughlin wrote, "He is an all-around rider with no weaknesses and is so consistent that his percentage of wins in different categories such as colts, fillies, dirt, turf, sprints and routes are between 16 and 19 percent. In 1985, he won 415 races at an incredible 23 percent win average. . . . In each succeeding year, his money total [earnings] had gone up while the number of rides has gone down, which indicates trainers are putting him on their best horses to win the big-purse races. . . .

"Romero is a gutsy rider who does what he has to [to] get the job done, but not at the risk of endangering his fellow riders. He is one of the least penalized riders in view of the large numbers of mounts he takes.

"You also have to like the way he doesn't abuse a horse needlessly. The next time Randy is in the lead down the stretch, notice how he will check the opposition around him and gage his horse's ability to win so he won't take too much out of the animal. Many of his mounts come back and either win, or give a good showing their next time out because Randy has left a little in the tank at the end of the race."

As hot as he had been in Florida, Randy took his game to another level at Keeneland, where he needed just the first seven days of the spring meet to set a new record for stakes winners. His five wins eclipsed a record co-held by Eddie Arcaro, Kenny Knapp, Don Brumfield, and Earlie Fires. On April 13, Randy won four races, including the $50,000 Fort Harrod Stakes on Yankee Affair.

The next day, Randy won the $50,000 Commonwealth Stakes on Sewickley, who was trained by Hall of Famer Scotty Schulhofer and would win three graded stakes under Randy later in the year. David Perry's beautiful half-page color photo of Randy winning the Commonwealth on Sewickley dominated page one of the *Lexington Herald-Leader* Sports Saturday section under the headline, "Another dandy ride for Randy."

Randy's ride had been instrumental in Sewickley's three-quarter length victory. Sewickley was squeezed at the start then had to overcome trouble at the five-sixteenths pole. "Around the five-sixteenths pole, Irish Open was on the outside and I thought he was getting out," Randy told Christy McIntyre of the *Lexington Herald-Leader*. "I started to go up in there. When I did, he came over and I had to get out and go around him."

The following day, Randy set out to win the $250,000 Grade 1 Blue Grass Stakes on Western Playboy, a colt who caught Randy's attention the year before. In just his second career start he had finished second under Pat Day to Dansil in the Iroquois Stakes at Churchill Downs on November 5, the first race on Breeders' Cup day. "He was a good-looking s.o.b.," Randy says. "I was working him before that race." Randy pestered Western Playboy's trainer, Harvey Vanier, all winter for the horse but landed the mount on Dixieland Brass instead.

Western Playboy was a son of Play Fellow, who was also trained by Vanier. Randy would have ridden Play Fellow in his victory in the 1983 Blue Grass Stakes had he not been burned in the Oaklawn Park sweatbox two weeks earlier. In 1984, Randy again could only watch as a mount that had been promised to him won the esteemed stakes. He had been set to ride Taylor's Special in the Louisiana Derby but broke his femur. Randy sat out as Taylor's Special won not only the Louisiana Derby, but the Blue Grass Stakes as well.

In 1989, Randy rode Feather Ridge to a second-place finish behind Western Playboy in the Jim Beam Stakes at Turfway Park. Pat Day rode Western Playboy that day, but he had already committed to trainer Shug McGaughey's Easy Goer for the Wood Memorial and the Kentucky Derby. So Vanier needed a new rider for Western Playboy and Randy, whose agent was John Gasper, got the mount. In his final workout before the Blue Grass Stakes, Western Playboy breezed a half-mile in a sharp :47⅗ seconds under Randy. "I think he's got a great, great chance," Randy told Jennie Rees of the *Herald-*

Leader. "I've been watching the colt since that race at Churchill."

In the Blue Grass, Western Playboy survived a hard early bump by Dispersal to win, giving Randy his elusive first Blue Grass Stakes. "He got bumped pretty hard," Randy said after the race. "He's so big, he overcame that really well. I got him back together again, and he went on and won easy by two lengths." But Western Playboy had injured his hock when he was bumped by Dispersal.

Randy finished the meet with a then-record six stakes wins and his fifth Keeneland riding title with twenty-eight victories.

Despite hurting his knee the day before, Randy rode Western Playboy in the Kentucky Derby. He did not make an impact, finishing last in the field of fifteen as the 9-1 fourth betting choice to Sunday Silence. "Western Playboy was hurting from that hock injury," Randy says.

Randy was hurting mentally. He still had not finished in the money in any of the Triple Crown races, the Kentucky Derby, Preakness Stakes, and Belmont Stakes. But that would change after Randy and Cricket went to France.

In leaving the country, though, he would lose the mount on Summer Squall, a two-year-old colt owned by Dogwood Stable whom Randy had ridden to a spectacular eleven-length debut maiden victory at Keeneland for trainer Neil Howard on April 20, 1989. "I knew he was special," Randy says of the colt. Randy told Howard he would be out of the country in France for Summer Squall's next start, a stakes race at Churchill Downs. Howard told him that Charlie Woods would ride in his stead and that Randy would get the mount when he returned. Instead, after Woods rode Summer Squall to an easy victory, Pat Day got the mount. Summer Squall then won three more stakes, including the $200,000 Grade 1 Hopeful Stakes at Saratoga, to finish 1989 five-for-five. At three, Summer Squall ran second to Unbridled in the Kentucky Derby, then defeated him in the Preakness Stakes.

That made Summer Squall eight-for-ten lifetime with two seconds. He won the Pennsylvania Derby in his next start before tailing off a bit, winning four of his final nine races. Day rode Summer Squall in all but one of his final eighteen starts, when Woods again got the mount.

On the plus side, Randy and Cricket took their first visit to Europe. Randy's invitation to France came from trainer Pat Biancone, who would eventually move to Hong Kong, then to the

United States. Biancone wanted Randy to work a three-year-old colt he was training in France, Le Voyageur, who had an exquisite pedigree. His sire was 1977 Triple Crown winner Seattle Slew. His dam was Calumet Farm's Davona Dale, who won the Filly Triple Crown in 1975.

"Calumet Farm owned Le Voyageur," Randy says. "They flew me and my wife in a private jet. We stayed ten days." Biancone, who hosted the Romeros for their entire stay in France—they also spent two days in England—asked Randy to work Le Voyageur on dirt. "I breezed him, and I said, 'Man, he did great.'" Then Randy asked Biancone how many Grade 1 stakes the horse had won. The answer was zero. Le Voyageur had only won one of his six starts, and that was a maiden race. "I almost fell over," Randy says. Regardless, on the basis of Randy's evaluation, the horse was shipped to Belmont Park to compete in the Belmont Stakes when Kentucky Derby and Preakness Stakes winner Sunday Silence attempted to complete the Triple Crown against his nemesis Easy Goer.

Randy placed Le Voyageur on the lead in the mile-and-a-half Belmont Stakes and, while he had no answer for Easy Goer, who won by eight lengths, Le Voyageur ran the race of his life, finishing third, just a length behind Sunday Silence in second. Le Voyageur's third-place finish in the Belmont was reported on page one in the June 14 issue of *Paris-Turf*. Finally, Randy had hit the board in a Triple Crown race.

Randy thought he had a horse who could compete in top stakes the rest of the year, but Le Voyageur never came close to duplicating that performance. Under Randy, he finished fifth in both the $500,000 Haskell Invitational at Monmouth Park and the $1 million Travers Stakes at Saratoga, and then an extremely distant eighth in the Super Derby. Randy never rode him again, and Le Voyageur would win only three of his final sixteen starts, all in allowance company.

Sewickley more than compensated for the poor finishes on Le Voyageur, adding victories in the $100,000 Grade 2 Tom Fool Stakes, the $100,000 Grade 2 Fall Highweight, and the $200,000 Grade 1 Vosburgh, all at Belmont.

By then, Randy had hooked up with a magical filly. Jane du Pont Lunger was the sixth generation of Pierre Samuel du Pont de Nemours, who emigrated from France to the United States, arriving on New Year's Day, 1800. His son founded the famed du Pont chemical company. Lunger, the matriarch of Christiana Stables, and her husband, Harry, devoted more than fifty years to Thoroughbreds. Harry, an attorney and stockbroker, was a graduate of Princeton University and Harvard Law School who did legal work for the Delaware State Legislature and was instrumental in bringing pari-mutuel racing to Delaware and in the opening of Delaware Park in 1937. "At that time, for someone to say we're going to have legal racing was like you saying, 'Well, come on, let's go to Mars for lunch,'" Mrs. Lunger once explained.

Harry told his wife that once racing began in Delaware, he would buy a horse. He did, but the Lungers' first horse, Brook, was awful. "He never beat a horse," Mrs. Lunger recalled. "He ran and ran forever, but he never beat a horse." Nonetheless, the Lungers went forward, despite Mrs. Lunger's paradoxical allergy to horses. Their devotion prompted Pulitzer Prize winner Red Smith to devote his syndicated sports column to the Lungers on September 18, 1961. The headline on that column in one newspaper read, "Although Brook Never Beat a Horse the Lungers Decided to Branch Out."

They raced under the stable name Christiana, the seventeenth-century queen of Sweden, which reflected the Swedish influence in the colonization of Delaware in the 1600s. Mrs. Lunger, who continued Christiana Stables after Harry passed away in 1976, became an expert in bloodlines and took great care and a long, long time in selecting her horses' names, offering friends and family a stipend if one of them came up with the name she liked the most. "I seldom name a horse before he's two. That just drives everybody crazy, but I want to get something I really think is appropriate. I want a real reason. I want to know a horse's personality before I name it," she stated.

In 1960, the Lungers purchased a colt at the Saratoga yearling sales for $34,000 and named him Cyane, the name of the ship Mrs. Lunger's grandfather commanded during the Civil War. Cyane won two stakes and earned $176,367 before being retired to stud. Cyane's first yearling, a filly, was purchased by the Lungers for $15,000 at the 1966 Saratoga yearling sale. The couple, who had once owned a house in Jamaica, named the Cyane filly Obeah after a West Indies myth that speaks of a frightening Obeah woman and Obeah man who cast spells. She won $387,299 on the track and was bred to Northern Dancer, one of the sport's most prolific sires. The Lungers bred Obeah to Northern Dancer five times, but his stud fee had risen from an original $10,000 to $100,000 when Obeah was bred to him for the final time. Obeah would subsequently be bred to other sires and became one of the most successful broodmares of her time, as ten of her eleven foals were winners, including stakes winners Dance Spell, Broom Dance, Salem, Tingle Stone, and Pumpkin Moonshine.

Obeah was twenty years old when she was bred to another top sire, Deputy Minister. The mating produced a striking filly who was born on April 6, 1987, with a long, narrow white blaze down her face. A friend of Mrs. Lunger's suggested a name based on the legend of the Obeah woman and Obeah man. To fend off the sorcery of these evil spirits, natives would use a wand. The name Mrs. Lunger chose was Go for Wand. She sent the filly to trainer Billy Badgett, who had been an assistant for legendary Hall of Fame trainer Woody Stephens. Billy's soon-to-be fiancée at the time, Rose, would become Go for Wand's exercise rider and best friend.

Rose knew right away that Go for Wand was extremely talented, intelligent, and curious: "It's not how fast they go; it's the way they hit the ground that's so different. You can have your hands down on her withers [shoulder] and relax. You don't move. You just seem to be floating across the ground. Hers seemed almost like a feminine way of moving. And then you'd see the other side, when you ask her, and she just pours it on. And you know it's there. It's always there. And you're waiting for it." Rose did not mind waiting. She would frequently let Go for Wand stand immobile at the eighth pole and watch the busy people and horses around her. When Go for Wand heard an airplane, she would actually look up at the sky. Rose supplied Go for Wand with carrots and grew so close to the filly that Go for Wand would allow Rose to lay down next to her in her stall. There was a price to pay. Rose always had a carrot for her, and Go for Wand would nuzzle her rider looking for it.

Go for Wand had a different relationship with Billy: she tried to bite him. Maybe it was because when Billy saw Go for Wand standing at the eighth pole, he would yell at Rose, "Come on, let's go!" He did have other horses to train. But he knew this one was special.

On an August morning of the third week of the Saratoga meet in 1989, Randy lucked out. Though Badgett's regular riders at the time were Jerry Bailey and Mike Smith, he also had ridden Randy and appreciated what he had overcome to continue his riding career: "He looked terrible on a horse, but horses just ran for him, probably because he had a tremendous attitude as far as being happy-go-lucky. Nothing ever bothered him, nothing. You can see a lot of people just getting down and affected by things that happen to them everyday, on a daily basis. But he never got that. He was always upbeat and happy. He loved his work. He loved his horses."

Randy happened to be hanging out at the Badgett barn as Go for Wand drew ever closer to making her career debut. Billy asked Randy if he would breeze his filly five-eighths of a mile and Randy was happy to comply. Go for Wand, an unraced two-year-old, went out and worked five furlongs in a very fast :59 and change. She did so with incredible ease. "She was so strong," Randy says. "You could tell she was naturally gifted. She was that special one. I said, 'Billy, if she stays sound, she'll win the Breeders' Cup [Juvenile Filly].' He said, 'Don't be telling that to nobody.'" Trainers can be superstitious, too, and Billy—who was likely as excited as Randy—wanted to take things one day at a time. Randy calmed down and said, "I'd really like to ride her." Billy said, "She's yours, Randy." No other jockey ever rode the magical filly.

"Randy was just in the right place at the right time," Billy said in an interview years ago. "And I'm kind of a loyal person as far as that goes. He was so pumped up about her. I couldn't let anybody else ride her in her maiden race." Randy is forever grateful. "There were a lot of riders trying to take her away from me, but Billy was a man of his word. He was loyal. I thank him so much for what he did. There are a lot of people who wouldn't have. He's loyal, and he's a friend."

Though Go for Wand was ready to race late in the Saratoga meet, Billy opted to wait until the Belmont fall meet for her debut on September 14, 1989. The word was out that the Badgett filly could run, and she went off at 2-1 in a field that turned out to be loaded. Go for Wand and two other fillies in the field of nine would win graded stakes.

When Go for Wand stepped into the starting gate, she announced her presence. "She grunted like a hog, like she was psyching herself up. I never heard a horse do that in my whole life," Randy relates. "She did it in every race. I rode twenty thousand, thirty thousand horses. She was the only one who ever did that.

She was one of a kind. She thought she was a stud." She ran like a stud in her first race, romping by four lengths in an extremely quick 1:10⅗ for six furlongs.

Go for Wand advanced to allowance company, and on a sloppy track at Belmont Park on October 2, she whipped eight rival fillies by an extraordinary 18¼ lengths, getting a mile in 1:36⅗ with a final quarter in :24⅘. According to Randy, "She just exploded. I knew that day she was something that doesn't come around every day."

Mrs. Lunger had to take Randy's word for it. She had missed Go for Wand's first two races. On the day of her debut, Mrs. Lunger and her daughter got caught in a vast traffic jam driving from Delaware to New York after a crane fell on a bridge. The second time Go for Wand started, Mrs. Lunger was accompanying her grandson to the University of St. Andrews in Scotland. But the whole family saw Go for Wand's third start in the Grade 1 Frizette Stakes at Belmont on October 14. Sent off the even-money favorite, Go for Wand could not get past Stella Madrid, finishing second by half a length, though she finished 5¼ lengths in front of Dance Colony in third.

Randy and Go for Wand win the 1989 $1 million Breeders' Cup Juvenile Filly at Gulfstream Park. (Photograph by Barbara D. Livingston)

Randy had no doubt Go for Wand could avenge her defeat in the $1 million Grade 1 Breeders' Cup Juvenile Filly at Gulfstream Park on November 4. In a field of twelve, which included Stella Madrid, Go for Wand was sent off at 5-2. Randy kept Go for Wand alternating in fifth and sixth early, then went after Stella Madrid, who had taken the lead. Under eight right-handed taps with the whip, Go for Wand edged past. Billy screamed, "Hang on there, Randy! Hang on there, Randy!" Rose yelled, "Mrs. Lunger, she's going to do it. She's going to win." She not only won, but she drew away to a 2¾-length victory over Sweet Roberta, who beat Stella Madrid for second. Go for Wand's margin of victory was the largest of the seven Breeders' Cup races that afternoon and locked up the Two-Year-Old Filly Championship.

"It was the ultimate," Randy says. "I said, 'I got me another monster.' I was so fortunate to be a part of it. It was overwhelming. This is what you work all your life for, to get this type, and I got two of them. In two years' time, I rode the two best fillies in the world."

Would Go for Wand be as good as a three-year-old? There is no guarantee that a top two-year-old will be just as good at three, but when Billy visited Wand at her winter home in Camden, South Carolina, he was delighted. Go for Wand had put on about one hundred pounds. According to Billy, "You always hope they can make the transition from two to three, and she did that unbelievably well." He mapped out her three-year-old campaign, targeting three Grade 1 stakes: the Kentucky Oaks at Churchill Downs in the spring, the Alabama Stakes at Saratoga in the summer, and the Breeders' Cup Distaff, which in 1990 would be on Go for Wand's home track, Belmont Park. Billy related, "I put her through probably one of the most rigorous campaigns you can put a three-year-old filly through, only because she seemed to come out of each race as good as she went into it."

Billy selected the seven-furlong, Grade 3 Beaumont Stakes at Keeneland for Go for Wand's three-year-old debut on April 10, 1990. She showed her intentions with a monster workout, six furlongs in 1:10⅗ just six days before the race. "I thought it might have been a little too fast, but she had done that before," Billy said. "She did it so easy. She got back to the barn and she ate up good."

Six days later, she devoured the competition. Despite racing on a muddy track, Go for Wand dusted five rivals by 8½ lengths in 1:26⅖, breaking the stakes record by a fifth of a second as the 2-5 favorite. Billy was relieved: "Any time you win a championship, winning the first race back is always a lot of weight off your shoulders."

Three days earlier, Randy made history at Keeneland, becoming the first jockey to ever win six races in a single afternoon there, a feat Randy had previously pulled off at the Fair Grounds in 1984 and at Churchill Downs the year after. His six-pack at Keeneland, which included winning five consecutive races, could have been seven. Randy was named on the winner of the fourth race, Kasran, but had been committed to ride Luiana Baby, who finished third. Regardless, Randy broke the record of five wins he shared with Eddie Delahoussaye, Manny Ycaza, and Pat Day, who did it three times.

Randy's first winner was Banana's Kin in the second race. After finishing third in the third race on Operative and third in the fourth race on Luiana Baby, Randy won five straight races, beginning with Muffinette in the fifth. He won the sixth on Nancy's Place and the seventh aboard Intown for the Day. The eighth race was the $55,450 Grade 3 Transylvania Stakes, and Randy rode Izvestia, a striking gray Canadian colt, to a two-length victory. Randy's historic sixth winner came on Slow Fuse for trainer Bert Sonnier.

On April 14, on the undercard for the Blue Grass Stakes, a race Randy did not have a mount in, he captured the $109,950 Grade 1 Elkhorn Stakes on Ten Keys by 1¼ lengths over Yankee Affair, the 2-5 favorite. "My horse ran super," Randy told Christy McIntyre of the *Lexington Herald-Leader.* A year earlier at Keeneland, Randy had ridden Yankee Affair to win the Fort Harrod Stakes. Ten Keys' victory gave Randy a meet-high fifteen wins. Craig Perret was second with nine and Jerry Bailey, third with five. Izvestia gave Randy another stakes victory at Keeneland, capturing the $75,000 Grade 3 Forerunner Stakes.

Next up for Go for Wand was the fifty-third running of the $224,100 Grade 1 Ashland Stakes at Keeneland on April 21, just eleven days after her three-year-old debut in the Beaumont. Randy, who would win four other races that afternoon, walked Go for Wand into the starting gate as the 3-10 favorite in a field of just five. The mile-and-a-sixteenth stakes would be contested on a drying-out track officially labeled "muddy." Go for Wand romped again, winning by five lengths and missing the stakes record by just two-fifths of a second. "She was just pulling me out of the saddle, and she was going easy," Randy said afterwards. "She's going to be something great. She's something special."

The day after the Ashland, Randy traveled to Dueling Grounds, a new track that opened for a one-day meet in Franklin, Kentucky, on April 22, 1990. The area around Franklin was once a famous dueling ground. In September 1826, Sam Houston, who would later become the governor of Texas, severely wounded his opponent, Gen. William White, in a duel there. Dueling was outlawed the following year. In 1997, the track would be renamed Kentucky Downs.

The opening day feature race at Dueling Grounds was the $250,000 Sam Houston Stakes, and Randy had a live mount on Slow Fuse. So did Hall of Famer Jacinto Vasquez on Two Moccasins. Randy has a vivid memory of that race: "We had no starting gate. They use a rope to drop the gate and we take off. Here we go for $250,000. Now we're going to the wire and it's me and Jacinto Vasquez. He beats me. It looked like the wire, so I stood up. So he stood up, too. But it wasn't the wire. I look up. There's two hundred more yards to go. I said, 'Damn!' And I lay back down on my horse. Can you believe it? I beat him. I beat him by a nose.

"The next morning, I ask the trainer, Tom Arnemann, where he was going to run Two Moccasins next. He said, 'I'm running him at Pimlico in the Dixie [Handicap].' I said, 'Can I ride him?' And he said, 'Yeah.' And I won the Dixie."

Back at Keeneland, Randy was on the way to a still-standing record thirty-two victories at the Keeneland spring meet, his sixth title there. He achieved the record despite missing the final four days of the meet while serving a five-day suspension. Randy had been cited for careless riding after his mount in a race, Muffinette, was disqualified from second and placed sixth for interference. The final day of his suspension prevented him from riding on opening day at Churchill Downs.

The spectacular performance by Go for Wand in the Ashland prompted the question: since she was obviously the best three-year-old filly in training, could she possibly beat colts in the Kentucky Derby? It was an option that was never seriously considered. "Mrs. Lunger is dead set against running fillies against colts . . . so we didn't even nominate her to the Triple Crown," Badgett explained to reporters.

Instead, Go for Wand's next start would be in the Grade 1 Kentucky

Oaks on May 4, 1990, the day before the Kentucky Derby. A field of ten would contest the 116th running of the Oaks on a muddy track. Randy knew he was in trouble early in the race. Go for Wand, just like Personal Ensign two years earlier, was having trouble handling the track surface at Churchill Downs. "She wasn't comfortable," Randy said after the race. "Usually, she's in the bit the whole time, but she fought me today. Six jumps out of the gate, I knew she was having trouble." Many times, the class of a great horse reveals itself in a loss, rather than in an easy victory. Though not at her best, Go for Wand finished second by three lengths to Seaside Attraction, three lengths ahead of the filly in third, Bright Candles.

Time offers perspective. Running second by three lengths in a ten-horse field in a Grade 1 stakes turned out to be the poorest performance of her career, a performance other horsemen would snatch in a second. But she was never just another horse, and she proved it when she shipped back to New York for the summer. In her next five starts, she would win five Grade 1 stakes and none of them were close.

On June 10, a month after the Kentucky Oaks, although Randy had to tap Go for Wand six times right-handed, twice left-handed, and four more times right-handed, she prevailed in the $200,000 Mother Goose Stakes at Belmont Park by a length and a quarter over Charon. Randy told reporters after the race, "I had no questions or doubts about her. I know what kind of mare she is. She's a super mare. Billy has done a great job with her. All I did was steer her. I can't take any of the credit."

A cough prevented Go for Wand from competing in the Grade 1 Coaching Club American Oaks at Belmont. "I thought she'd get over it quicker than she did, but it lingered on for a couple of weeks," Billy told *Saratogian* columnist Mike Veitch. "I had to walk her for about ten days. I probably could have made the Coaching Club American Oaks, but it would have been asking a lot. That would have been putting an awful lot of pressure on her."

Instead, Billy focused on the Grade 1 Alabama Stakes at Saratoga—a stakes Mrs. Lunger had won with Broom Dance in 1982—and chose the traditional prep for the race, the $122,400 Test Stakes nine days earlier, for Go for Wand's next start. The Test was seven furlongs; the Alabama a mile-and-a-quarter. Go for Wand's performances in the two Saratoga stakes was nothing short of spectacular.

Go for Wand signaled her readiness for the Test when she drilled five furlongs in :59⅖ four days before the August 2 stakes. She would go off the 6-5 favorite in a field of ten. Go for Wand broke eighth from the two post, fell back to ninth for an instant, then dragged Randy along a clear path on the inside to engage speedy Forest Fealty through a first quarter of a mile in a quick :22⅕. "They just out-footed her," he says. "They were too quick for her early. I wasn't concerned. I rode her like she was unbeatable. Every time I rode her, I made sure there wasn't a straw in her path, because, when I did call on her, she would always accelerate. That day, she exploded. I wasn't going to fight her and mess up her stride. Go for Wand battled Forest Fealty head-to-head through an extremely fast half-mile in :44⅗ and took the lead by a head. Forest Fealty countered and stuck a nose in front midway on the turn. Go for Wand did not like that and quickly surged, opening a length-and-a-half lead.

Such a speed duel should have left Go for Wand vulnerable to the closers in the race, but she just kept going, passing six furlongs in 1:08⅕, just one-fifth of a second off Spanish Riddle's still-standing 1972 six-furlong track record. She crossed the wire two lengths in

Randy on Go for Wand before they captured the Grade 1 Test Stakes at Saratoga in 1990. (Photograph by Barbara D. Livingston)

front of Screen Prospect in 1:21, matching Very Subtle's 1987 stakes record, which was just three-fifths of a second slower than Darby Creek Road's 1978 still-standing seven-furlong track record of 1:20⅖. "I'll tell you one thing," Randy proclaims, "she tied a stakes record. If I'd have just hit her one time, I would've broken it."

So powerful was Go for Wand's performance that Screen Prospect's trainer, Peter Vestal, was delighted to finish second. "She ran the race of her life," he told reporters. "She got beat by the best three-year-old filly in America. The time is fantastic. She ran a heck of a race. I'm proud of her."

Screen Prospect, however, would not test Go for Wand again in the $200,000 Alabama Stakes on August 11. Only two fillies would: Charon, who had finished second to Go for Wand in the Ashland and Mother Goose, and Pampered Star. A crowd of 32,480 at Saratoga sent Go for Wand off as the 1-2 favorite over a drying-out track that was labeled "muddy" for the first race before being upgraded to "good."

Go for Wand was a lot better than good. Randy, sitting motionless on his brilliant filly, allowed her to take the lead and she coasted around Saratoga Race Course, setting comfortable fractions while Randy barely moved his arms. Through the stretch, Randy checked behind his right shoulder twice to make sure she was clear, then, right before the wire, stood up. She had won the historic Alabama by seven lengths over Charon in 2:00⅖, breaking Love Sign's 1980 stakes record of 2:01 and only four-fifths of a second slower than General Assembly's 2:00 track record, set when he won the 1979 Travers. Only one other Travers winner, Honest Pleasure, who won in 2:00⅕ in 1976, ever ran a faster mile and a quarter at Saratoga than Go for Wand. She did it under wraps. Returning to the winner's circle, Randy held up his left index finger, indicating number one. "Incredible," he says. "It was no contest. She was in a league of her own."

Mrs. Lunger again confirmed that Go for Wand would not race against colts when she announced that she would not run in the Travers a week later. "I don't want her to do it," she said. "She'll meet the colts in the stud barn in two years." She never made it.

When New York racing shifted back to Belmont Park, Go for Wand faced older fillies and mares in the $100,000 Maskette and $250,000 Beldame. Neither race was close. In the Maskette, Go for Wand overhauled Feel the Beat to win by 2½ lengths. The margin

Randy on Go for Wand in the post parade of the 1990 Alabama Stakes at Saratoga. She would win the Grade 1 stakes impressively. (Photograph by Barbara D. Livingston)

was not spectacular, but the way she won was. She won effortlessly. "She scares me," Randy said at the time. "She's so good. She's unbeatable now; she's a champion."

On the day after the Maskette, Randy journeyed to Chicago to ride Super Abound to a three-quarter length victory over his Kentucky Derby-winning stable-mate, Unbridled, in the $250,000 Grade 1 Secretariat Stakes on grass at Arlington Park. Hall of Fame trainer Carl Nafzger trained both horses for ninety-two-year-old Frances A. Genter. Earlier in 1990, Nafzger had provided one of the sweetest moments in racing history, describing for Mrs. Genter, who had trouble seeing and following her horse during the race, how Unbridled was about to win the Derby. The Secretariat was Unbridled's first start on turf, and he would return to dirt to win the 1990 Breeders' Cup Classic. Super Abound had won four of eight grass starts previously and received twelve pounds from his famous stable-mate. By winning, Super Abound became the first Minnesota-bred to capture a Grade 1 stakes, according to Bentley Smith, Mrs. Genter's son-in-law, who ran her stable and lived in Minnesota.

Randy also won a pair of $75,000 Grade 3 stakes at Arlington, the Arlington Matron on Degenerate Gal and the Arlington Oaks on Overturned, before Go for Wand returned to action in New York. Go for Wand backed up Randy's growing confidence in her, crushing her four opponents in the Beldame by 4¾ lengths as the 1-10 favorite. Her winning time in the mile-and-an-eighth stakes was a stakes record 1:45⅗, just two-fifths of a second off Secretariat's 1973 track record. It may have been the fastest mile and an eighth ever run by a filly in New York. "I never uncorked my stick that day," Randy relates. "I knew she was really running, but she was doing it so easily. If I would have pushed her at all, she could have broken Secretariat's track record. But it would have been stupid to do that with another big race coming up. I didn't want to mess her up. I thought that was her best race ever."

She climbed to the number one spot in the weekly Thoroughbred Racing Communications Poll and pushed her earnings to more than $1.37 million from ten victories and two seconds in just twelve starts.

Go for Wand would make just one more start in 1990: the $1 million Breeders' Cup Distaff at Belmont Park on October 27. Waiting for her was Bayakoa, the Argentine mare trained by Hall of Famer Ron McAnally who won the 1989 Breeders' Cup Distaff after her owners

Randy after winning the 1990 Beldame Stakes at Belmont Park on Go for Wand.
(Photograph by Barbara D. Livingston)

Frank and Jan Whitham supplemented her for $200,000. Bayakoa was named Champion Older Filly in 1989 off her nine wins in eleven starts. In 1990, Bayakoa won six of nine starts and the Whithams again put up $200,000 to run her in the Breeders' Cup.

The buildup to the race garnered unusual levels of attention in the media. The day before the Beldame, on October 6, Billy and Rose, who were engaged before the 1989 Breeders' Cup, were wed in Howard Beach in Queens. They planned a honeymoon four days after the 1990 Breeders' Cup. Word leaked out about Rose and Billy's honeymoon plans, and between that and the matchup of Go for Wand and Bayakoa, everyone seemed to be interested in the Distaff. A photo of Go for Wand reaching down to nibble a carrot Rose held in her left hand ran in the *New York Daily News* on October 23. The next day, an Associated Press picture of Go for Wand standing between Rose and Billy was picked up by newspapers around the country. That same day, *Newsday* ran a large picture of Go for Wand rolling in dirt. "It was just like a whirlwind, the attention that she got and that we got," Rose would later comment. "They said this is the human interest story of the decade."

The story was better than most people know. Rose was pregnant with the Badgetts' first child. "We'd been together for several years, and we were excited about it. We already had bought a house and we were planning on children. But we weren't going to tell anybody until after the Breeders' Cup," Rose continued. Rose galloped Go for Wand up until the Breeders' Cup, knowing that she might never have that opportunity again. "I knew, win, lose or draw, that it would be the last time. She was going to South Carolina. She wouldn't race again until next year and I was going to have a baby."

The Distaff would be the third Breeders' Cup race that cold afternoon at Belmont Park. A crowd of 51,236 braved the forty-three-degree temperature to be there. Millions more watched NBC-TV's coverage. An isolated camera was set up in Mrs. Lunger's box, where she and Rose would watch the Distaff together. Billy would watch from the clubhouse. "From the day Go for Wand broke her maiden, we never watched the race together, me and Mrs. Lunger," Billy recalled in an interview.

The first Breeders' Cup race that afternoon was the $1 million Sprint. Fourteen horses started, but only twelve finished. Mr. Nickerson suffered a heart attack during the race and fell to the track on the far turn. He never got up. Long shot Shaker Knit fell over him and was humanely euthanized. Shaker Knit's jockey, Jose Santos, escaped serious injury and returned to win the second Breeders' Cup race, the $1 million Juvenile Filly, with the undefeated Meadow Star, who completed a perfect seven-for-seven season as the 1-5 favorite.

One of the top contenders in the Distaff, Gorgeous, missed the race because she chipped a bone in her left knee the day before while galloping. That left a field of seven. All eyes were focused on Go for Wand, who would go off the 1-2 favorite under Randy, and Bayakoa, who would be ridden by Laffit Pincay, Jr., and would go off at even money (1-1). She would carry four pounds more than Go for Wand.

Starting at the two post, Go for Wand broke in the middle of the pack but quickly rushed up on the inside to take the lead with Bayakoa, settling in as a tight second alongside her. "I thought if Go for Wand broke well, I'd take advantage of it. I really felt Laffit thought I was going to follow him all the way around. But she broke good. I said, 'He's going to follow me.' I wasn't going to let him take me all over the racetrack and carry me out. I wanted to be in control," Randy says.

The two champions then went at each other head-to-head, nose-to-nose. Biding his time, Randy talked to his filly, then urged her at the five-eighths pole. Pincay did the same. At the five-sixteenths pole, Go for Wand had a half-length lead. Pincay was urging Bayakoa to give more. "When he came up to me, I moved away from him again," Randy relates. "Then he urged his horse again. I really had to set Go for Wand down, but I had some horse left."

Rose, watching from Mrs. Lunger's box, recalled, "Turning for home, I could see Randy had more horse. Then they both hit another gear. I knew she was going to be in it until the wire."

Though Go for Wand was still clinging to a narrow lead at the eight pole, the two horses' strides were absolutely synchronized. When they reached the sixteenth pole, Go for Wand was still in front by about a head. "Pincay was tapping Bayakoa on her shoulder and was moving in close on me because he knew he was beaten," Randy told Clark Spencer of the *Miami Herald*. "That's when I said to myself, 'I've got him. I beat him.'"

Then, in her next stride, Go for Wand reached out with her right front leg. Her ankle shattered when her foot struck the track. She fell, catapulting Randy over her neck, and tumbled on the ground, her legs flailing as she rolled on her back. She fought her way back up and struggled forward to the finish line, her broken right ankle swinging like a pendulum in a ghastly image imprinted for life on anyone who saw it. She reached the finish line and collapsed. Randy, who had landed hard, was prone on the track.

"After I fell down, I looked out of the corner of my eye," Randy recounts. "I was on my side, and I picked up my left arm, and I looked underneath my arm. I could see her leg flopping and I said, 'Oh, my God.' I put my head down. They picked me up in the stretcher."

Nine-year-old Randy II, watching the race with his mother in a clubhouse box seat, yelled, "Daddy!" when Go for Wand went down. "A guy next to me lifted me up so I could see over everybody who had stood up," Randy II remembers. "I looked over to my mom. She always kept her head down. She looked up and that's when we ran down to the track. When we got down there, they let us through, and we're running towards where Go for Wand fell. My mom made it to my dad. Angel Cordero [who had finished fifth on Luthier's Launch] grabbed me. He kept me away. He said, 'I talked to your dad. It's okay.'" In 2009, Cordero explained, "It looked very bad. There's no reason he [Randy II] had to see that."

As Go for Wand staggered the last steps of her life, outrider Steve Erck did his thankless job. After reaching her, he wrapped his arms around the filly's neck and steered her to the ground. "There's always a chance a horse might be saved," he told Jay Hovdey, then with the *Los Angeles Times*. "By the time I got her down, it looked to me like she'd broken both legs. But I couldn't really tell. All I saw was a lot of blood. And all the horse is thinking about is the pain— and getting it over with as soon as possible."

Rose ran onto the track to her filly. "I wanted to hold her," she would explain. "She was looking at me. I was trying to talk to her and I was hysterical. Then, when I knew what they had to do, I said, 'Okay, okay.'" They ended her pain by euthanizing her on the track.

Billy was not a stranger to unexpected tragedy. When he was working for Woody Stephens, Billy said experienced the tragic death of Swale. Eight days after Swale had added the 1984 Belmont Stakes to his victory in that year's Kentucky Derby, Billy walked Swale back to the barn after a morning gallop. "The horse was doing tremendous," Billy said. The colt was cooled out and led from the barn for his bath. Billy was sitting on a nearby fence, watching him. With no warning, Swale suddenly jumped into the air and literally dropped dead from either a seizure or a heart attack.

But this, in front of a crowd and while millions watched on television? Even when the brilliant, undefeated filly Ruffian snapped her leg in her 1975 match race against Kentucky Derby winner Foolish Pleasure and was eventually euthanized, the injury occurred on the backstretch. "The worst part about the whole thing was you never see horses break down where she broke down in deep stretch," Billy says. "If a horse is going to break down like that, they usually do it down the backside where they're changing leads, or on the turn. But there?"

Randy was in considerable pain, physically and mentally. "The happiest day of my life was Personal Ensign when she won, beating Winning Colors," Randy says. "The saddest day of my life was to see Go for Wand break her leg." Randy told the *Miami Herald*'s Clark Spencer, "The man who taught me to ride said, 'Don't fall in love with a horse,' but I couldn't help it. I fell in love with her. God almighty, what a great filly."

Yet two hours later, Randy, who had hairline fractures in eight ribs and a shoulder as a result of his fall, found the strength to mount Izvestia for the $3 million Breeders' Cup Classic for trainer Roger Attfield. "The adrenaline was flowing in my blood," he says. "I wish I never did it. I regretted it. I don't think it was wise, and I didn't do justice to the horse. I didn't do justice to myself. You look back and regret what you do sometimes.'" Sent off the 5-1 third choice in the Classic, Izvestia finished sixth, ten lengths behind the winner, Unbridled.

Back at the Badgett barn, Go for Wand's groom, Joe Schonstein, told reporters, "She's like my best friend. It's not like she's an animal; she's a person." Go for Wand's death also sucked all of the joy of winning out of Bayakoa's connections. She had won by 6¾ lengths. "They give their lives for our enjoyment," Debby McAnally said. Her husband, Ron, mourned, "I can't cope with this . . . That other filly . . ."

About that other filly, Go for Wand was buried at Saratoga, the scene of two of her most impressive victories. Recalling only the magical filly's public death robs her of all her victories. And if that horrible image of the Breeders' Cup is overwhelming, remember that she died on the lead.

17

Repercussions

Randy was sore the day after the Breeders' Cup but once again figured that his discomfort was nothing to be concerned over. "I wasn't hurting that bad," he told John Nelson of the Associated Press weeks later. "I guess I was in shock."

Randy, Cricket, and Randy II took off that evening for a brief, unplanned two-day vacation in Fort Lauderdale, where they had a home in addition to ones in Louisiana and Kentucky, before Randy was scheduled to ride at Churchill Downs. But that Monday morning, he was so stiff he called his doctor. He was told that the X-rays were negative and the pain was due to sore muscles. He visited a doctor in Florida and was given pain medication. Three days later, he flew to Kentucky to ride three horses. "I felt kind of decent, but I knew something was wrong because I couldn't pull up my horses," Randy told Nelson. "I decided then to stop and see what was wrong before I hurt myself or somebody else."

A second doctor performed a second set of X-rays, which were also negative, and the doctor advised Randy to undergo physical therapy. That did not go well. He told Nelson, "I called the doctor and said, 'I don't know what you're doing, but the therapy is killing me.' I couldn't sleep at night, and I was hurting more than ever." Randy went to see a different doctor. That one ordered a bone scan. The scan revealed he had broken eight ribs, one of them in two places, and had suffered a hairline fracture of the tip of his shoulder. "I was lucky I didn't break my neck or puncture a lung riding those three horses," Randy said to Nelson. "It could have killed me trying to ride." So, under doctor's orders, Randy stopped riding. He planned to come back to ride at the Gulfstream Park winter meet, then head to Keeneland, and finally return to New York. Even though he missed the final two months of 1990, Randy still finished twenty-second in earnings with more than $4.75 million.

During his time off, Randy followed through on a favor. In doing so, he reconnected with his roots. On the eve of the 1990 Breeders' Cup, Randy had dined with Bill Greely, president of the Keeneland Racing Association. Greely mentioned that he would like to spend a day seeing the bush tracks of Louisiana. Randy told him, "Sure, we can go anytime you want, Bill," Ed Madary wrote in a story in *Racing Action*. "Sure enough, he [Bill] called me around Christmas time. We met him at the Fair Grounds and flew down to Lafayette on a Sunday for the match races."

Randy; Greely and his wife, Norma; and Dell Hancock, the sister of Claiborne Farm president Seth Hancock, made the trip. "It worked out perfect for me, while I was healing up," Randy told Madary. "It was a lot of fun going back to the matches. It had been years since I'd been and it was really fun taking them with me. They couldn't believe it—they loved it." Greely sure did: "We went to a place called Cajun Downs, stood on the rail, drank beer, ate boudin balls and watched the races. I think everybody who likes racing should do this at least once."

Randy enjoyed his brief vacation, but when he returned to Florida, he had work to do: "I had to hire a coach to get back in shape. I was overweight. I had gained like five or six pounds." He worked diligently to get back in racing shape, but as he was nearing his return, Randy injured his right arm working out a horse at Gulfstream Park when the horse slammed him into the starting gate. That cost him ten days. Randy then worked a horse owned by Mrs. Lunger for Billy Badgett at Gulfstream Park. The horse suffered a heart attack and died but Randy, this time, escaped injury.

When Randy finally did return to racing, he struggled. For the first time in his entire career, he struggled—badly. At Calder Race Course on January 15, he went zero for three there before racing switched to Gulfstream Park. He won just one race at Gulfstream from his first thirty-eight mounts. That made him one for forty-one. "It was the first slump I ever had, and I took it bad. I came back too quick. I rushed back from all my accidents, every one of them."

Clark Spencer of the *Miami Herald* wrote in a February 11, 1991, story, "The slump was starting to take a toll on Romero's spirits. He smiled less often and spoke in somber whispers." Randy told Spencer, "I was expecting to have a real good meet here. I wasn't depressed, but I guess I still was kind of heartbroken."

How could he not be? Go for Wand was an eighth of a mile away from giving Randy a victory in a Breeders' Cup race for the fourth consecutive year. And Mrs. Lunger was planning to run Go for Wand as a four-year-old. Who knows how good she would have been at four?

Randy needed a big win, and he got it on February 10 riding Rigamajig to a two-length victory in the $50,000-added The Very One Handicap for trainer Richard Destasio. "I'm so happy," Randy said after leaving the winner's circle. "From the day the mare [Go for Wand] got hurt and I got hurt, it has been tough. I rode with a lot of confidence, and now, I hope to continue with it."

He could not. Six days later, he broke his elbow and almost all his front teeth. "This was the worst, the elbow," Randy says. "This was a nightmare." It was a nightmare that would last nearly eighteen months.

"I rode a filly on the grass for David Whiteley," Randy says. "There was a horse at the half-mile pole who comes out and hits my horse in the shoulder. He spins my filly out and I fell on my elbow." The accident occurred in the eighth race on a Friday afternoon on February 15. Randy was riding My Gal Shall on the far turn in the mile-and-a-sixteenth allowance turf race when she clipped heels. As My Gal Shall was going down, For You, ridden by Jerry Bailey, got tangled with My Gal Shall's hind legs and fell to the ground with her. Challenge Me, who was ridden by Chris Antley, was following For You and also went down.

Randy lay unconscious for three minutes. He had broken his left arm and several of his front teeth, which would be replaced with implants and dentures, and suffered a small cut on the bridge of his nose. Bailey, who suffered a bruised back, walked away but was taken to the hospital for tests, which confirmed he had only minor injuries. Antley also escaped serious injury and he helped carry Randy on a stretcher to the ambulance, which took him to Hollywood Memorial Hospital.

"I didn't sedate him because he was unconscious for a full three minutes," attending physician O.V. Carr told sportswriter David Joseph. "Neurologically, he was stable." At the hospital, Randy's condition was listed as "guarded."

"He doesn't even remember what happened," Randy's wife, Cricket, told Clark Spencer of the *Miami Herald*. "He doesn't even know where he's at right now."

Despite the initial scare, he was able to resume riding in less than three months. Three screws were inserted into Randy's elbow, and Randy returned to New York to begin working horses in mid-May. "I worked four hours a day in the gym five times a week. I just drove myself. I took a lot of pain pills and medicine."

Randy returned to riding with a new agent, Juan Dominguez, who replaced John Gasper. Gasper had picked up another rider, Corey Black. "When I got hurt, I understood that he still had to make a living, and he went with Corey Black," Randy told Fran LaBelle, Jr., of the *Daily Racing Form*. "We parted, but it was a friendly parting. We did well together."

Randy began riding again at Belmont Park on May 23 but won only one of his first thirteen starts. Out of town, Randy won the $60,000 Grade 3 Vineland Handicap at Garden State Park on Christie Cat, May 25, though he was still hurting.

Doctors removed one of the three screws. After ten days, they took out the other two, and still, Randy was in tremendous pain: "I [was] taking bottles of pain medicine a week. Bottles. I said, 'Doc, there's something wrong with my arm. I could hear it—click, click, click.' I could hear my arm cracking. They said they were the adhesions dissolving. It wasn't. It was bone against bone. I tried acupuncture. I did it for about a month. It helped. It killed the pain. But the arm felt like it was still broken."

He could only wince when he watched Hansel win both the Preakness Stakes and Belmont Stakes under Jerry Bailey. Randy had ridden Hansel to two victories in his first two starts for trainer Frankie Brothers in 1990. A scheduling conflict cost Randy the mount when he rode Go for Wand to win the Test Stakes at Saratoga the same day Hansel ran in the $200,000 Sapling Stakes at Monmouth Park in New Jersey. Pat Day picked up the mount, and Hansel finished third in the Sapling. Day rode Hansel in his next four starts but won just one of them, the $150,000 Arlington-Washington Futurity. In his first two starts as a three-year-old with Day aboard, Hansel finished fifth in the Grade 2 Fountain of Youth and third in the Grade 1 Florida Derby.

When Day chose to ride another horse in the Grade 2 Jim Beam Stakes at Turfway Park, Brothers needed another rider. He would have gone with Randy had the jockey been healthy. Instead, he used Jerry Bailey. The trainer asked Randy to offer Bailey his advice on how to ride Hansel. "Pat Day wasn't riding him right," Randy says. "Hansel was very timid. He liked to be in the race and be clear of horses. We went to dinner—me, Bailey, Joe Riccelli, who was my good friend, and Frankie. Frankie said, 'Why don't you tell Jerry how to ride him?'" Randy did and Jerry worked Hansel until he was comfortable on the mount.

With Bailey aboard, Hansel won the Jim Beam Stakes by 2½ lengths and the Grade 2 Lexington Stakes by nine. Though Hansel finished tenth of sixteen as the 5-2 favorite in the Kentucky Derby, he rebounded to win the Preakness Stakes by seven lengths and the Belmont Stakes by a head. To Randy, who had never won a Triple Crown race, it was tough to watch. "But I wanted him to win for Frankie. He was a beautiful horse," Randy says. Hansel then finished a distant third in the Grade 1 Haskell Invitational and second by a neck to Corporate Report in the Grade 1 Travers Stakes when he suffered a career-ending injury right before the finish line.

On July 5, a year after winning the Grade 3 Tremont Stakes on Hansel, Randy won the Tremont again on Salt Lake for trainer D. Wayne Lukas. "I broke his maiden, then I come back and won the Tremont with him." Randy describes, "I rode him with one arm."

Trainer Todd Pletcher, the Eclipse Award-winning trainer from 2004 through 2007, was an assistant working for Lukas at the time. He had known Randy since he was a teenager because Randy rode some of Todd's father's horses. "I've known him since, probably, I was thirteen or fourteen years old, when Randy was in Louisiana," Todd Pletcher says. "He was dominant. He was one of those guys whose wins were double the guy in second. He was a dominant force there. Then he moved on to the highest level in New York and did well. Nobody has gone through more setbacks than Randy. To keep coming back like that, to have that love of the game—you can't say enough good things about Randy."

But Randy could not keep riding this time. He had re-fractured his elbow in the same location. Then his arm became infected. He stopped riding after July 18. He knew then he would miss the entire prestigious Saratoga meeting. "Randy's elbow is broken again, and there is an infection in the bone," Randy's wife, Cricket, told Fran LaBelle, Jr., in a story in the *Daily Racing Form* of July 24, 1991. "If the infection has messed up the bone, we'll just have to take it from there. There is nothing definite at this time, as far as his career, except that he's definitely out at Saratoga."

With help from Jockeys' Guild director John Giovanni, Randy consulted New York specialist Dr. James Parkes. "He put it in a cast because he didn't want to do more surgery," Randy told Kimberly Herbert of *Blood-Horse Magazine.* With his elbow in a cast, he finished the year with twelve victories from 154 starts. The cast would not be removed until January 1992.

On a lighter note, in a lengthy story on Randy in the August 4, 1991, edition of the *Daily Racing Form,* writer Ed Fountaine described Cricket as "a pretty blond who could pass for the actress Meg Ryan." And with his off time, he was able to spend more time with his wife, as well as the rest of his family and friends. Randy's spirits were also buoyed when he was inducted into the Fair Grounds Hall of Fame. "You have to take the good with the bad," he told *Blood-Horse Magazine's* Herbert. "The Hall of Fame picked me up a lot. I did a lot of hunting and fishing in Alabama. Tony Foyt, A.J. Foyt's son, is a good friend and he took me deer and turkey hunting in Texas. I watched *Good Morning America* and *Regis and Kathie Lee,* and I worked with my son on his baseball game."

During this period, Randy's weight ballooned to 140 pounds, 25 more than his riding weight, and he began extensive daily therapy to get back in shape, working three hours a day as well as swimming and running five miles. That allowed him to begin breezing horses for Scotty Schulhofer, D. Wayne Lukas, Don Combs, and other trainers in New York in late March, even while he sought to strengthen his biceps. With yet another new agent, Cory Moran ("I was hurt so many times that nobody wanted to touch me," Randy says), Randy resumed riding in New York in late April, winning his first race back at Aqueduct on April 25. But he was still experiencing tremendous pain in his elbow.

Randy traveled to Churchill Downs to ride Sir Pinder for Manny Tortora, a Florida trainer, in the 1992 Kentucky Derby. He finished fifteenth in the Derby, but Randy did finally get help with his still aching arm. As Randy relates, "I'm in the Louisville airport that same night going home to New York. Laffit Pincay, Jr., is with me [he was going to California]. I'm almost crying. He says, 'What's the matter, Randy?' I said, 'My arm, and it's hurting so bad. I have three doctors working on the s.o.b.' He says, 'Come to California and I'll get you a good doctor. Go back home to New York. Get your stuff together.'" It was the best advice of Randy's life. "I thought my arm was gone," Randy admits. "I thought I might never ride again."

Pincay admired Randy's courage: "There are some riders who, despite all their problems, broken bones and sickness, know they have a job to do and they face it. Randy was one of those riders. A lot of riders would have just given up and taken some time off, but Randy liked horses and he liked to win. He loved to ride and did anything to be out there riding." Pincay could identify with that. "I broke my collarbone many times, and I always came back before I should have. I still had a lot of pain, but there were horses I didn't want to miss. Other times I was so sick from the flu and things like that, and I still rode because I didn't want to miss anything. I felt sorry when he got burned and then he broke his elbow. And he still came back. He had a lot of courage."

Randy went to California and stayed with Jeff and Linda Lukas. The doctors, including Dr. Robert Kerlan, who had previously operated on Pincay, operated on Randy's arm successfully, but they had difficulty believing Randy had ridden in the Kentucky Derby before the surgery. "The doctor says, 'There ain't no way you rode in the Derby,'" Randy shares. "I said, 'Doc, I did.' He said, 'No way, Randy. You know what you got? Instead of your arm bending at the joint, it's bending at the break. You wore out three inches of bone in your arm.'"

Before the operation, the doctors told Randy he might lose his arm. The surgery lasted four hours. "They took three inches of bone out of my left hip, and put it in my arm with plates and screws," Randy describes. The surgery was successful, but had it been performed immediately after he broke his elbow, he would have missed five to six months instead of eighteen months.

Cricket spoke of Randy's frustration, one she shared with her husband, in a May 8, 1992, story by Fran LaBelle, Jr., in the *Daily Racing Form*. Cricket said, "Neither Dr. Kerlan or his associate [Dr. Robert Chandler], could believe that the surgery wasn't done before.

"Randy heard this and was just devastated. He followed the advice of the other doctors because he really wants to make it back. And I've got two releases staring me in the face telling me

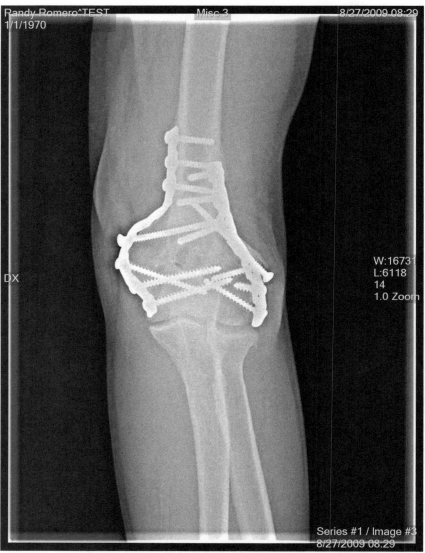

An X-ray of the elbow injury that ultimately ruined Randy's career. With three pins in his arm and the bone not yet healed, doctors gave him a release to continue to ride. This premature release lead to the wearing off of three inches of bone at the break.

that his arm was completely healed. All of a sudden, he goes to a doctor who is considered the best, and he tells him he should have had surgery last year.

"He won't be back until he's healed. . . . It's not fair because Randy did everything he was told to do, and now it's going to wind up costing him almost two years."

Randy could have taken legal action but chose not to. "They told me I could sue the previous doctors. I didn't want to do it. I wanted to ride. I just didn't want to go through the trouble. And I should have. I was finished," Randy says. "My arm strength was never the same. I started and stopped riding several times. It was hurting all the time. I took a lot of medication, which hurt my liver and kidneys."

Immediately following the operation, Randy stayed with the Lukases, and then he commuted for several weeks back and forth from his home in Garden City, Long Island, to California. "I stayed in Jeff and Linda Lukas's home when I was out there," Randy said in a September 6, 1992, story in the *Daily Racing Form*. "And I can't thank them enough for their help."

A month later, Randy was finally able to ride again, though he did not win a stakes race until October 25, when he captured the $80,000 New York Stallion Stakes on Rush Chairman Bill. That was Randy's fourth stakes victory in two years. Four years earlier, he had won six stakes in two days at Gulfstream Park.

Randy would do his best to make up for his dearth of winnings in the coming days. He won the $75,000 Grade 2 Young America Stakes at the Meadowlands on Mischievous Music on October 30 and then the $350,000 Grade 1 Brooklyn Handicap on Chief Honcho, November 21, one of three winners he rode that afternoon at Aqueduct. "I needed a day like that to show people that I'm willing and able to ride and can get horses to win races," Randy told Fran LaBelle, Jr. "Since I've come back, I feel that I'm stronger, and my sense of timing is better than ever. But it's not enough that you believe it, you have to have other people who believe in you."

He lost one of those people a few days before the Brooklyn when Cricket's mother, Shirley McKean, died. "She died of cancer and was only 57 years old," Randy told LaBelle. "My wife, Cricket, took it real hard, and I felt bad because she was like a mother to me, too. I really feel bad for my wife. She's been through so much in the last year and a half or so—her mother being sick and a couple of other deaths in her family and me being hurt. At the funeral, I kept telling my wife that she had to keep her faith. As hard as things are, it was going to change. We've had enough bad times; things have to get better."

He did his part. Slowly, Randy rebuilt his business, finishing 1992 with 30 wins from 298 starts and earnings of just more than $1.2 million. He headed for Florida for the winter, hoping for a better year in 1993.

18

Oh, Brother

Randy and Gerald Romero are more than brothers. They are friends, and they have been their whole lives. "My brother and me are real tight," Randy says. "After my grandfather died [in 1978], he was like a father to me. I talk to Gerald every day." That is easy to do. Today, the brothers live in the same apartment complex in Metairie, a suburb just outside New Orleans.

Ideally, Randy would like to train horses one day with his brother, who is three years older and the oldest of the five Romero brothers. Gerald briefly tried making it as a jockey, then began training quarter horses before switching to Thoroughbreds when he was nineteen. Midway through 2008, because of a dwindling number of clients, Gerald began working full-time for one of his owners, Mike Munna, who also owns a trucking/demolition company. In the spring of 2009, Gerald abandoned construction to become Munna's full-time private trainer. Gerald is also a partner on three broodmares, three weanlings, and two yearlings with his friends Nathan and Chris Meyers in Texas. "The business has really changed the last few years," Gerald says. "You have to have people that can afford the game. You can't have champagne with a beer budget."

Part of the growing expense of running a Thoroughbred is the cost of medication. Gerald continues, "I think that medication plays a great part in the racing industry that I dislike. If it would be up to me, there would be no medication. It's a mess. It's like chemical warfare. Back in the old days when I was training horses, you put your horse on ice and took care of him. They didn't have all these drugs. Years ago, you gave a horse maybe two, three months off a year. People don't do that anymore. I think medication is overused. It's gotten away from really taking care of the animal." Gerald and Randy grew up taking care of the horses they raced. They had to. Their family owned most of them.

As a teenager Gerald was a sharp enough horseman to realize

that his younger brother had incredible natural talent as well as courage and an unerring work ethic. "I've never seen anyone since he was nine years old devote his whole life to horse racing as he has," Gerald says. "A lot of Randy's life has been a roller coaster. He's a free-spirited guy. Randy was an aggressive rider, but he is a gentle type of guy. Randy's always been a very likable person, down to earth, no airs about him."

Like most people, Gerald marvels at the obstacles Randy has overcome in his career and his life: "He's a miniature Muhammad Ali. You think he'll never come back, but he always does. He's had so many comebacks.

"One of his greatest assets, and one of his greatest faults, was that he was aggressive. He took a lot of chances. He'd do anything he could do to win. He would cut the corner. Go through a hole with little room. Stuff like that. It cost him a lot of injuries."

Although, like Randy, Gerald is a dedicated horseman, he struggled early as a trainer. "I started with nothing, and I didn't know I was going to make it, either." His career took off when he and his new bride, Mona, who is now the executive director of the Louisiana Horsemen's Benevolent & Protective Association—where Randy's wife Cricket works—moved to Shreveport to race at Louisiana Downs in 1977. "It was the best move we ever made," Gerald states. "The track was just starting then. We were there the second year, Mona and I. We were just married. I guess it took four or five years of struggling before we finally got in with a guy who owned movie theaters in Houston, Dick Ott [who owned Pepperrera, Randy's comeback horse after he was burned]. We started claiming horses and we did very well together. When we got rolling, why, we got outside clients."

Randy, of course, was a direct beneficiary, riding the best of his brother's horses when he was in town. He had already benefited from Mona's father, Eldridge Hebert, Jr., who owned Randy's first and second Thoroughbred stakes winner, Oil Patch Pappa.

Gerald and Randy were doing well enough together that, at Gerald's suggestion, they went to the 1981 Keeneland yearling sale and purchased a gray son of Hail the Pirates, out of Proper Pickings, by Groton, for twenty-three thousand dollars. They named the horse Hail to Rome to honor their grandfather, whose nickname, "Rome," was short for Romero. In his first start as a two-year-old at Keeneland, Hail to Rome finished second at 9-2 under Pat Day. Randy was aboard for the colt's second start, another maiden race at Keeneland, and Hail to Rome finished second by a neck as the 3-2 favorite. "I dropped the whip," Randy confesses. That was Randy's only ride on Hail to Rome, who then won his next three starts, climaxed by his one-length victory in the Evangeline Downs Futurity as the 6-5 favorite. "It meant everything in the world to us," Randy shares. "My grandfather was my hero, and it was the first horse we ever bought. And to have him do well meant so much."

He did well up to a point. Hail to Rome won just one of his next nine starts extending into his three-year-old season, yet Gerald and Randy sold him for $250,000 to Hall of Fame trainer Jack Van Berg. Hail to Rome won just one of six starts and was switched to trainer Paul Grenon's barn, going winless in his final six starts. Getting $250,000 for the horse would have made their grandfather smile.

Two years later, Randy and Gerald bought MischiefinMind, who won a prep for the Louisiana Derby. But Randy and Gerald's most successful collaboration was on a horse they did not own: Dixieland Heat.

Once before, when Randy desperately needed a lift following his sweatbox accident, Gerald gave him Pepperrera, who carried his brother to the winner's circle less than fifteen weeks after he nearly burned to death. In 1993, Randy's career was slowly dying as he tried to rebuild his once-thriving business after missing so much time the previous two years. And once again, Gerald helped his kid brother.

There is nothing more intoxicating to a jockey, a trainer, or an owner than having a promising two-year-old win his first few races, raising the possibility that he will take all of them to the promised land, the Kentucky Derby, the following year. Leland Cook, a businessman from Corsicana, Texas, purchased Dixieland Heat, a son of Dixieland Band out of Evening Silk, a daughter of Damascus, for $77,000 at the 1991 Keeneland fall yearling sale and gave him to Gerald to train. Cook had claimed his first horse in 1987 with Gerald.

Dixieland Heat's debut came on the very last day of 1992 at the Fair Grounds and just about everyone knew this two-year-old could run. He would go off the 3-5 favorite and trounce his ten rival maidens by 7½ lengths under E.J. "Elvis" Perrodin, who would ride Dixieland Heat in his first three starts. "I was in Florida and Gerald was in New Orleans," Randy says. "Gerald told me he was a nice horse."

Dixieland Heat followed up by winning an allowance race by three lengths at 1-2 and then captured the $33,000 Lecomte Stakes by 2¼ lengths at 4-1. His first two wins had been at six furlongs, but the Lecomte was at one mile (eight furlongs), suggesting that he just might be able to stretch out to a mile and a quarter in the Kentucky Derby. That is when Gerald reached out to his brother. They decided that Randy would split any money he earned in Dixieland Heat's next two starts at the Fair Grounds, the $25,000 Risen Star Stakes and the $300,000 Grade 3 Louisiana Derby, with Perrodin. "That was only fair since he would have had the mount," Randy says. "We're fair people."

The Risen Star Stakes, which was split in two divisions that year, was named for the Louisiana-based colt trained by Louis Roussel III who won the 1988 Preakness and Belmont Stakes. Earlier in Randy's career, Roussel tried talking Randy out of shifting his tack to Florida and leaving Louisiana. "He said, 'Stay here, I'll buy you a house, a $250,000 house.' But I had done everything I could in Louisiana," Randy relates. Except win the Louisiana Derby. Ironically, Risen Star had won the 1988 Louisiana Derby under Shane Romero, who is unrelated to Randy.

Dixieland Heat was dominant in the mile-and-a-sixteenth Risen Star Stakes. Sent off at 3-5 in a field of seven, Dixieland Heat won by 3¼ lengths, making him four-for-four lifetime. "I was very impressed," Randy says. "He did that within himself, with ease. I was very excited. That it was my brother made it even better. I was so happy that my brother was training him."

The Louisiana Derby was next and a mammoth field of thirteen would contest the mile-and-a-sixteenth stakes on a sloppy track. While Personal Ensign's victory in the 1988 Breeders' Cup was his greatest ride, the 1993 Louisiana Derby would be Randy's signature ride, one that typified his persona and his success. It is a ride that neither Randy nor Gerald will ever forget. "If it wasn't for Randy, he [Dixieland Heat] wouldn't have won," Gerald stresses. "It rained like all get out. The track was sloppy, sloppy, sloppy. The horse is starting to make his run. He's sitting fifth or sixth. And turning for home, there's no room. And, finally, the last eighth of a mile, Randy manages to get him on the inside. Because if he has to go around [the horses in front of him], he don't win. Well, he tries to go on the inside and the jockey on the lead was pushing him into the fence. Don't want to let him through. I quit looking. I thought he was beat. And then, zoom! He goes right through and he wins going away. When he gets back to the winner's circle, he's as white as a ghost. I say, 'Randy, what's wrong with you?' He said, 'If you weren't my brother, I would have never did that.'

"The side of his boot was all white where he hit the fence. He was rubbing [against] the fence. The horse almost went over the fence. The stewards gave days [a suspension] to the other jockey [Bruce Prideaux], the jockey that tried to run him into the fence."

More than sixteen years later, Randy vividly remembers the decision he made in the Louisiana Derby in mid-stretch. "They were four horses abreast in front of me. There was no way I could go around and win the race. So I took my chances and I stayed in there. The rail opened up. And my horse pulled me up there."

But was there enough room to get through? And would his horse comply? Many experienced horses dislike passing other horses on the inside, and Dixieland Heat was only making his fifth lifetime start. Randy had to decide in a flash. "It was a quick decision, a split second, and I went through," Randy says. "My boot split in half from hitting the fence. The other jockey bumped me several times. It was really close and he [Dixieland Heat] was a baby. I didn't know if he had the courage to go through there. But he pulled himself through there. My horse got through and won. I wouldn't have done it if it wasn't for Gerald. It was really, really tight, the narrowest hole I ever went through."

Dixieland Heat had won by 2¼ lengths, giving Gerald his first graded stakes victory, improving Dixieland Heat's record to five-for-five, and stamping his ticket to the Grade 2 Blue Grass Stakes at Keeneland and, the Romero brothers and Cook hoped, to the Kentucky Derby on the first Saturday in May.

"We're heading towards Kentucky—that's where I told them we were heading when we started in 1987," Cook told Mark Gordon of the *Daily Racing Form*. "That's the way we wanted to try to go. We started with the claimers, but we were going to move on." Cook, who was recovering from a blocked artery in his leg, said of the Louisiana Derby, "I may get bigger wins from a standpoint of ownership, but this is the one that lit the rockets. This is going to always rank as a giant leap forward."

Would there be another in the Blue Grass? A field of nine entered

Randy on Dixieland Heat, who was trained by Randy's brother Gerald, and groom David Wallace. Dixieland Heat would win the Louisiana Derby when Randy courageously shot his horse through a narrow opening to remain undefeated in 1993. (Photograph by Barbara D. Livingston)

the mile-and-an-eighth Blue Grass Stakes at Keeneland on April 10, 1993, exactly three weeks before the Kentucky Derby. Bettors made Dixieland Heat, who was stretching out to nine furlongs for the first time, 7-2. Racing sixth early, Dixieland Heat was roughed up a bit. "He had a little traffic trouble, but it wasn't that bad," Randy remembers. Randy made a bold middle move and was third by a neck when the horses hit the top of the stretch. Dixieland Heat had the two horses in front of him beat but could not hold off Prairie Bayou. He finished in a tight photo for second with Wallenda, two lengths behind Prairie Bayou, who would go on to finish second in the Kentucky Derby and win the Preakness Stakes before suffering a fatal breakdown in the Belmont Stakes. The photo went to Wallenda, who had finished a nose ahead of Dixieland Heat.

But his third-place finish was better than it looked. Jennie Rees of the *Louisville Courier-Journal* wrote, "Even in the Blue Grass defeat, the Romeros were encouraged. The colt was roughed up early, looked like a winner leaving the far turn, only to give way to Prairie Bayou by two lengths and Wallenda by a nose. Dixieland Heat came out with the hair and hide rubbed off three of his heels despite bandages, a condition known as 'running down.'" Gerald told Reese, "You really have to be in the horse business to understand how much that bugs a horse. But he didn't stop. The horse fought, showed a lot of heart." Randy was concerned, however. "He actually had run down on all four legs," Randy relates. "It was bleeding through the bandages on all four legs. He was raw after the race."

It is easy now to look back and say that Dixieland Heat would have been better off skipping the Kentucky Derby, but opportunities to run a legitimate horse in the world's most famous race are rare, particularly for horsemen at smaller tracks with small stables. And this would be the Romero brothers' sole chance to win or even finish in the money in the Kentucky Derby together. They would be the first jockey-trainer brothers to have a horse in the Kentucky Derby since 1964, when Mr. Moonlight, ridden by Jimmie Combest and trained by his brother, Nick, finished seventh.

Eight days before the Derby, Randy and three of his contemporaries, jockeys Jerry Bailey, Don Brumfield, and Pat Day, went to the Lexington Thoroughbred Park to see a statue immortalizing them. Sculptor Gwen Reardon's bronze masterpiece depicts seven Thoroughbreds straining for the finish line in an imaginary race.

The jockey on the lead horse is Randy, who was blown away by the sculpture.

"They even got the horseshoes and everything, huh? You see that?" he asked in Robert Kaiser's story in the April 23 *Lexington Herald-Leader*. "It's got everything." Bailey was also impressed: "I think it's pretty neat. She did a great job. Everything looks authentic." Day noted, "That's my nose" when he saw his likeness.

The men's reactions thrilled Reardon, who had invited the jockeys to see her work. "I wanted to meet them, and I wanted to see how they felt about this," she said in Kaiser's story. Day, Bailey, and Brumfield were disappointed not to be on the lead horse, but Reardon put it into perspective: "There aren't an awful lot of people on this planet that are cast in bronze."

Though he would not race again for nine months, Dixieland Heat ran in the 1993 Derby. He drew post fifteen in the nineteen-horse field, was eighth early, and then faded to twelfth, beaten 14¾ lengths by the winner, Sea Hero, who would also win the Grade 1 Travers Stakes at Saratoga later that year. "My horse showed a little fight," Randy says. "His feet must have been bugging him."

Randy had decided to stay in Kentucky after the 1993 Derby and ride that summer at Churchill Downs, where he signed on again with agent Doc Danner. "I was out for two years and lost so much contact with my big clientele in New York," Randy told Jennie Rees in her May 5, 1993, story in the *Louisville Courier-Journal*. "I just couldn't get back into the outfits I wanted to get back into. And I got tired of the hustle and bustle. Life here is so relaxing. You get spoiled.

"The money is good, and you can ride good horses. The people like me here; they treat me like something special."

First, though, he returned to Japan to ride Lotus Pool, a horse trained by Burt Kessinger, in the $1.59 million Grade 1 Yasudo Kinen Stakes on May 16. Though Randy had ridden the horse in just one of his thirty-two starts, a sixth-place finish in his United States debut on October 13, 1990, Kessinger reached out to him because he had ridden at Tokyo Racecourse on My Big Boy.

Randy thought he had Lotus Pool in great position in the sixteen-horse field in the Yasudo Kinen. "I thought he was going to win, but he bowed [pulled his tendon] in his leg right before the finish line," Randy says. Lotus Pool finished fifth but only lost by a length and a half. He only missed second by a neck.

Randy returned to Kentucky but did not last the year. His business was slow—he won just four stakes in five months after the Louisiana Derby—and Randy accepted a contract to ride in Hong Kong for six months, leaving a day after he and Lady Tasso captured the $60,000 Audubon Oaks at Ellis Park in Kentucky on August 22. "I just wanted a change. I wanted to do something different. It was a good opportunity for me, one I got through Bill Greely [the president of Keeneland had been contacted by friends in Hong Kong looking for a rider]. They offered me $250,000, with $50,000 up front, and paid all my expenses. I did well at the beginning of it, but I was so far from home. I was by myself, and the only TV channel they had in English was CNN. I had to eat out with the owners lunch and dinner every day. They treated me very well, but I got homesick."

After reaching a fair agreement with his contract holder, Randy returned to the United States, having spent three months abroad. He had an unwanted souvenir: torn cartilage in his knee, which would require surgery. "A horse ran off with me during a workout and threw me," Randy states. "I saw a doctor there and they tapped the knee, removing all the fluids. But it needed surgery, and I didn't want to have it over there." Back home, Randy had the surgery in December.

Any momentum he had generated before he went to Hong Kong had vanished, and he struggled in early 1994. One of his first rides back was on Dixieland Heat on February 2, 1994, at the Fair Grounds. Wearing blinkers for the first time, Dixieland Heat finished seventh in an allowance race as the 3-2 favorite.

Randy had decided to race that winter at Oaklawn Park, hoping to stay the full season there for the first time since 1981. But riding mostly long shots, he won just two of his first thirty-five mounts. In the Grade 2 Razorback Handicap on March 26, he rode Dixieland Heat to a fourth-place finish in a field of eight on a sloppy track. Dixieland Heat had finished third in his prior start, the $51,000 Whirlaway Stakes at the Fair Grounds, under E.J. "Elvis" Perrodin while Randy was in Florida. Randy rode Dixieland Heat twice more in 1994 at Keeneland, winning the first, an allowance race, by a head in the horse's first start on grass before finishing sixth in the Grade 3 Fort Harrod Stakes, also on grass.

Randy planned to ride at Keeneland and Churchill Downs in the spring, at Ellis Park in the summer, then ride at Keeneland

and Churchill Downs during the fall and winter before returning to Oaklawn the following January. After Randy moved his tack to Churchill Downs for its spring/summer meet, he suffered a broken knuckle in mid-May when a horse threw him in a barn. Randy acknowledges, "He messed up my left knee, too, the same knee." Randy needed another surgery on his knee and announced his retirement. Then he changed his mind. "It was a premature move," Randy explains.

After recovering from knee surgery, he flew to Arlington Park in Chicago to ride a horse for trainer Bob Hess in a stakes race. Randy finished second but was disqualified. He received a seven-day suspension for careless riding and spent the time back in Louisiana fishing and thinking about his future. He had won just three races at the Churchill Downs meet. He was thirty-six years old, and he was, once again, riding in pain. At that point, he had endured twenty-three surgeries.

When his suspension ended, he returned to Kentucky and worked a horse on Monday morning, July 11, at Churchill Downs. When he got off the horse, he decided he had had enough. Even though he was listed to ride a horse at Ellis Park the next day, he again decided to retire.

"It [riding] was really hurting my bad knee," he told Jennie Rees in her July 13 story in the *Louisville Courier-Journal*. "I said, 'That's enough. It's time to stop.' I'm tired of getting beat up. My joints aren't working like they're supposed to. I can't perform like I want to. I go by [the barns] and try to hustle [mounts], and people see I'm having problems with my limbs. I don't want to put the trainers in a bad position. I don't want no hard feelings. They're trainers, but they're friends of mine."

In a telling quote in a 1998 *Breeders' Cup Souvenir Magazine* story by Gary West, Randy mused, "You never lose your talent; only your clientele."

Reflecting on his decision to retire, Randy says, "I was having problems with my knee. It kept blowing up on me. My business had gotten bad. I was getting depressed. I'm trying to ride and my knee is hurting. So I stopped riding."

Randy hoped to become a bloodstock agent, specializing in pin hooking, the purchasing of yearlings at sales, training them early the following year, and selling them at two-year-olds-in-training sales. "I only made one deal, and it wasn't a good deal for me," Randy says. "It didn't work out. I bought a filly for $60,000. I trained her and put her in a two-year-old sale, but she chipped her ankle in a workout on the day before the sale. I had to take her out of the sale. I trained her and she chipped the other ankle. I tried breeding her to Dixieland Heat and she couldn't get in foal. I had about $90,000 in her, and I gave her away to a friend. It was very frustrating. I decided to go back to riding again. It was real slow, but I got going again."

First, though, he had to have his twenty-fourth surgery, this one on his bothersome knee, in August. When that healed, he began working out with the University of Louisville football team in September. "Dr. Shea out of Louisville set me up with the team. He was my orthopedic doctor. I just worked with them with weights in the gym and I really enjoyed it. They treated me like a king. They were a lot bigger than me," Randy says.

He was fit to ride in November and tried to jump-start his career at Churchill Downs, then went to the Fair Grounds with a new agent, Rick Mocklin, who had been an announcer at Jefferson Downs in Louisiana. Randy's final, abbreviated numbers in 1994 were 25 wins from 417 starts and earnings of $847,458.

In 1995, however, his brother Gerald came through for him one more time. Randy rode Dixieland Heat in his final career start in the $104,000 Pelletier Handicap at the Fair Grounds, March 25, 1995, and they won the six-furlong stakes by a nose at 2-1. That gave Dixieland Heat a career record of nine wins, one second, and three thirds from eighteen starts and earnings of $426,749. As hard as it was to believe, it was Randy's first stakes win since Lady Tasso's victory in the Audubon Oaks at Ellis Park in August a year and a half earlier.

Randy added the $60,000 Fairway Fun Stakes at Turfway Park in Kentucky on April 2, then headed to Keeneland, where he had once been a dominant rider. In 1995, he rode twenty-two horses there without a single win. And then Randy showed one more time just how good a rider he was with big money on the line.

Randy landed the mount on speedy long shot Wild Syn, who was trained by Tom Arnemann and owned by his father, Jurgen, in the $500,000 Grade 2 Blue Grass Stakes. In his previous start under Julie Krone, Wild Syn finished third in the restricted Holy Bull Stakes at Gulfstream Park at odds of 5-1. In a field of just six in the Blue Grass, he would go off 30-1. Taking full advantage of the rail in the field of six, Randy put Wild Syn on the lead, then let him roll through moderate fractions in the mile-and-an-eighth stakes: a half-mile in :49 and three-quarters of a mile in a dawdling 1:13⅕. When the five horses behind Wild Syn went after him, Randy's long shot had more than enough left, running his final eighth of a mile in a snappy :11⅘ to complete the mile and an eighth in 1:49⅕, 2½ lengths in front of Suave Prospect in second. Tejano Run was third. Favored Thunder Gulch, under Pat Day, was fourth, beaten by nearly five lengths.

"Randy rode a beautiful race," Day told *Lexington Courier-Journal* columnist Rich Bozich. "He got away out there, settled nice and easy and waited for the rest of us to come after him. When nobody did, he had plenty of horse left and did a good job finishing. Randy has been through a lot. It's nice to see him get a big win like this."

Randy acknowledged how meaningful this victory was in Bozich's story: "It's been a long road to get here. I wake up every morning happy to be alive. You just can't imagine how good this feels. I'll be honest with you. It's been tough to get people to believe in me again." He never doubted himself, however. "I just needed to get myself right," he told Bozich. "My mind wasn't right. My body wasn't right. I needed some time away. But it was a premature retirement."

Suddenly, Randy had what he hoped was a live mount in the Kentucky Derby. In the field of nineteen, Wild Syn went off at 18-1. Randy rated him in second through a rapid half in :45⅘ and three-quarters of a mile in 1:10⅕. Wild Syn, though, had nothing left and finished last, 40 lengths behind Thunder Gulch. Thunder Gulch lost the Preakness, then headed to New York for the Belmont Stakes. Wild Syn skipped the Preakness and would go off at 13-1 in the Belmont Stakes' field of eleven, running without the anti-bleeding, potentially performance-enhancing medication Lasix. Again, Randy had Wild Syn forwardly placed early, and again Wild Syn had nothing left, finishing last by 38½ lengths to Thunder Gulch, who would also win the Travers Stakes and be named Three-Year-Old Champion.

Randy never rode Wild Syn again, and the horse never came close to winning a race. His best finish in ten starts after the Belmont Stakes was a third in an allowance race. Still, Wild Syn had given Randy a much-needed lift: "It got me going again a little bit, but I still didn't have full strength in my arm."

That did not affect his innate ability to recognize equine talent when he saw it. One morning at Keeneland, he saw an impressive young filly. Randy had journeyed from Louisville to Lexington to work Homing Pigeon, a horse trained by Harvey Vanier who was scheduled to run in a stakes race at Churchill Downs. "While I was there at Keeneland, I saw this unraced two-year-old filly, Tipically Irish," Randy says. "She was beautiful. Bill Cinsari, an exercise rider and jockey, was on her, and I said, 'Who owns her?' He said Bill Helmbrecht, a trainer and owner. I ran over to Bill Helmbrechts' barn. I asked Bill about that filly. He said, 'Randy, she's for sale. I want twenty-five thousand dollars.' I asked Bill, 'When are you going to work her again?' He said next week. I said, 'Can I work her? I want to buy her.'" Helmbrecht agreed.

At twenty-five thousand dollars, Randy could have afforded to buy her, but if her price skyrocketed, Randy thought his brother Gerald's client Leland Cook might be interested. And he was. But a week later, it rained. "So I couldn't work her," Randy says. "But I went to the barn again. He said, 'She's running next week at Churchill Downs and you can ride her.'" In the interim, Randy learned from Joe King, a clocker and outrider, that Tipically Irish had twice worked five furlongs in under one minute, exceptional for an unraced two-year-old filly.

Randy was aboard Tipically Irish when she made her debut at Churchill Downs in a 5½-furlong maiden race on June 4. She would go off at 8-1 in the field of ten. Randy bet $200 to win on her. "She broke dead last, and she won by a head," Randy recounts. She paid $18.60. Randy had just made a profit of $1,660 on his bet. It was going to take a lot more money to buy this filly who had just won her debut, suggesting limitless potential. "In the winner's circle, Bill said I had first shot. My brother was ready to buy her for Leland Cook, but we didn't know how much she cost. I told Gerald that I thought she was worth $200,000. We went to the barn and the owner wanted $250,000."

When Cook said he could not go that high, Randy found another buyer. "I approached D. Wayne Lukas, and Michael Tabor [one of Lukas's clients whose Thunder Gulch had just won the Kentucky Derby] bought her for $250,000," Randy says. "I made a commission when she was sold to Lukas." Randy never rode her again.

How good was the filly? After running third and sixth in a pair of stakes, Tipically Irish finished second in an allowance race, then she won an allowance race by twelve lengths, the $100,000 Kentucky Jockey Club Juvenile Filly by a length and a half, and the grade 1 Oak Leaf Stakes at Santa Anita by a neck. She went off at 9-1 in the $1 million Breeders' Cup Juvenile Filly at Belmont Park and was an extremely distant sixth to My Flag. Following a sixth in the grade 2 Demoiselle Stakes and a ninth the following February in the grade 3 Davona Dale Stakes, she was retired. The filly Randy had spotted on the Keeneland track had won four of ten starts, with one second and one third and earnings of $231,995.

There is an interesting note about Tipically Irish. In her ninth career start in the Demoiselle, she was ridden by Robbie Davis, her ninth different jockey in nine starts. After Randy, she was ridden by Shane Sellers, Donna Barton, Herb McCauley, Pat Day, Gary Stevens, Laffit Pincay, Jr., and Mike Smith. Davis was number nine. Sellers, her second jockey, rode her in her finale. As a broodmare, Tipically Irish produced Killenaule, a son of 2000 Kentucky Derby winner Fusaichi Pegasus who had four wins, four seconds, and seven thirds in twenty-seven starts and earned $238,934. Killenaule is a stallion in Indiana whose 2009 stud fee was $3,500.

Randy decided to ride the rest of the summer of 1995 at Arlington Park, where he picked up another new agent, Jay Fedor. Randy finished second on Upper Noosh in the Pucker Up Stakes of July 1 and second the next day in the Ribbon Stakes with Mastery's Gamble. "I'm looking forward to the day that I win a stakes here, and I don't think that's too far off," he told *Daily Racing Form*'s senior writer John McEvoy in his July 9 story. Randy was prescient. On that very afternoon, he captured the $40,000 Office Wife Stakes on Go Go Jack. Randy won two more stakes at Arlington and finished the meet as the fourth leading jockey, a huge leap forward.

On the road, he won a stakes at Fairmount Park, one at Turfway Park, one at Keeneland, and then the $112,800 River City Handicap at Churchill Downs on November 13. He rallied Homing Pigeon from last to beat favored Hawk Attack by a neck for Chicago-based trainer Harvey Vanier, whose wife, Nancy, owned the five-year-old. Randy had never ridden Homing Pigeon in a race before, though he had been beaten by him at Arlington Park. "I was racing against him in Chicago; he was beating me all the time," Randy told Jennie Rees of the *Courier-Journal*. "Now I'm mentally focused on riding, trying to get my career back on the map again. Now I'm pain free. I hadn't been pain free in five years, I guess. Now I'm really down on my belly and trying to get people to believe in me again, to give me that one chance. Harvey has given me that chance."

When the Churchill Downs meet ended in late November, Randy moved on to the Fair Grounds, where he won two December stakes, the second on Valid Expectations in the $40,000 Sugar Bowl Handicap on December 31. He finished 1995 with healthy numbers: 79 wins from 723 mounts and earnings topping $2.8 million. That set him up for an even better year in 1996.

Though he won just one stakes race in the first four months of '96 and suffered a broken pelvis in a barn accident, he won a pair of grade 2 stakes in Chicago, taking the $500,000 Illinois Derby on Natural Selection at Sportsman's Park on May 11 and the $150,000 Pucker Up Stakes at Arlington Park aboard Ms. Mostly on June 29.

As the summer continued, Randy began closing in on a milestone, his 4,000th career victory. Getting it was not a piece of cake, at least not a piece of the same cake. With Randy zeroing in on 4,000, Arlington Park went all out to promote it. When Randy reached 3,996, Arlington began handing out cards each day asking fans to guess the mount who would be Randy's 4,000th winner. Fans who chose the right horse would receive two Breakfast at Arlington coupons and qualify for a drawing to win a day in a Sky Suite for a party for ten people.

When Randy recorded number 3,999 on Sunday, August 18, Arlington prepared a festive cake for the next day of racing, the following Wednesday, in order to commemorate number 4,000. Cricket flew in from Kentucky for the occasion. Only Randy did not win a race that Wednesday. Arlington made a new cake on Thursday. Randy had another winless day. Arlington baked a new cake on Friday. Randy did not win a race. Cricket went home. Arlington baked another cake on Saturday, August 24, and Randy ended an eighteen-race losing streak on La Chatte, who won the sixth race, a maiden race for fillies, Randy's 4,000th winner. Although Cricket was not there, many out-of-town high-profile jockeys who were Randy's friends were, thanks to Arlington's International Festival of Racing, highlighted by the Arlington Million. "It took me a while to get that race won," Randy said thirteen years later. "My wife wasn't there. She waited three days. I did it without her, but all the jockeys were there for the Million."

Randy hoped his 4,000th winner would give him momentum into the fall and it did. Southern Playgirl, a two-year-old filly, carried Randy to two more Grade 2 stakes victories, capturing the $150,000 Arlington-Washington Lassie on September 29 and the $250,000 Alcibiades Stakes at Keeneland eleven days later. Randy's final stakes win in 1996 was at the Fair Grounds, where Bucks Nephew won the $40,000 Louisiana Handicap, December 29. Randy finished the year with 138 victories from 1,070 starts, up considerably from the year before. His earnings of more than $3.3 million was nearly half a million more than the previous year's.

Bucks Nephew also gave Randy his first stakes winner in 1997 by taking the $60,000 Diplomat Way on January 26. A week later at the Fair Grounds, Dancing Water won the $60,000 Tiffany Lass Stakes.

But in early March, Randy was finishing a workout with a filly, Miss Beaupiece, at the Fair Grounds when she stopped suddenly and threw him to the ground. "I was pulling her up, and she started bucking and playing," Randy told Byron King of the *Daily Racing Form*. "I lost my balance and fell." Randy chipped the other side of his pelvis in the fall. He did not need surgery for this injury, but he lost time, a precious commodity for a jockey trying to reestablish himself. "People quit riding me; I kept getting hurt," Randy states.

Randy missed the Keeneland spring meet he had been targeting and wound up spending the summer, fall, and winter at Calder, where he won three stakes with Vivace—the $250,000 Miami Beach Sprint Handicap, the $250,000 Princess Rooney Handicap, and the $28,000 Maggies Pistol Handicap—for trainer Cam Gambolati, who had won the 1985 Kentucky Derby with Spend A Buck. But the trainer who orchestrated Randy's successful invasion of Calder was Eddie Plesa.

"We won a lot of races," Plesa says. "He rode for me in New York. It was an easy decision to use Randy because in our business, we talk about back class. Randy is the ultimate professional. Not only did he have natural ability, he worked at his craft. Sometimes, when the natural ability is compromised because of injury, if you don't have the other things going for you, like smarts, you can't make up for it. Randy did. Randy had a fire in him that he wanted to win. He had the desire. He certainly had the skill. He was as good as it gets. To be able to take advantage of his skills in Florida in the summer, it was a no-brainer.

"Another thing with Randy was when he got off a horse, he could tell you something about a horse. It's not something you hear a lot from riders. He had an instinct. When he told you something about a horse, you paid attention."

Plesa was one of countless trainers who marveled at Randy's ability to overcome injuries. "Most people would be home with a crying towel saying, 'Why did this happen to me?' Randy never complained. He's a Hall of Famer not only in his profession, but in his spirit, too."

But the injuries kept coming. Randy lost nearly four weeks in the summer when he was kicked in the chest by a young horse. He credits a new, mandatory safety vest with saving his life. "Thank God, the vest was on," Randy says. "I had three broken ribs. She kicked me with her back leg. I was lucky that I had the vest on. We had just started using them at Calder." Despite the missed time, his 1997 numbers were respectable, 120 victories from 851 mounts and more than $2.6 million in earnings.

In 1998, his last full year of riding, he won 111 of 885 starts and over $2.3 million in purses. His last graded stakes victory was on Banshee Breeze in the $200,000 Grade 2 Bonnie Miss Stakes at Gulfstream Park on March 16 for Hall of Fame trainer Carl Nafzger. In her lone start as a two-year-old in 1987, Banshee Breeze had finished seventh at 11-1 in a maiden race at Churchill Downs under Brian Peck. She did not race again at two, and Randy picked up the mount for her three-year-old debut in a maiden race at Gulfstream Park. Sent off at 6-1, she won by 3¾ lengths. She followed that with a powerful eight-length allowance win before stepping up to the grade 2 Bonnie Miss. Sent off the 9-5 favorite, she won by a length and a half.

But after Banshee Breeze finished third in the Grade 1 Ashland Stakes at Keeneland, Nafzger replaced Randy with Jerry Bailey for the Grade 1 Kentucky Oaks, and she finished second by a neck to Keeper Hill. Bailey maintained the mount, and after finishing third in the Grade 1 Mother Goose Stakes, she won three consecutive Grade 1 stakes, the Coaching Club American Oaks by a neck at Belmont Park, the historic Alabama Stakes at Saratoga by six lengths, and the Spinster Stakes at Keeneland by 12 lengths as the 4-5 favorite. Sent off the same odds against older fillies and mares in the Grade 1 Breeders' Cup Distaff at Churchill Downs, she was nosed by Escena.

Randy would win just one stakes race in 1999, the $65,000 Spinning World Stakes on Ayrial Delight at Keeneland, April 18, 1999. Not long after, Randy announced his decision to retire. This time it stuck.

19

A Grand Goodbye

Randy announced his retirement on June 4, 1999, without providing an exact date. He wanted to ride through the end of the Churchill Downs' summer meet, concluding June 27, then finish his Thoroughbred riding career at Evangeline Downs in his native Louisiana, where he had begun riding Thoroughbreds twenty-six years earlier. "I wanted to end my career where it started," Randy explains.

He also wanted to honor other Cajun riders that night. After speaking with Shane Sellers and Robby Albarado, and getting verbal commitments from them, Randy approached Evangeline Downs president and general manager Charles Ashy, Sr., with the idea. Ashy was more than willing to put together a Cajun Jockey Night and a Cajun jockey race, which would be the final ride of Randy's magnificent, bittersweet career.

Randy then revealed that he would become an agent for Louisiana native Marlon St. Julien, at that time one of the top riders at Lone Star Park in Texas. Randy planned on taking St. Julien, one of the few African-American riders in the country, to Ellis Park later that summer to begin his ascent to the top level of racing in Kentucky.

Before Randy left Churchill Downs for his final night in Louisiana, the Louisville Kentucky Thoroughbred Club honored him with a celebrity roast at the Kentucky Derby Museum. Among those in attendance were Sellers, Albarado, trainer Dallas Stewart (who had been Randy's valet so many years earlier), and trainers Bernie Flint and Pat Byrne. "It was a special night," Randy remarks. "Ronnie Ebanks was there and all my friends. I've got some really, really good friends. I'm a lucky, lucky man. It really meant a lot to me."

Randy's final ride would be on Monday evening, July 12, in the $30,000 Cradle of Jockeys Invitational Stakes at one mile for three-year-olds and up. Joining Randy in the race were Sellers, Ron Ardoin, E.J. "Elvis" Perrodin, Corey Lanerie, Ray Sibille, Mark

Guidry, and Marlon St. Julien. Albarado wanted to participate, but he had already committed to a vacation in Hawaii with his family. Albarado had encouraged St. Julien to sign Randy as an agent.

Sellers, who had helped plan the event, told Jeff Taylor of the *Daily Racing Form,* "Today is all about Randy Romero. It's not about Shane Sellers or any of the other riders who came in. Randy paved the way for us younger riders to leave Louisiana and do some good. I'm happy to be able to help put this together, because there will never be another Randy."

Ardoin said in Taylor's story, "Randy and I grew up riding the bushes together. We both got our starts professionally right here in Lafayette. I believe he was a year ahead of me when I had my bug [apprentice allowance]. I felt really honored that he called and asked me to be part of this."

So was St. Julien, who told Taylor, "Randy has changed the way I look at things. He has me believing in the plan we have laid down. We are both very confident in the future."

First, though, Randy celebrated the past. Although it rained heavily before the 6:30 P.M. card began and intermittently throughout the evening, a crowd of 2,686, some 1,700 more than a typical Monday night, showed up. "This is the greatest thing since opening night [in 1966]," Ashy told Bob Fortus of the *New Orleans Times-Picayune.* "The interstate was backed up with people trying to get here."

The evening began with an autograph session, allowing Randy to speak with fans who had followed him his entire career, who had seen him try to squeeze out every ounce of his talent every time he rode and come back from a series of injuries and accidents that would have stopped most athletes. "Tonight comes right from the heart," he told Taylor. "I couldn't be where I am today without the people that are here tonight."

Some came from far away. Melissa Ward drove seven hours from her home in Little Rock, Arkansas, to say goodbye to Randy. "When I saw that Randy was having his last ride, I had to come here," she told Patrick Courreges of the *Lafayette Daily Advertiser.* "I wanted to be here for this historic occasion. He's so nice, and he smiles and wins races. He's a special person."

Randy's son interrupted his vacation in Panama City, Florida, to surprise his father. "It's sad, but it's exciting," he told Courreges.

Randy rode in two races on the undercard, finishing second and third. He was then honored by Evangeline Downs management between the seventh and eighth races when he was presented an inscribed glass trophy. Given a microphone, Randy addressed the crowd: "I just want to thank everyone for being here. This was a wild ride."

Then he joined Sellers, who had begun a singing career, in a musical number. "We sat in the winner's circle and he sung to me," Randy laughs. "It was on the TV monitors." Then Sellers made a dedication to Randy before the jockeys took their mounts for the featured ninth race, the final one of Randy's life. Randy was aboard Awesome Explosion, who opened as the 2-1 favorite before drifting up to 10-1.

Randy finished sixth. St. Julien won the race on Oscar Magic, followed by Gran's Halo, who was ridden by Sellers. Randy went into the winner's circle for the photo and told St. Julien he owed him 30 percent (agents usually get 25 to 30 percent). They both laughed.

Randy's final year of riding had produced just 17 winners from 251 mounts and earnings of $620,257. His career numbers were among the best of any jockey in racing history: 4,294 victories, 3,744 seconds, and 3,304 thirds from 26,096 mounts and earnings topping $75 million.

In a lengthy interview with Jennie Rees of the *Louisville Courier-Journal* before his final night, Randy shared his thoughts and his feelings about retiring: "Some of my dreams came true; some didn't. Now, maybe the others can through Marlon. He's the next star. I really feel that way." Rees also wrote of St. Julien's decision to sign a rookie jockey agent. "I'm going with my gut feeling," he told her. "He knows everybody it would take to get me to the top. I'm gambling as far as he's never been an agent, but he knows what it takes to be one, I think. He's accomplished a lot; he's been a lot of places. He knows a lot of the bigger people, people I'd love to ride for, that I need to ride for to get to the top."

Randy had ridden at the top—more than once. "My career has been so good, and I want people to remember me as being a top rider, and not riding until I'm 50 years old," he told Rees. "As long as I had the people who believed in me, they used me. But when they quit believing in you, they quit using you. And they don't believe in me anymore.

"I never lost my heart. Never. I lost my reflexes. I probably wish I'd have lost it [his heart] 10 years ago. I probably wouldn't be as hurt as I am now. I took some chances. Whatever it took, I did it. Didn't think twice. I could ride maybe another two years and be profitable—but not riding top horses. They've got to go through eight riders before they get to me. I just can't wait that long anymore."

Two weeks before Randy retired, Penny Fitch Hayes, Randy's final jockey agent, told Randy that she had been contacted by his estranged father, Lloyd, to see if Randy wanted to ride Hallowed Dreams, a promising, unraced two-year-old filly he trained and co-owned. Randy declined. Though Hallowed Dreams would win her first sixteen starts, Randy today is at peace with his decision: "I was retiring and I was tired of getting hurt."

Soon after he retired, Randy was presented the 1999 Courage, Spirit and Triumph Award by the Louisville Thoroughbred Club. "Day in and day out, he performs with professionalism, enthusiasm, courage and dignity," the club's president, Manny Cadina, told Dan McDonald of the *Daily Advertiser.* "He's the kind of person who makes you proud to be a part of Thoroughbred racing."

20

Agent Romero

Becoming Marlon St. Julien's jockey agent was an easy career change for Randy. He had hustled for his own mounts even when he had top agents working for him; his enthusiasm for his mounts was second to none. "He had P.R. like no one else, I thought," one of Randy's younger Cajun jockey contemporaries, Robbie Albarado, said in a Jennie Rees story in the *Louisville Courier-Journal* just before Randy retired from riding. "That's why he's going to make a great jockey agent."

Before taking on St. Julien, Randy had wanted to become Albarado's agent. "When he was riding in Louisiana, I wanted to get his book and take him to New York," Randy says. "But he didn't want to go to New York yet. We became good friends. He's a good person. I admire the guy." So do many others. Albarado rode two-time Horse of the Year Curlin flawlessly in 2007 and 2008 for trainer Steve Asmussen. Even so, he still needs and uses an agent. Randy used nearly two dozen of them.

"When I was riding, I appreciated the agents I had, but I was my own agent," Randy says. "I just took care of my business. I knew what I had to do. It was automatic to me being an agent. It was like hustling for me, but I was hustling for another rider. My job was to get him [St. Julien] mounts. I'd see fifteen, twenty trainers every day because I had a top rider. I thought he was and I knew he was."

Early in his new career, Randy received a huge assist from his former agent, Doc Danner: "Doc Danner taught me a lot when I started. He took me around and he taught me a lot about the condition book [a book at each racetrack listing future races], and how to handle people, which I knew already. But he was helping me through it."

Randy had not discovered St. Julien's name in a phone book. He had been following the young jockey, who was twenty-seven when

Randy took his book, for some three years before becoming his agent. St. Julien had been the leading rider at Lone Star Park in Texas in 1997. As Randy neared retirement, he began calling St. Julien every week at Lone Star Park, then began calling him daily. St. Julien was reticent, explaining to Maryjean Wall of the *Lexington Herald-Leader*, "You're scared to go to the big time. You're scared you might starve."

Growing up in rural Louisiana, St. Julien had been torn between two loves: horse racing and football. His uncles had owned horses, and his mother, a schoolteacher, was a racing fan. "I didn't know if I'd be too big to ride or too small to play football," he told Wall in her October 15, 1999, story. He topped out at 140 pounds and played football through the tenth grade before he decided he had a more promising future at a racetrack. "I lost 25 or 30 pounds and it came off quickly." He told her that he would don a sauna suit in the bathroom, turn up the heat, and close the door to lose weight and that he would practice riding in his house on the floor, connecting a couple of belts to simulate reins.

St. Julien got a job on a farm near Evangeline Downs and began riding at the same track that had launched Randy's career. Randy was impressed the first time he saw him ride there, telling Wall, "He was the strongest finisher I've ever seen, and I mean including Pincay and Antley. And another thing, he was a likable guy. He was first class."

With Randy's help, St. Julien started strong in 1999 and made a quick impression at Keeneland, winning five races in just two days. That left him tied with Pat Day in the rider standings early in the meet. St. Julien would finish 1999 with 165 victories and $5.1 million in earnings, $800,000 more than he had made the previous year.

The following spring, St. Julien became the first African-American jockey to compete in the Kentucky Derby since Henry King in 1921. St. Julien's horse, Curule, finished seventh in the field of nineteen, which was the highest finish Randy ever had in America's most famous race. In an interview in *Jet Magazine,* St. Julien said, "I just want to be considered one of the best riders in the country, whether black, white, purple, blue or brown. I also want to leave the game with a lot of respect and say I accomplished a lot in my career."

Randy relates, "Marlon was doing really good. He was a very good rider. Pat Byrne rode him, won a stakes with him. Billy Mott rode him. Dallas Stewart used him. I was enjoying every minute." That would change. "He was only good for about a year and a half," says Randy, who had picked up a second rider, apprentice Faustino Orantes. "Marlon stayed with me for about a month, him and his wife, Denise. He had a little baby girl, Jasmin. We were living in Louisville. The kid was just getting started. After the Churchill Downs meet ended [in the summer of 2000], I wanted to go to Saratoga, and I took him there. Everybody told me I was stupid, but I knew what I was doing. I believed in him. I knew he could produce. We won thirteen races. Then we stayed in New York for a little while. Then we left and we went to Turfway Park. We had some winners. Got back to Keeneland and Churchill Downs. He was the second or third to Pat Day. Then we went about sixty races without winning a race. We were at Churchill. I mean I was putting him on so many favorites."

St. Julien's career quickly deteriorated. "He wasn't showing up to work mornings and afternoons," Randy remembers. "I was putting him on horses and he wasn't showing up to ride them. I knew there was something going on. I called him and I called him. I called my wife and said, 'Go get that s.o.b. I think he's still sleeping.' My wife runs over there and she knocks on the door and told him, 'You missed the first two races.'" Randy was livid. "He has to ride all day. He was on drugs. It got worse and worse."

But soon Randy would have more pressing concerns.

21

Is This the End?

Randy was in Hot Springs, Arkansas, in January 2002, working at the Oaklawn Park meet for his two jockeys, Marlon St. Julien and apprentice Faustino Orantes, when he became terribly ill. His kidneys were failing. "It came suddenly," Randy says. "I was hustling mounts for Marlon and Faustino. I just kept on throwing up. The wife of the guy I was staying with, a commodities broker named Dwight, was a nurse. They took my blood pressure. My blood pressure blew up. She said, 'Randy, you really need to go to the hospital. You're really sick.' And I could feel it. So I went to the hospital. They wanted to admit me right away. I hate Hot Springs [the location of his sweatbox accident]. I said, 'No, I'd rather go back to Louisville and see my doctor, Don Duff. They didn't want to let me out of the hospital. I had to sign a piece of paper to get out of there. I called Cricket. I told her, 'I'm dying.' I flew back to Louisville."

Cricket, who was in Louisville, had already endured a lifetime of bad phone calls concerning Randy, but this one really hit home. "It was devastating," she says. "He was in Hot Springs and he called me up. He was at the hospital and he was in kidney failure. I mean, it was scary. I had a step-grandfather that died of kidney trouble. He had gone in for a kidney transplant years ago. I was very young, probably six or seven. And he opted for the kidney transplant because he didn't want to live on dialysis. And, of course, he didn't make it. At that time, I was so young. I didn't know what they were talking about." This time she did.

She sought to comfort her husband when he got to Louisville. "I'm one of these—I don't know if it's just from being with him for so long all these years that we're probably the most optimistic people— if there's a will, there's a way. If it can be fixed, we're going to fix it," Cricket says. "It was something we had to deal with. We both had our crying spats, and then, it's like, okay we can deal with it."

But the news just kept getting worse. After tests, Duff told Randy that his kidney was functioning at eight percent capability. He needed a transplant immediately.

Randy's older brother, Edward, a quarter horse trainer who has the same blood type as Randy, volunteered one of his kidneys. "You don't want to see your brother die," Edward told Liane Crossley of *Thoroughbred Times*. "If you love your family, you do what you got to do."

The cost of the transplant was expected to exceed two hundred thousand dollars. Because he had suffered so many injuries, Randy was never able to get health coverage. He was, however, partially covered by Cricket's insurance. At the time she was working at a drug company in Louisville. "I have some insurance through Cricket's work, but we were told that it would not cover the entire cost of the transplant," Randy told Leslie Deckard of *Blood-Horse Magazine*. "I have a lot of friends who are helping me out. I've never asked for anything, but it's nice to know people are so caring."

Jockey/singer Shane Sellers, who was from Randy's hometown of Erath, Louisiana, and whose riding career was put on hold because of reconstructive knee surgery (he would return to riding later in 2002), jumped into action, establishing the Randy Romero Transplant Fund at National City Bank in Louisville. He also announced that he would hold concerts to raise money for Randy and was amazed by the response he received. "I have been overwhelmed by their [the public's] generosity and love for Randy," Sellers said in Crossley's *Thoroughbred Times* story. "He's done a lot for the game. We can't afford to lose a guy like him."

The Fair Grounds held a benefit in Randy's name, donating a seafood dinner and entertainment afterwards, which sold three hundred tickets. Combined with the sale of Fair Grounds Spring Festival of Racing beer steins and an earlier auction of a framed print of Randy aboard Personal Ensign, the event raised nearly fourteen thousand dollars. Arlington Park, thanks to the leadership of Chairman Richard Duchossois, established a Rally for Randy Fund and donated the initial two thousand dollars. Arlington officials invited other tracks to join in. Many did, including Louisiana Downs; the New York Racing Association, which operates Saratoga, Belmont Park, and Aqueduct; Churchill Downs; and Gulfstream Park.

Randy's close friend, restaurateur Tommy Walters, held a fundraiser for Randy at his Furlongs Restaurant in Lexington on

April 21. "I wanted to raise $10,000 dollars," Walters says. "I invited one hundred of our friends and charged $100 a plate. Then, I got a call from Brereton Jones. He's a good friend of ours. I had done some fundraisers for him." Jones, who was the governor of Kentucky from 1991-1995, and his wife, Libby, own Airdrie Stud in Old Frankfort Pike near Midway, Kentucky. "I called to invite them to eat, he and his wife, Libby," Walters says. "He said, 'Tom, this is what I want you to do. I'm going to donate a season of Mazel Trick [a stallion he owned].' Then it snowballed," Walters continues. "Johnny Jones, who owns Walmac [Farm], offered a [breeding] season to Salt Lake. Then, the lady who owns Kentucky Eagle Beer here in Lexington, Ann McBrayer—her husband ran for governor—donated a golf bag and bought it back." Walters did not raise close to the $10,000 he wanted. "I raised $125,000," he states. "I've got two daughters, but the best thing I ever did was raise that money for Randy. I'm proud of it. It made him happy. Even if it was only for one day."

Another fundraiser for Randy was held at Coyotes, a nightclub in Louisville, on May 2. At Coyotes, Sellers and his band provided the entertainment. Two guitars donated by country music star George Strait were auctioned. Hall of Fame trainer Nick Zito, who could not be at the event, had Randy's old protégé, Ronnie Ebanks, buy one of the guitars. Richard Duchossois bought the other. "Mr. Duchossois flew to Coyotes on his private jet," Randy says. "Bill Thayer, the vice president [of Arlington Park], came too. Mr. Duchossois, I love the guy to death. He's a very good man. He's really a special guy." Other trainers, including Kenny McPeek, Dale Romans, Frankie Brothers, Neil Howard, Pat Byrne, and Carl Nafzger, bought items at the auction to support Randy.

In a *Thoroughbred Times* story by Arien Schweiger on April 6, Sellers said of Randy, "I talk to him two to three times a day, every day. It's not only for financial support. I make him remind himself how strong he's always been mentally."

Randy was overwhelmed by the support he received. "I never imagined I had so many friends," Randy told Leslie Deckard of the *Blood-Horse*. "People have been so good to me. I just don't know how to thank everyone." In a story in *Thoroughbred Daily News*, Randy said, "I'm blessed to have as many good friends who have been on my side all through this. So many people have been so helpful."

Why would so many friends do so much to help Randy? Tommy Walters, a native of Lafayette, Louisiana, got to know Randy in 1982, when Randy began eating at his restaurant. "I had watched him while he was riding in Louisiana and admired him," Walters explains. "He was a hero from Louisiana. I have his pictures on the walls. One is A Toast to Junius.

"He has such a passion for the game. I have horses. On May 5, 1995, Randy rode my $15,000 claimer, Bien Fu, which means 'good' and 'crazy' in Cajun French, at Churchill Downs and won. In the winner's circle, he hugged me and kissed me on the cheek, and I kissed him. And he said, 'Neg, I've won three Breeders' Cup races, but this is the best win in my career.' He had tears in his eyes. So did I. Randy's helped me tremendously. If I could have given him my kidney, I would have."

But Randy's kidney transplant was put on hold. A full day of tests revealed that Randy had Hepatitis C, a virus that causes chronic liver disease. He may have been infected from one of the blood transfusions he received when he was burned in the sweatbox in 1983. "We never knew before then," Cricket says. "They determined that he had Hepatitis and that he had this for nearly twenty years without knowing. And they told us at that point, the liver took priority over the kidney. So that stopped the kidney transplant.

"So now we had the liver to deal with. That's very scary because you can live on dialysis, but you can't live without a liver. There's no machine that can keep you alive if your liver goes. So they went and did biopsies and then they said that he had 25 percent of his liver that was actually working."

The doctors recommended that Randy try an experimental drug to put the Hepatitis into remission. If it worked, Randy could then have a dual transplant of a kidney and a liver. Both would have to come from the same donor to reduce the chance that the organs would be rejected by Randy's body. But the drug did not work. "It came back more rapid than before," Cricket says. "That's why he can't have a kidney transplant still."

Dr. Duff had placed Randy on dialysis immediately after discovering the kidney failure. His first treatment was at Norton Suburban Hospital in Louisville on Sunday evening, January 27, 2002. "At first, they put me on something like chemo to try to kill the virus in my blood, but it's still there today," Randy says. "My kidney wasn't functioning. I was so sick. I had too much potassium in my body. I couldn't pee. Too much potassium in your body can kill you."

Randy would require three four-hour dialysis treatments a week for the rest of his life. After his first one in 2002, he told Jennie Rees of the *Louisville Courier-Journal* that he felt better. She asked Randy if his riding career was worth it. "No, if you look at it now," he said. "I never knew this would happen." When she asked him about Personal Ensign, though, he quickly changed his mind and said, "I just loved it. I would do it again."

If he had been able to do it the first time without daily flipping—self-induced vomiting to keep his weight down—he might not have suffered from the extent of problems he will face the rest of his life. "I'm not going to say all of that is the reason for my kidney problems now, but it contributed," Randy told Deckard in the *Blood-Horse*. "I was hurt a lot and I abused my body trying to make weight. I started watching my weight as a nine-year-old, and at the end of my career, I was pulling seven pounds per day just to ride."

Mainstream America learned of Randy's plight in a lengthy feature in *USA Today*'s July 31, 2002, issue. The story was promoted on the upper left-hand corner of the front page with a picture of Randy and an unnamed horse. The promo was labeled, "Racing's deadly secret: Randy Romero nearly died trying to lose weight. Other jockeys have similar tales. Cover story 1C." On the front page of the Sports Section, the world got to see Randy's reality: a large color photo of him hooked up to the dialysis machine that was saving his life. The photo by *USA Today*'s Robert Deutsch was taken from above, showing Randy reclined in a chair, his left arm hooked up to the machine at Norton Suburban Hospital in Louisville. Underneath the photo was a headline: "Jockey riding for a fall." Beneath the headline was another photo of Randy taken on the backstretch at Churchill Downs. Randy is sitting down, talking on his cell phone, working as a jockey agent.

Tom Pedulla's insightful, well-written article interwove the issue of jockeys flipping to make weight and the details of Randy's dire health dilemma, which was caused, at least in part, by his daily flipping. He noted that Randy only retained an average of two meals a week while he was riding. "When you see your husband and friend have to throw his guts up five or six times a day to do something they love, that's a hard thing," Cricket told Pedulla. "Could you imagine never having anything in your stomach? I couldn't." Randy's son told Pedulla, "I don't think it's necessary for them to kill themselves to do something they love." Randy, though, told Pedulla that after he was burned he abused alcohol and overate: "I had no control. I was hungry all the time. I'm not proud of what I did. I should have been a lot smarter."

By 2002, he was. He had finally stopped flipping. He quit "cold turkey." And, with dialysis supplementing his weak-functioning kidneys, a better diet, and exercise, he continues to live an otherwise normal life.

Randy's spirits soared in mid-March 2003, when he learned that he was one of three jockey finalists for induction into the National Museum of Racing Hall of Fame in Saratoga Springs, New York. "Wow, that's great," Randy told Jennie Rees of the *Louisville Courier-Journal*. "I'm so happy to hear that. That was one of my goals when I was riding: to be in the Hall of Fame." The other two finalists were two of Randy's contemporaries in New York, Eddie Maple, who had recently retired, and Mike Smith, who is still riding. Smith was chosen for induction. When Smith learned that he had been chosen over Randy, Smith called him and apologized, saying Randy deserved it more. "That was first class," Randy confirms.

Randy was a finalist again in 2004 but again did not make it. He told Marcus Hersh of the *Daily Racing Form* in a May 29, 2004, story, "I feel like Susan Lucci," referring to Lucci's nineteen Emmy nominations for her role in the daytime television show *All My Children* before finally winning the award. Randy told Hersh, "Sure I'd like to get in. I'd like to have a chance to enjoy it while I'm still around. I hope they don't wait until I die."

In 2009, Randy again was one of the three finalists. The other two were Eddie Maple and Alex Solis, still a top California jockey. Maple edged Randy to earn induction. Randy called and congratulated him. Randy would have to wait at least another year for his deserving enshrinement.

"In my book, he's a Hall of Fame jockey and a Hall of Fame guy," Hall of Fame trainer Shug McGaughey says of Randy.

Although the Hall of Fame nomination had temporarily raised his mood, in the summer of 2003, Randy was having trouble coping with the reality that his body needed a kidney and liver transplant, one that he might never receive. Once again, a friend stepped forward to help. Neil Hopkins, a Connecticut technology sales executive and horse owner, met Randy several years ago. His wife, Wendy, was friends with Sarah Dunham, the daughter of New York trainer Bob Dunham. "They [Wendy and Sarah] grew up together in New Orleans," Neil relates. When Neil was introduced to Randy by Sarah Dunham, they quickly became friends. "I love him like family," Hopkins says. "He's an amazing person. When I met him, he was going through a low point in his life. He was bloated. I did a ton of research and sent him to the Mayo Clinic in Jacksonville, Florida. I had him going through a series of tests and an evaluation. Coming out, he knew where he stood in life. He was scared he was going to die."

Randy left the Mayo Clinic in a better frame of mind, and in late June 2003, for the first time in nearly eighteen months, he visited the backstretch at Churchill Downs. He told Marty McGee of the *Daily Racing Form* in a July 2 story that he was still hopeful that the medicine he was taking would eliminate the Hepatitis C virus in his bloodstream, clearing the way for a kidney transplant at the end of the year. That never happened. To this day, Randy's liver is operating at 25 percent efficiency, but that number has been stable, and Randy's blood is tested every week to monitor his liver function.

At the Fair Grounds in December 2003, Randy returned to work as a jockey agent, representing Jose Martinez, Jr. When Martinez went to Arlington Park the following summer, Randy went with him and added a client, Liz Harris.

In 2004, thanks mainly to Randy, the entire nation learned about flipping, one of racing's dirty secrets. Randy had nothing to gain by speaking out against flipping in a Home Box Office documentary, filmed mostly in Kentucky, which aired on April 26, 2004. Originally, Randy was told the piece would be about his recovery from his many accidents as well as about his flipping. But he went ahead with the show anyway. The film was called "Jockey" and focused on Randy, Sellers, and apprentice rider Chris Rosier. A follow-up piece, which aired in 2007, featured a brief group interview of Sellers and Hall of Famers Chris McCarron and Laffit Pincay, Jr., as well as brief interviews with Hall of Fame trainer D. Wayne Lukas and Hall of Fame jockey Pat Day.

In the HBO documentary, Sellers, McCarron, and Pincay said that they rarely talk about flipping with anybody. "I don't want my kid to know what I'd done," Sellers said. "I don't want some kid to think that I'm condoning it. I think it's horrible." McCarron said, "The only person who ever knew was my wife." Pincay admitted that he was "embarrassed" he did it. Randy called flipping "a way of life" and estimated that out of ten jockeys, five or six flip. "Two or three pounds is a lot of weight to a jockey," Randy said.

The goal of the featured riders was to increase the minimum weight requirement for jockeys from 110 pounds to 116. Lukas and Day spoke out against changing the weight. Lukas said that when a horse carries more weight, the chances of sustaining an injury increase. He said that the weight requirements for jockeys come with the territory. "They're going to have to make some of those sacrifices to perform or they should find another job," he said. "That's cold, but that's the reality." That may be Lukas's reality, but he does not speak for all trainers.

Day said raising weights will not eliminate the problem. When he was asked if he thought jockeys were being lazy by flipping instead of controlling their weight through diet and nutrition, Day said, "Absolutely, absolutely. Randy—bless his heart, I love him dearly— when he was riding, and riding successfully, he was in one of three places. He was on the track riding, at the kitchen eating, or in the bathroom flipping. Now, I don't believe that that was necessary. I believe that he hasn't treated his body very fairly." Day's statement deeply hurt Randy. Had Randy not kept his body in great shape, he would not have survived nearly being burned alive in 1983.

However, Randy does admit the damage he did to his body. In the documentary, Randy said, "I was so hungry all the time." When asked how flipping affected his current health and how he deals with the consequences, he said, "Sometimes it gets tough." He teared up for a second, then added, "I'm going to be on dialysis for the rest of my life."

Randy's longtime friend Mark Guidry, now a trainer after a highly successful riding career, was asked if he admired Randy for speaking up about flipping in the documentary. "Well, sure. You have to throw it out there," Guidry says. "He was trying to get racing changed. He handled it well. He didn't jump up and down or curse someone out. He did it the right way.

"He never blamed anybody for what he went through. He blamed himself for it. He was trying to make a point of what riders have to go through every day. I've seen other people do the same thing and not handle it as well as Randy did. He didn't put any blame on anyone. That's what makes him unique."

The HBO documentary generated stories around the country. The *Chicago Daily Herald*'s May 14 package of two stories and a sidebar began on the front page of the Sports Section, which featured a large photo of Randy standing in front of the clubhouse turn at Arlington Park looking away from the track. The headlines were "Taking life for one more ride" and "Randy Romero, Arlington Park's newest jockey agent fights for his life and for jockeys everywhere." The front-page story jumped inside, where Randy's stories commanded an entire page. A sidebar labeled, "Randy at a glance" listed his size, family, career highlights, memorable races, statistics, and his major surgeries—shoulder, femur, elbows, ankle, jaw, pelvis, both knees, and cheekbone—and noted that Randy needed a kidney and liver transplant from a single donor.

"I think God has put me here to send the message, I really, really believe that," Randy told Mike Spellman, who wrote the main story and a sidebar. "Maybe it can change the way jockeys live their lives and be more professional in the way they eat and the way they handle their bodies."

Randy shared his feelings about being a jockey agent: "I love doing this. If I can't ride, this is what I want to do. I love seeing the people in the morning and going out to hustle. I hate staying in the house and just thinking about what's coming up. If I'm going to die, I'm going to die working at the place I love doing the things I love to do."

22

Juiced

By 2005, Randy's health had received an unexpected boost. Randy not only felt better, but he was also able to stop taking two medicines controlling his blood pressure. He credits his improved health to a Himalayan juice he learned about from Hall of Fame trainer Billy Mott's wife, Tina.

Tina Mott had come across Himalayan GoChi (originally Goji) juice while trying to help her aunt, who was suffering from arthritis. "I heard about it twenty years ago," Tina says. "My aunt had arthritis badly, and six months later, she was much, much better." After watching the impact of the juice on her aunt, Tina began buying and using it for her own family, their dog, and even their horses. She then became a distributor for the company that produces the juice.

The juice comes from the tiny red goji berry that grows in the Himalayas. "Chi" is the ancient Chinese term for vital life force. Regarded as the first natural healers, Himalayans have an unusually long life span and their use of the berry may contribute to the longevity of the population. More than fifty studies of the berry have been published in various health journals, including the *Journal of Alternative and Complementary Medicine,* the *British Journal of Nutrition,* the *Journal of Chinese Herbal Medicine,* and *International Immunopharmacology.* Scientists believe that the berry's unique polysaccharides, when synergized together, induce cells in the human body to work better and more cohesively. "They increase cell-to-cell communication, so your cells wake up and start to act normally again," Tina says.

The Motts have known Randy and Cricket for some twenty-five years, and it pained them to watch Randy's deteriorating health. "He's just the sweetest," Tina says. "He's got an innocence that you don't find. It's extremely rare. He's a doll. He's kind. He'd give you the shirt off his back. That's the way he's always been."

"Occasionally, he'd show up at Saratoga, and Bill would say how bad he looked. It was real sad. A year later, he showed up at out barn at Saratoga. He had somebody's book at the time. I almost didn't recognize him. He was all bloated. His eyes were all yellow. I asked how he was doing and he said that he was feeling really bad and had no energy. I said, 'You should try this juice I sell.' He said, 'What is it?' I told him what it is. He said that a lot of people told him to take different things and he didn't do it. He said he feels different about this. He said, 'You know what? I'm going to try this stuff.'"

To Randy, it was a no-brainer. "Well, I didn't think about it too much," he admits. "I was going to do anything and give it a shot. Absolutely. If drinking it could make you better, why not? I believed in it after about four months. I knew it was working because the doctors said my blood count was better than ever. And it got me off my two blood pressure medicines."

The Motts could not have been happier. "He looks like he looked twenty-five years ago," Tina says. "He's not bitter. He's happy to be alive, to be in the life that he loves."

In April 2005, Randy was doing so well that he was able to take advantage of an unexpected vacation from his friend Neil Hopkins. "I said, 'Randy, you need a break,'" Hopkins recalls. "I'm going to take you blue marlin fishing for a week in Kuna, Hawaii. I took Randy and six other close friends, and we rented two charter fishing boats for a week. He was in heaven. The first night we were there, he said, 'Which ocean is this?'" Hopkins told him it was the Pacific and they both laughed. "He had the time of his life," Hopkins says.

He was able to enjoy himself despite the realities of his health. While they were on the boat, one of Randy's stints stopped working. "He had to go one hundred miles and stay in the hospital for two days," Hopkins says. "The guy never complained. He said, 'That's the most beautiful ride I ever had.'" At the hospital, doctors discovered Randy had a blood clot in an artery in his arm. They put a new stint in Randy's neck. "I was hurting like an s.o.b., but I enjoyed going back on that boat," Randy remembers.

The next day, he caught a mahi-mahi. "A real nice one," Hopkins says. Hopkins did even better, catching a huge marlin. Randy says it was 450 pounds; Hopkins says it was 800 pounds. Who knows how big it will be when Hopkins tells his grandchildren? "We had the time of our lives," Hopkins states.

Just as he had done when he sent Randy to the Mayo Clinic two years earlier, Hopkins picked up the tab. "I love him," Hopkins concludes. "He needed help. And I was able to help him."

Randy felt good enough in the summer of 2005 to begin working with horses at Churchill Downs for trainer Dallas Stewart, his former valet and close friend. "It's the happiest I've been in five years," Randy told Kathleen Adams of the *Blood-Horse* in a July 9, 2005, story. Randy, who was spending an hour and a half in the gym every other day, began hot-walking horses for Stewart in April, then riding them under tack in the shed row a month later before working three or four horses a day. "I'm going to take it really slow," he told Adams. "I'm being very careful."

He had to be. Randy had shunts in both arms. Stewart, of course, was concerned that Randy would do too much too soon, telling Adams, "I told him, 'I don't want you to get hurt.' Good riders know how to make it easy on themselves. He's very intelligent about young horses." Randy, who continued to do three four-hour sessions of dialysis every week, told Adams, "He [Stewart] was the only person I would have approached."

On Saturday night, June 25, Randy was one of eight inductees elected to the Louisiana Sports Hall of Fame. He was the fourth jockey to earn that honor, following J.D. Mooney, Eric Guerin, and Eddie Delahoussaye. "It's one of the biggest thrills of my life," Randy told the *Daily Racing Form*'s Marty McGee. "To go back home and be with my family and to be honored like this, there really are no words to describe how good it makes me feel."

Randy was introduced at the Hall of Fame ceremony at Northwestern State University's Prather Coliseum by his close friend and hunting buddy Carroll Angelle: "Hollywood had Red Pollard [Seabiscuit's jockey]; we are so proud we have Randy Romero."

Angelle knew first-hand of the price Randy paid for his success. Now a business development director for Aramark, one of the world's largest catering companies, Angelle ran the Restaurant Angelles right across the street from Evangeline Downs in the 1970s. "Randy started coming in after the races to eat," Angelle says. "We became friends. Cricket, at the time, was fifteen years old. I asked Randy if he was babysitting her. He said, 'That's my girlfriend.'"

Angelle had advised Randy to stop flipping. "When he flipped, I said, 'Neg, that's not good for you.' But that's the only way he could do it. He'd blow up. Then I got the job at the Fair Grounds in 1983. When Randy broke the record, I presented the trophy to him and Cricket. When they split up, he lived with me."

Of course, Angelle has stories about Randy's enormous appetite. "Randy was a big eater," he says. "Anytime he wanted something special, he'd call me. When he moved in with me, my icebox was full with stuff, and the first night I could hear him in the kitchen. I said, 'What the hell's going on?' He's eating cornflakes and milk at two o'clock in the morning. And he had eaten half a gallon of ice cream. I said, 'Randy, what are you doing?' He said, 'I'm hungry.' My grocery bill went from $150 a week to $800.

"One night on his birthday at Ruth's Chris (Steakhouse in New Orleans), we had each ordered a porterhouse steak and spinach, broccoli, cream potatoes, and potatoes au gratin. Randy ate all his

Randy at trainer Dallas Stewart's barn at the Oklahoma Training Track in Saratoga Springs in 2008. (Photograph by Barbara D. Livingston)

steak. I ate half of mine. He said, 'I'll be right back.' He went to the bathroom, came back and said, 'Neg, can I have that steak?' I said 'Sure.' He ate that. Then we had dessert. The bill with just him and me and a couple glasses of wine was $300."

Angelle's admiration of Randy is genuine: "He's a survivor. He never gives up. If he gave up, he would have died a long time ago. He's a fighter. He's a hard worker and he likes to accomplish things."

He did, even as a jockey agent. In the fall of 2005, Randy began booking mounts at Churchill Downs for his sixteen-year-old third cousin, Randall Toups, who was also from Erath and had also begun riding at Evangeline Downs. "I watched him ride a couple of races," Randy says. "I liked him. I really liked him." Randy became Toups' agent and Toups finished as the leading apprentice rider at Churchill Downs and fifth in the overall standings in the 2005 fall meet. On November 10, Toups brought home a long shot claimer named Are You Save, who paid $190.20 for a $2 win ticket.

In an article about Randy and Toups in the December 2005/ January 2006 issue of *Post Time USA,* two-time Eclipse Award winner Bill Mooney wrote: "When he talks, Toups sounds like he's 19 or 20. He addresses men as 'sir,' ladies as 'ma'am,' and had a firm handshake. But Toups is only five feet tall and weighs 93 pounds, and, at a glance, he appears to be about 11. 'My wife, Cricket, and I took him to a restaurant the other night,' Randy said. 'The waitress gave us menus, but she gave Toups a coloring book.'"

Joking aside, Randy thought Toups could ride anywhere: "I wanted to take him to New York. We talked and he came with me to New York for the Aqueduct winter meet. And I got him with Rick Dutrow [one of the nation's top trainers] and his brother Sydney. So we got first call for them, and we kept on running a bunch of seconds." But Toups injured his back in a mid-February accident when his mount broke down in a race at Aqueduct, and he returned to Louisiana.

Randy remained in New York and hooked up with eighteen-year-old Panamanian jockey Fernando Jara for a sensational run, one which ended bitterly. Randy became Jara's agent on February 5, 2006, purchasing a one-year contract from Jose Rivera for fifteen thousand dollars. "I really thought he was special," Randy says. "I watched him. I saw he was so talented. I'm a jockey. I rode for forty years. He was patient. He rode smart. He was smooth. He wouldn't get upset. He seldom sulked. Pleasant kid." But he barely spoke English. "Very little," Randy says. "I'd draw diagrams and make notes for him on a piece of paper and make him understand."

Everyone understood how truly gifted Jara was. "He was winning a bunch of races. He was winning stakes for Kiaran McLaughlin, for Billy Mott, for everybody. He rode for Shug," Randy continues.

In the 2006 Belmont Stakes, Jara gave Randy a thrill he had only dreamed of enjoying. Randy had never finished better than third in a Triple Crown race, but Jara won the Belmont Stakes on late-running Jazil, who was trained by McLaughlin. Jara rode a brilliant race. "It was exciting for me," Randy says. "It was a pleasure because I had never won it. My wife was there. I flew her in. We had a blast. It was unbelievable."

The fun was just starting. Jara enjoyed a dazzling Saratoga meet later that summer, winning the Grade 1 Whitney Handicap on Invasor, also trained by McLaughlin, and the Grade 1 Diana Handicap on Angara, trained by Mott. Invasor followed up with a stunning victory over heavily favored Bernardini in the Grade 1 Breeder's Cup Classic, earning 2006 Horse of the Year and Champion Older Horse honors.

Jara earned $8.6 million with Randy as his agent in 2006 before taking the final two weeks of the year off to return to Panama. Before he left, he fired Randy. Jara wanted to be represented by Gatewood Bell, the son of Darley Stable USA president Jim Bell, who worked part-time for McLaughlin. "I'm upset, but what are you going to do?" Randy said in a December 1 story in the *Daily Racing Form*. "It's life and you got to go on. I hope the best for the Bells and for Kiaran and for Fernando."

But to sign with Bell, Jara had to wait until his one-year contract with Randy expired. They eventually settled on a fee of fifteen thousand dollars. Randy, typically, took the high road with the media. "We left on good terms," Randy told the *Daily Racing Form* in a December 16 story. "He won some races for me I never won. It was a blast and I had a lot of fun. I was lucky to have him."

Maybe it was the other way around. Invasor won the 2007 Grade 1 Donn Handicap at Gulfstream Park and the 2007 Dubai World Cup before suffering a career-ending injury. Jara went into a miserable slump when he returned to New York in the spring, one so bad that he left in the middle of the Saratoga meet to try California. The change of scenery did not help. Jara was struggling to get mounts, and he returned to Panama. He rode there and then in Dubai in the winter of 2008-2009. He returned to the United States in the summer of 2009 to ride at Arlington Park.

Randy returned to Kentucky and acquired a new client, another Panamanian jockey, Aldo Arboleda, who began riding for Randy at the Arlington Park summer meet in July.

In an August 4, 2007, story by Steve Bailey in *Thoroughbred Times,* the headline was "Former jockey Romero is re-energized by health drink and a new rider." In the story, Randy told Bailey he was feeling better than he had in fifteen or twenty years and he gave much of the credit to GoChi juice. "It's been a miracle for me," Randy said. "I feel younger and stronger than I have in years. My doctors can't believe how much I've improved. It's totally turned my life around. I almost feel like I could ride again, but my doctors have asked me not to because of the risks."

Bailey asked him about the life milestone he would hit on December 22, 2007. "The big 5-0," he said, with a laugh. "I'll tell you something. The way I'm feeling now, I think I'm going to be here for years to come."

Instead, a month after his fiftieth birthday, Randy began urinating blood. "The kidney burst and I almost caught ptomaine poisoning," he says. "I was peeing blood for ten days. The doctors said I had a kidney stone in my penis. They put a stint in my penis. I went to the doctor in his office in New Orleans. I said, 'Doctor, I'm still peeing blood.' He said, 'Don't be scared.' I said, 'You're damn right I'm scared. I think I'm dying. I think you're killing me."

Randy, who had also been representing jockey E.T. Baird at the Fair Grounds, flew to Louisville to see another doctor. His damaged, enlarged kidney needed to be removed immediately. To access it, surgeons had to remove one of Randy's ribs. "I was really, really sick," Randy says. But then he got better. He began walking the halls of the hospital. "I'll tell you what, I couldn't even walk at first," Randy says. "All the damn sicknesses and accidents. It's just so hard for me to get going again. But I got myself in good shape. I got myself strong."

In May, he began getting on horses again for Dallas Stewart. By August, he was exercising as many as eight horses each morning at Saratoga. Stewart's exercise rider and assistant trainer, Kenny

"Chopper" Bourque, a former jockey who won more than twenty-four hundred races and is also from Erath, was not surprised Randy could do that despite undergoing dialysis three times a week. "He has great determination," Bourque says. "He does everything to win and compete. It didn't matter if his horse was 100-to-1 or 1-to-1. He thought he could win. He always thought he was going to win that race. And that's how he was all his life."

But in late August at Saratoga, he got thrown when his horse propped, injuring his back. He recovered, and in January 2009, when he was approached by jockey Pat Valenzuela at the Fair Grounds, Randy, who had dropped Aldo when he got sick, briefly became a jockey agent again. Valenzuela, an incredibly talented rider, had been one of the leading riders in the country more than once before repeatedly succumbing to his inner demons and substance abuse problems. He was at the Fair Grounds because Louisiana was the first state to renew his jockey license after yet another failed drug test and/or unexplained absence. In mid-February, Randy and Valenzuela split. Randy could not handle Valenzuela's reluctance to work horses every morning, something Randy had done his entire career, healthy or not.

23

Still Kicking

Randy may be the fastest walker and the worst driver in the state of Louisiana. Either way, he wants to get to his destination quickly. He drives over a curb and goes the wrong way on a one-way street in the span of two minutes. He seems to interpret "Do Not Enter" signs as "Please Come This Way." Cricket says, "He drives like he's the only one on the road."

On a December Sunday, Randy and Gerald, who live in the same apartment complex in Metairie, a suburb of New Orleans, visit the Fair Grounds. Randy, when he visits the jockeys' room, is greeted warmly by every jockey coming out for the last race of the day.

On the way home, he and Gerald get lost, which is hard to do. It's a five-minute drive from their homes.

Back at home, the hierarchy of Randy's family is readily discerned by a sign in the bathroom: "If mama ain't happy/Ain't nobody happy." There's another sign in the house: "Sing like no one is listening/Love like you've never been hurt before/Dance like no one is watching/Live like heaven begins tomorrow."

When he is home, Randy watches Fox News constantly, especially if Bill O'Reilly is on. He also likes to watch football. So does Cricket. Naturally, both are fans of the New Orleans Saints. Randy rode horses for Saints owner Tom Benson. When he is driving in his car, Randy listens to Rush Limbaugh on the radio.

Cricket, who handles workers' compensation for the Louisiana Horsemen's Benevolent & Protective Association, comes home after Randy returns from the track and tells him that the daughter of a trainer whom they are friends with has suffered an aneurysm. Randy immediately calls the trainer and, when he gets voicemail, leaves a comforting message.

There is a beautiful print in the living room by Christine Picavet of Personal Ensign and Winning Colors' epic battle in the 1988

Breeders' Cup Distaff in deep stretch. Personal Ensign, saddle cloth 6, is on the outside. Randy, with his right hand holding the right rein, wears black boots, white pants, the black shirt and red cap of the Phipps' stable, and the numeral 6 on his right arm. His head is down. The whip is held straight up in his right fist, not being used. Personal Ensign, her powerful muscles rippling, is looking straight ahead, all four of her legs off the ground in mid-stride. Winning Colors, her head cocked slightly to the right, sees Personal Ensign a nose behind. She is steel gray with a big white blaze down the middle of her face. Jockey Gary Stevens has a blue right sleeve and yellow silks. The whip is in Stevens' left hand. Randy walks past the painting every night on his way to bed.

The following morning, Randy is scheduled for dialysis, one of three four-hour sessions he must endure every week to remain alive. It is a sunny, clear blue morning. On the way to dialysis, Randy stops at a strip mall on Robert E. Lee Boulevard to pick up a prescription at Walgreens. At the other end of the mall is an old, unused movie theater, the very theater where Randy and Cricket watched *Casey's Shadow*. On the top of the building, very large block letters proclaim the theater's name: ROBERT E. LEE. The glass exterior displays a huge sign announcing that the space is for lease. An anonymous message has been taped on one of the doors: "Walk, Mediate, be Kind: Create a happy life. 25 steps."

Randy's dialysis is scheduled for 11:30 A.M. He arrives at 11:05. "Some people are so weak afterwards they almost fall down," Randy comments. He has brought along a blanket, explaining, "When they take the blood out of you, you get cold." There are thirteen people waiting. In the waiting room, there is a television set and vending machines. There is a sign in the office asking, "How much sodium is in that?" One of the people waiting is a lady who has no legs. "I feel pretty damn good," Randy says. "It could be a lot worse."

He is no celebrity here, just a common patient who chats with the others. "Most of the people don't work; they're on disability," Randy says. One of them, a man with a walker, rode a bus here. He tells Randy that he recently did eight hours standing. Another patient asks Randy, "Are you in pain after?" He answers, "Sometimes, if they pull five pounds. One time they pulled thirteen when I was real sick. It gets your heart jumping."

Hundreds of residents in New Orleans rely on dialysis to stay alive. Randy says, "There are a lot of dialysis centers around New Orleans and they're all full. A lost of dialysis patients died from Katrina. They got most of them out, but they didn't get all of them. I was in New York.

"You can go one day without dialysis, but another day could kill you. Too much potassium can give you a stroke. It's one of five bad things. [Sodium is another.] It can give you a hard time breathing, and fluid can flood the heart and give you a heart attack."

At 11:37, Randy goes into a huge room where twenty patients sit at individual dialysis stations. The staff is professional and friendly. Randy settles in a reclining chair, his feet up, the blanket covering his legs. Randy is given a tranquilizer before the procedure begins. "To calm you down," Randy explains. "It kills the four hours pretty quick." Depending on how he feels during the four-hour session, Randy will watch television, listen to music, read, talk on his cell phone, talk to his nurses and doctors, do paperwork, or doze. Today, he quickly nods off.

His right arm is hooked to the machine that is saving his life by cleaning his blood. A tube inserted into an artery in one of Randy's arms redirects his blood into the machine, which separates blood and water, which contains waste and poison. The machine then sends Randy clean blood through another tube inserted into a different artery in his arm. "The blood just goes around," Randy says. The machine produces a steady, rhythmic sucking noise that repeats every five seconds.

Linda Wilson, a dialysis technician, is one of the staff who works with Randy. "He's doing well," she says. "It can get a little chaotic. My job is to make sure my patients are safe, that they don't go out on you [pass out]. The blood pressure can drop. If it's too, too low, it's a problem. Then I contact a nurse [there is one on each side of the room]."

Asked about Randy, she says, "I've known him for about two years. He basically takes one day at a time. Everybody likes him. He brings in the TV [three months earlier, a Spanish television crew was allowed access to Randy's dialysis for a story they were doing].

During the session, Randy's alarm goes off twice, indicating a problem with his blood pressure. Both times, a nurse comes in and simply resets the machine. Later, Dr. Jill Lindberg comes in with Randy's notes and says, "Everything's fine, no changes."

Randy pulls ten pounds this day. When he gets home, he is drained and a bit disoriented. He sorts out his pills for the upcoming two weeks. He eats a light dinner and goes to bed at 6:30. Two days later, his dialysis session is easier. They only pull four pounds.

He is at peace with dialysis being a permanent part of the rest of his life: "I don't feel sorry for myself. I know dialysis is very hard, but you have to be tough. This is our last chance. This is our lifeline. It's better than the alternative, being dead. At first, I used to cry a lot. Then they gave me some medicine, Prozac. It helped me out a lot. I don't have a problem with dialysis anymore. You just have to accept it. I do, I really do."

His son, Randy II, accepted his reality long ago: that his father was a famous jockey and prone to potentially fatal accidents. And he wanted to be just like him. "Ever since I was little," he states. "I'm going to say I was about three or four and I would get a saddle and pair of boots and ride the arms of the couch. I rode both arms off the couch. Rode them off." His father's reaction? "He was fine with it," Randy II says.

Cricket says Randy "has been a good dad. They butted heads all the time, but they're very close." One disagreement was about Randy II settling on a career. Randy told his son, "I knew what I wanted to be when I was eight years old." Randy II countered, "But I'm not you and I'm never going to be you. If I was born weighing six pounds . . ."

Today, Randy II, who has a tattoo on his chest that reads, "Only the Strong Survive," calls his father "the greatest person on this earth. You couldn't find a better person or a better dad. He's like a best friend. He'd do anything for you, and if he can't, he'll find a way. Both my parents have been so good for me. Yes, they've been on my butt, but more or less, we talk about everything."

In contrast, Randy II has very limited contact with his grandparents. He has only seen his grandfather, Randy's father, twice in his life. "I only met Lloyd once when I was young," Randy II says. "I remember a little bit of it. We went to this farm. He had this pistol. He let me shoot it at a yellow feed bucket. He said it would be mine someday. Other than that, I've never met him." However, he did catch sight of him one more time. "At the Fair Grounds, when my daddy went to ride there," Randy II recalls. "I saw him in the paddock and said to my mom, 'That guy looks familiar.' She said, 'It's your grandpa.' I was in high school. We didn't talk. I did talk to him once on the phone when I was Randall Toups' agent at Hawthorne [in Chicago]. Randall had been practically raised by Lloyd. He got him on the phone for me."

Randy II excelled in baseball as a pitcher, first baseman, and third baseman for Eastern High School in Louisville. He batted .435 one season and still holds the school's record for home runs in one season. He was good enough to get a tryout with the Cincinnati Reds in his junior year of high school but did not make it.

Like any other teenager, Randy II was nearly fatally embarrassed by his mother and father. Cricket, who at the time was working at Randy II's high school bookstore, was with her fifteen-year-old son on a spring break in Sarasota, Florida. At the beach, upon seeing two girls from his high school that she recognized—one of them a girl Randy II was enamored with named Donna—Cricket yelled, "Hello!" Randy II cringed. "She's hollering at them, and I was trying to hide under the beach towel," he remembers.

A year later, Randy II and his parents were having dinner at Garrett's, a restaurant in Louisville. Donna was working as the hostess. Randy II told his father, "Man, she's hot," a statement he would soon regret. Randy asked, "You like her?" Randy II said, "Yeah." So Randy called the waiter over and told him to bring Donna to their table. "So here she comes to our table," Randy II relates. "She said, 'Can I help you?'" Randy II responded, "My dad's being an idiot. I'm sorry.'"

Then he and Donna met through friends and married. "Pretty crazy," Randy II says. Like his parents, they separated briefly before reuniting.

Too big to become a jockey, he tried following his father to the racetrack as a jockey agent, first in Kentucky. "It was real hard for me at first," he says. "They said, 'That's Randy's son.' It's not easy to live under the shadow of a great man in the industry. Nobody wants to live under his name. They want to make it on their own. That's why I went to Chicago." Randy II was a jockey agent in Chicago, representing Miguel Mena, Emanuel Cosme, Toups, and Francisco Torrez at various times over four years there. But he gave it up, moved back to Louisville, and began a new job as a waiter at Furlongs while he reunited with his wife, Donna, a nurse.

In the summer of 2009 with the help of his father, Randy II found a new career and, he hoped, a comfortable niche in horse racing. After completing a course in equine dentistry at Louisiana State University he began working as a dentist for horses. He and his father traveled to Arlington Park, Florida, Kentucky, and across Louisiana through the fall and winter of 2009 to work on horses for trainers Randy used to ride for. "I love it," Randy II exclaims. "It's the greatest thing I've ever done. I help the horse. I help the trainer. I love the racing game and I can stay attached to it." His father is delighted: "He's good at it. I'm so excited for him."

In January 2010, Randy and his friend Jimmy Lafont took a four-day religious retreat, one observed in complete silence. A few days later, they screamed their lungs out in the Louisiana Superdome, watching the New Orleans Saints win their first National Football Conference Championship and earning the franchise's first trip to the Super Bowl. They were guests of Saints owner Tom Benson. Randy's only wish was that he could have brought his son with him to the game. They have become closer than ever thanks to their journeys together as Randy II built up his new career.

Unlike Randy, Randy II's two children have easy access to their grandparents. Asked how his father is with twelve-year-old Tyler and seven-year-old Mia, Randy II says, "He's the best. My daughter and my stepson love him more than me." Cricket is amazed at Randy's relationship with Mia. "He's a great grandfather," she says. "I never thought anybody could whip him, but she has him whipped. To be around any little girl—Randy hasn't been—I was curious how he was going to handle it, a girl. She'll go to the track with him, baseball cap on. They're buddies. She gets anything she wants. It's funny. She and I are very close. It is really weird with Randy. She's very protective of him."

She is too young to know how many serious accidents nearly killed her grandfather. Randy II lived through them. "Let's face it, with some of these accidents, how is he not dead?" Randy II wonders. "We've all asked ourselves that. To me, he's a medical mystery. He's almost not human. He's got a heart the size of the world. He's a fighter. He's a soldier. He won't give up. He still gets up every morning with the same attitude: go get it." Cricket agrees, "He's a medical miracle. What can I say? He is something special."

Even special people need a hero. In times of deepest darkness in his life, when he wanted to die after being burned, Randy thought of his grandfather and of one particular time: "My grandfather had sugar diabetes. At one time, he was foreman and working on a refinery. He fell off a grain elevator and broke his right leg. I'll never forget it. I was five years old. He had sugar diabetes and his leg was turning purple. And I could see it. And, in fact, they wanted to amputate his leg, and he wouldn't let them.

"As it went on, his leg wasn't set right. He didn't want nobody to operate on it and he was a tough s.o.b. And all of a sudden, I'm sitting by him and he takes his knife out and he starts picking some pieces of bone out of his knee. He's cutting little pieces of skin and gets little pieces of bone out of there. I'm sitting there. I say [in Cajun French], 'Grandpa, what are you doing?' He says, 'I got to get that out. It's hurting me.' I said, 'Why don't you go to the doctor?' He didn't want to go to the doctor. He didn't want to spend the money. That's how he was. He was hard-headed and he was tough. That's where I get my toughness from, my grandpa. No pain medicine. Nothing. He didn't say nothing and he was hurting like hell.

"After the burn, that's what I thought about. I thought of my grandpa. He was my strength. He carried me. Whenever I had a problem or got hurt, he was my hero. You understand that? He was the toughest s.o.b. I ever met."

His grandson was even tougher.

Appendix

Randy Romero's Thoroughbred Statistics

Year	Starts	1sts (rank)	2nds	3rds	Earnings (rank)
1973	95	9	9	5	$16,484
1974	657	101	110	83	$184,435
1975	781	130	111	107	$208,493
1976	1,123	173	144	147	$441,635
1977	1,123	193 (30)	167	125	$505,991
1978	1,417	241 (14)	211	150	$920,044
1979	1,391	257 (13)	213	186	$1,844,350 (29)
1980	1,502	283 (6)	257	192	$2,662,873 (23)
1981	1,269	249 (13)	180	163	$2,722,051 (24)
1982	1,584	295 (7)	225	228	$3,857,936 (15)
1983	690	110	86	67	$1,486,660
1984	1,052	250 (15)	171	146	$2,365,196
1985	1,828	415 (2)	327	229	$5,343,767 (14)
1986	1,401	224 (25)	194	166	$8,082,352 (6)
1987	1,370	242 (19)	175	179	$7,937,455 (8)
1988	1,229	174	181	164	$7,966,436 (8)
1989	1,164	171	157	164	$6,605,222 (13)
1990	1,021	153	149	138	$4,758,299 (22)
1991	154	12	16	12	$454,289
1992	298	30	43	36	$1,205,479
1993	730	92	79	83	$2,801,002
1994	437	25	55	48	$847,458
1995	723	79	88	91	$2,869,282
1996	1,070	138	140	120	$3,345,971
1997	851	120	126	137	$2,637,481
1998	885	111	100	117	$2,345,008
1999	251	17	30	21	$620,257
TOTALS	26,096	4,294	3,744	3,304	$75,035,906

Randy Romero's Riding Titles

Arlington Park: 1982 (record 181), 1985 (159)
Belmont Park: 1986 fall (54), 1987 spring (61)
Delta Downs: 1976, 1977
Evangeline Downs: 1976 (107), 1977 (135), 1978 (141 ties state record)
Fair Grounds: 1979-80 (122), 1980-81 (104), 1983-84 (record 181), 1984-85 (167)
Gulfstream Park: 1986 (41)
Hialeah: 1987 (56 wins tied with Julio Pezua)
Jefferson Downs: 1977
Keeneland: 1980 spring (20), 1981 fall (25), 1982 spring (24), 1985 spring (17), 1989 spring (28 including a record 6 stakes), 1990 spring (record 32)
Louisiana Downs: 1979, 1980

223

Randy Romero's Six Wins in One Day
Churchill Downs: May 8, 1985
Fair Grounds: February 8, 1984
Keeneland: April 7, 1990

Randy Romero's Stakes Victories

Stakes	Horse	Track	Date
$10,000 Lafayette Futurity	Oil Patch Pappa	Evangeline Downs	Sept. 6, 1976
$5,000 Lake Front Futurity	Oil Patch Pappa	Jefferson Downs	Nov. 13, 1976
$15,000 Feliciana Stakes	Dr. Box	Louisiana Downs	May 28, 1977
$5,000 Texas Breeders Sales	Chateau Mark	Evangeline Downs	June 12, 1977
$5,000 Delta Downs Derby Division	Shimmy Sham	Delta Downs	April 2, 1978
$5,000 Delta Downs Derby Division	Solon Springs	Delta Downs	April 2, 1978
$8,000 Lone Star Derby	Blue Jet King	Evangeline Downs	April 30, 1978
$5,000 Texas Breeders Sales	Ideal Mame	Evangeline Downs	June 11, 1978
$10,000 Southwest La. Futurity	A Toast to Junius	Evangeline Downs	July 4, 1978
$10,000 Jefferson Futurity	A Toast to Junius	Jefferson Downs	Aug. 12, 1978
$8,000 La. Breeders' Futurity	A Toast to Junius	Delta Downs	Oct. 29, 1978
$10,000 St. Tammany Handicap	Port Eads	Jefferson Downs	Nov. 11, 1978
$5,000 Texas Thor. Breeder Sale	Fly Johnny Fly	Evangeline Downs	June 10, 1979
$20,000 Arcadia Stakes	All Bob's Fault	Louisiana Downs	July 22, 1979
$15,000 Glamour Stakes	Proven Val U.	Louisiana Downs	Aug. 4, 1979
$20,000 Jefferson Futurity	Bold and Active	Jefferson Downs	Aug. 11, 1979
$15,000 Rampart Stakes	All Bob's Fault	Louisiana Downs	Aug. 11, 1979
$25,000 Vantage Stakes	Memory Garden	Louisiana Downs	Sept. 2, 1979
$10,000 Lafayette Futurity	Bold and Active	Evangeline Downs	Sept. 3, 1979
$20,000 Seneca Stakes	Irish Salute	Louisiana Downs	Sept. 29, 1979
$25,000 Envoy Stakes	Avenger M.	Louisiana Downs	Oct. 13, 1979
$150,000 Louisiana Downs Handicap	Incredible Ease	Louisiana Downs	Oct. 21, 1979
$50,000 Crystal Stakes	War Party	Louisiana Downs	Nov. 3, 1979
$25,000 Barksdale Handicap	Incredible Ease	Louisiana Downs	Nov. 24, 1979
$12,500 Jeanne d'Arc Prep	Sweet n Pretty Too	Fair Grounds	Dec. 8, 1979
$50,000 Jeanne d'Arc	Sweet n Pretty Too	Fair Ground	Dec. 16, 1979
$30,000 Louisiana Handicap	A Letter to Harry	Fair Grounds	Jan. 19, 1980
$25,000 Battler Star Handicap	War Party	Fair Grounds	Feb. 2, 1980
$28,000 Red Camelia Handicap	Fairly Right	Fair Grounds	Mar. 1, 1980
$50,000 Ashland Stakes (G2)	Flos Florum	Keeneland	Apr. 19, 1980
$40,000 Bewitch Stakes	Jolie Dutch	Keeneland	Apr. 25, 1980
$10,000 Penelope Stakes Division	Smooth Bore	River Downs	May 18, 1980
$10,000 Penelope Stakes Division	Mardi Gras Maid	River Downs	May 18, 1980
$20,000 Cajun Stakes	Turbulence	Louisiana Downs	June 15, 1980
$15,000 Pioneer Stakes	Contorsionist	Louisiana Downs	June 21, 1980
$20,000 Fantasia Stakes	Greenback Gert	Louisiana Downs	June 21, 1980
$20,000 Dixie Miss Stakes	Inyala's Goody	Louisiana Downs	June 28, 1980
$20,000 Seneca Stakes	Greenback Gert	Louisiana Downs	July 5, 1980
$25,000 King's Court Stakes	Turbulence	Louisiana Downs	July 13, 1980
$20,000 Chapel-Belle Stakes	Hey Mama	Louisiana Downs	Aug. 16, 1980
$25,000 Cosmah Handicap	Shawn's Gal	Louisiana Downs	Aug. 31, 1980
$25,000 Vantage Stakes	Hey Mama	Louisiana Downs	Sept. 7, 1980
$50,000 Pelican State Stakes	Shiskabob	Louisiana Downs	Oct. 12, 1980
$30,000 Minstrel Stakes	Yo Solo	Louisiana Downs	Nov. 7, 1980
$17,500 Louisiana Futurity Restr.	Reason's Tattoo	Fair Grounds	Dec. 13, 1980
$15,000 Jeanne d'Arc Prep	Joy Returned	Fair Grounds	Dec. 14, 1980
$27,500 Claiborne Handicap	Turbulence	Fair Grounds	Mar. 21, 1981
$30,000 Suthern-Accent	Graceful Landing	Louisiana Downs	May 10, 1981
$25,000 Cajun Stakes	Turbulence	Louisiana Downs	May 10, 1981

$25,000 Aristeia Stakes	Derrick's Lady	Louisiana Downs	May 23, 1981
$25,000 Swan Isle Stakes	Rose Judge	Louisiana Downs	May 30, 1981
$25,000 Garnet Stakes	Turbulence	Louisiana Downs	June 13, 1981
$25,000 Rebel Stakes	Rose Judge	Louisiana Downs	June 27, 1981
$30,000 Independence Stakes	Not Tomorrow	Louisiana Downs	July 4, 1981
$11,600 D. S. Young Mem. Futurity	Homemade Lovin	Evangeline Downs	July 5, 1981
$30,000 Mimosa Stakes	Spare the Queen	Louisiana Downs	July 11, 1981
$30,000 Old South Stakes	Of Royal Blood	Louisiana Downs	July 19, 1981
$25,000 Lady-Luck Stakes	Lady Christal	Louisiana Downs	July 25, 1981
$25,000 Land of Opportunity Futurity	Lady Christal	Louisiana Downs	Aug. 1, 1981
$30,000 Sequoia Stakes	Noodle Ruler	Louisiana Downs	Aug. 2, 1981
$30,000 Crystal Stakes	San Worth	Louisiana Downs	Aug. 8, 1981
$25,000 Beau Brummel Stakes	Shiskabob	Louisiana Downs	Sept. 5, 1981
$50,000 Pelican State Stakes	Restless Navajo	Louisiana Downs	Sept. 6, 1981
$10,000 Lafayette Futurity	Cherokee Circle	Evangeline Downs	Sept. 7, 1981
$40,000 Chrysanthemum H'cap (G3)	Cannon Boy	Laurel Park	Nov. 14, 1981
$50,000 Kentucky Jockey C (G3)	El Baba	Churchill Downs	Nov. 21, 1981
$25,000 Pontalba Stakes	Rose Bouquet	Fair Grounds	Nov. 28, 1981
$5,000 Mississippi Futurity	Hugo Farr	Fair Grounds	Dec. 4, 1981
$25,000 Tenacious Handicap	Dr. Riddick	Fair Grounds	Dec. 6, 1981
$50,000 Essex Handicap	Plaza Star	Oaklawn Park	Mar. 6, 1982
$50,000 Magnolia Stakes	Jasmine Jule	Oaklawn Park	Mar. 12, 1982
$50,000 Louisville Stakes	Bobrobbery	Churchill Downs	Apr. 27, 1982
$30,000 Churchill Downs Handicap	Top Avenger	Churchill Downs	Apr. 29, 1982
$50,000 Shecky Greene Handicap	Straight Flow	Arlington Park	May 22, 1982
$40,000 Real Delight Handicap	Touch of Glamour	Arlington Park	May 30, 1982
$75,000 Equipoise Mile Handicap	Summer Advocate	Arlington Park	June 5, 1982
$30,000 Jefferson Cup	Wavering Monarch	Churchill Downs	June 12, 1982
$10,000 Athena Stakes	Murlesk	River Downs	June 13, 1982
$30,000 Cleopatra Handicap	Pretorienne	Arlington Park	June 16, 1982
$35,000 Colfax Maid Stakes	All Sold Out	Arlington Park	June 26, 1982
$35,000 Isaac Murphy Memorial	Noted	Arlington Park	June 26, 1982
$50,000 Fairmount Derby	Northern Majesty	Fairmont Park	June 27, 1982
$100,000 Ak-Sar-Ben Gold Cup (G2)	Wavering Monarch	Ak-Sar-Ben	July 3, 1982
$20,000 Banquet Belle Stakes	Dancing Partner	Thistle Downs	July 11, 1982
$30,000 Old South Stakes Division	Pretorienne	Louisiana Downs	July 18, 1982
$30,000 Old South Stakes Division	Lacey	Louisiana Downs	July 18, 1982
$50,000 Ak-Sar-Ben Juvenile (G3)	Highland Park	Ak-Sar-Ben	July 23, 1982
$50,000 Pucker Up Stakes (G3)	Rose Bouquet	Arlington Park	July 24, 1982
$200,000 Haskell Invitational	Wavering Monarch	Monmouth Park	July 31, 1982
$9,000 Fairmont Juvenile	Decision	Fairmont Park	Aug. 14, 1982
$15,000 Rosebud Stakes	Maritza	Fairmont Park	Aug. 28, 1982
$50,000 Fayette Handicap	Rivaleo	Keeneland	Oct. 9, 1982
$50,000 Clark Handicap (G3)	Hechizado	Churchill Downs	Nov. 27, 1982
$60,000 Bolsa Chica Stakes	Dedicata	Santa Anita	Feb. 22, 1983
$25,000 Southland Stakes	I'm Driven	Louisiana Downs	Aug. 28, 1983
$30,000 Minstrel Stakes	Tivo	Louisiana Downs	Sept. 10, 1983
$25,000 Pontalba Stakes	Pretty Prospect	Fair Grounds	Nov. 26, 1983
$17,500 Louisiana Futurity	Cruzin Smooth	Fair Grounds	Dec. 24, 1983
$50,000 Jeanne d'Arc Stakes	I'm Driven	Fair Grounds	Dec. 26, 1983
$20,000 Bicker Stakes	Top Princess	Fair Grounds	Dec. 30, 1983
$25,000 Black Gold Handicap	Taylor's Special	Fair Grounds	Feb. 4, 1984
$100,000 Fair Grounds Classic (G3)	Police Inspector	Fair Grounds	Feb. 19, 1984
$25,000 Sixty Sails Handicap	Freeway Folly	Fair Grounds	Feb. 26, 1984
$25,000 Mardi Gras Handicap	Monique Rene	Fair Grounds	Mar. 6, 1984
$50,000 Bayou Handicap	Freeway Folly	Fair Grounds	Mar. 11, 1984

$35,000 Sugarland Stakes	Monique Rene	Louisiana Downs	Aug. 24, 1984
$150,000 Ruffian Handicap (G1)	Heatherten	Belmont Park	Sept. 30, 1984
$40,000 Fife 'N' Drum Stakes	Dramatic Desire	Louisiana Downs	Oct. 5, 1984
$30,000 Folklore Stakes	Temerity Prince	Louisiana Downs	Oct. 6, 1984
$25,000 Bayou Stakes	Bertha Fay	Louisiana Downs	Nov. 3, 1984
$100,000 Ladies Handicap (G1)	Heatherten	Aqueduct	Nov. 24, 1984
$25,000 Old Hickory Stakes	The Royal Freeze	Fair Grounds	Nov. 25, 1984
$25,000 Hits Parade Intl. Futurity	Little Biddy Comet	Fair Grounds	Dec. 16, 1984
$40,000 Furl Sail Handicap	Sefa's Beauty	Fair Grounds	Jan. 19, 1985
$25,000 Whirlaway Handicap	Rapid Gray	Fair Grounds	Jan. 27, 1985
$50,000 Hot Springs Handicap	Taylor's Special	Oaklawn Park	Feb. 16, 1985
$25,000 Mardi Gras Handicap	Sefa's Beauty	Fair Grounds	Feb. 19, 1985
$40,0000 Pelleteri Handicap	Taylor's Special	Fair Grounds	Mar. 2, 1985
$25,000 Matchmaker Handicap	Gerrie Singer	Fair Grounds	Mar. 17, 1985
$50,000 Pippin Handicap	Heatherten	Oaklawn Park	Mar. 23, 1985
$50,000 Lafayette Stakes	Proudest Hour	Keeneland	Apr. 6, 1985
$100,000 Count Fleet Sprint H'cap	Taylor's Special	Oaklawn Park	Apr. 18, 1985
$100,000 Ashland Stakes (G2)	Koluctoo's Jill	Keeneland	Apr. 20, 1985
$50,000 Derby Trial (G3)	Crème Fraiche	Churchill Downs	Apr. 27, 1985
$125,000 Hempstead Handicap (G1)	Heatherten	Belmont Park	June 9, 1985
$30,000 A.L. Oxford Stakes	All of a Sudden	Fairmont Park	June 29, 1985
$30,000 H.J. Hardenbrook Memorial	Honey Mac Dan	Balmoral	July 4, 1985
$15,000 Dolly Val Handicap	Madame Secretary	Balmoral	July 20, 1985
$50,000 Swoon's Son Handicap	Stay the Course	Arlington Park	July 27, 1985
$25,000 Mademoiselle Stakes	In Full View	Arlington Park	July 28, 1985
$150,000 Omaha Gold Cup (G3)	Flare Dancer	Ak-Sar-Ben	Aug. 3, 1985
$75,000 Arlington Matron (G2)	Heatherten	Hawthorne	Aug. 7, 1985
$20,000 Balmoral Handicap	Exit Five B.	Balmoral	Aug. 17, 1985
$15,000 Whirlaway Stakes	Gibakook	Balmoral	Aug. 18, 1985
$125,000 Bassinet Stakes	In Full View	River Downs	Aug. 25, 1985
$25,000 Arch Ward Stakes	Bar Tender	Hawthorne	Aug. 31, 1985
$25,000 Majestic Light Stakes	Hopeful Word	Hawthorne	Aug. 31, 1985
$150,000 Secretariat Stakes (G2)	Derby Wish	Hawthorne	Sept. 2, 1985
$30,000 Chief Illiniwek Stakes	Days of Yesteryear	Hawthorne	Sept. 15, 1985
$75,000 Louisiana Downs Oaks	Just Anything	Louisiana Downs	Sept. 22, 1985
$100,000 Hawthorne Derby (G3)	Derby Wish	Hawthorne	Oct. 5, 1985
$50,000 Devon Handicap	Spectacular Spy	Philadelphia Park	Nov. 11, 1985
$40,000 Unknown	Bold and Vibrant	Fair Grounds	Nov. 28, 1985
$50,000 Warminster Handicap	Spectacular Spy	Philadelphia Park	Dec. 28, 1985
$25,000 Diplomat Way Stakes	Silent King	Fair Grounds	Dec. 29, 1985
$300,000 Gulfstream Park H'cap (G1)	Skip Trial	Gulfstream Park	Feb. 22, 1986
$30,000 Hibiscus Stakes	I'm Splendid	Hialeah Park	Mar. 17, 1986
$50,000 Prima Donna Stakes	Double Derby	Oaklawn Park	Apr. 15, 1986
$200,000 Garden State Stakes	Fobby Forbes	Garden State Park	Apr. 19, 1986
$175,000 Sixty Sails Handicap (G3)	Sefa's Beauty	Sportsman's Park	May 24, 1986
$200,000 Coaching Club America (G1)	Valley Victory	Belmont Park	July 6, 1986
$250,000 Michigan Mile & 1/8 (G2)	Ends Well	Detroit	July 12, 1986
$100,000 Ballerina Stakes (G2)	Gene's Lady	Saratoga	Aug. 8, 1986
$250,000 Bud-Haw Gold Cup (G2)	Ends Well	Hawthorne	Aug. 16, 1986
$100,000 Arlington Classic (G1)	Sumptious	Arlington Park	Aug. 19, 1986
$50,000 Leixable Stakes	Fama	Belmont Park	Sept. 20, 1986
$50,000 Cliff Hanger Handicap (G3)	Explosive Darling	Meadowlands	Sept. 20, 1986
$100,000 Rutgers Handicap (G2)	Fred Astaire	Meadowlands	Sept. 26, 1986
$150,000 Cowdin Stakes (G1)	Polish Navy	Belmont Park	Sept. 27, 1986
$75,000 Queen Charlotte Division	Vacumette	Meadowlands	Oct. 3, 1986
$75,000 Queen Charlotte Division	April Again	Meadowlands	Oct. 3, 1986
$750,000 Jockey Club Gold C (G1)	Crème Fraiche	Belmont Park	Oct. 4, 1986

$100,000 New York Stallion Stakes	Royal Value	Belmont Park	Oct. 11, 1986
$50,000 Engine One Stakes	Red Wing Dream	Belmont Park	Oct. 11, 1986
$30,000 Budweiser Breeders' Cup	Pine Tree Lane	Meadowlands	Oct. 11, 1986
$200,000 Frizette Stakes (G1)	Personal Ensign	Belmont Park	Oct. 13, 1986
$50,000 Bold Princess Stakes	Spectacular Bev	Belmont Park	Oct. 18, 1986
$250,000 Champagne Stakes (G1)	Polish Navy	Belmont Park	Oct. 18, 1986
$200,000 Ladies Handicap (G1)	Life at the Top	Aqueduct	Nov. 16, 1986
$50,000 Holly Stakes	Grecian Flight	Meadowlands	Nov. 26, 1986
$100,000 Long Look Handicap (G2)	Life at the Top	Meadowlands	Nov. 29, 1986
$60,000 Joe Palmer Handicap	H.T. Willis	Aqueduct	Dec. 10, 1986
$60,000 Montauk Stakes	Grecian Flight	Aqueduct	Jan. 4, 1987
$20,000 Joseph O'Farrell Mem.	Phantom Jet	Hialeah	Jan. 28, 1987
$25,000 Miami Beach Stakes	Ten Thousand Stars	Hialeah	Jan. 31, 1987
$30,000 Gulfstream Park Breeders' Cup	Bolshoi Boy	Gulfstream Park	Mar. 7, 1987
$50,000 Shirley Jones Handicap	Life At the Top	Gulfstream Park	Mar. 25, 1987
$250,000 Gulfstream Park H'cap (G1)	Skip Trial	Gulfstream Park	Mar. 29, 1987
$35,000 Suwanee River H'cap (G3)	Fama	Gulfstream Park	Apr. 1, 1987
$100,000 Razorback Handicap (G2)	Bolshoi Boy	Oaklawn Park	Apr. 4, 1987
$100,000 Rampart Handicap (G3)	Life at the Top	Gulfstream Park	Apr. 5, 1987
$50,000 Best Turn Stakes	Java Gold	Aqueduct	Apr. 18, 1987
$50,000 Fort Lauderdale Handicap	Skip Trial	Gulfstream Park	Apr. 19, 1987
$250,000 Carter Handicap (G2)	Pine Tree Lane	Aqueduct	May 2, 1987
$100,000 Fort Marcy Handicap (G3)	Dance of Life	Belmont Park	May 9, 1987
$50,000 Olympic Handicap	Skip Trial	Gulfstream Park	May 17, 1987
$50,000 Pearl Necklace Stakes	Doubles Partner	Laurel Park	June 28, 1987
$50,000 Sweet Tooth Stakes	Doubles Partner	Belmont Park	July 11, 1987
$150,000 Tidal Handicap	Dance of Life	Belmont Park	July 11, 1987
$60,000 Empire Stakes	Fourstardave	Saratoga	Aug. 28, 1987
$150,000 Hopeful Stakes (G1)	Crusader Sword	Saratoga	Aug. 29, 1987
$500,000 Woodward Stakes (G1)	Polish Navy	Belmont Park	Sept. 5, 1987
$100,000 Cotillion Handicap (G3)	Silent Turn	Philadelphia Park	Sept. 12, 1987
$30,000 Half Moon Stakes	Bold Lady Anne	Meadowlands	Sept. 25, 1987
$75,000 Rare Perfume Stakes (G2)	Personal Ensign	Belmont Park	Oct. 10, 1987
$250,000 Beldame Stakes (G1)	Personal Ensign	Belmont Park	Oct. 18, 1987
$75,000 Jamaica Handicap (G3)	Stacked Pack	Aqueduct	Oct. 21, 1987
$200,000 Spinster Stakes (G1)	Sacahuista	Keeneland	Oct. 31, 1987
$1,000,000 Breeders' Cup Distaff (G1)	Sacahuista	Hollywood Park	Nov. 21, 1987
$75,000 Queens County H'cap (G3)	Personal Flag	Aqueduct	Nov. 26, 1987
$60,000 Bold Princess Stakes	Girl Powder	Aqueduct	Dec. 6, 1987
$175,000 Widener Handicap (G1)	Personal Flag	Hialeah	Dec. 26, 1987
$100,000 Appleton Handicap (G3)	Yankee Affair	Gulfstream Park	Jan. 9, 1988
$75,000 Coaltown Stakes	Mining	Aqueduct	Jan. 24, 1988
$50,000 Golden Grass Stakes	Tanzanid	Gulfstream Park	Feb. 24, 1988
$40,000 Fort Lauderdale Division	Lordalik	Gulfstream Park	Mar. 4, 1988
$40,000 Fort Lauderdale Division	Kings River	Gulfstream Park	Mar. 4, 1988
$50,000 Swale Stakes	Seeking the Gold	Gulfstream Park	Mar. 5, 1988
$500,000 Florida Derby (G1)	Brian's Time	Gulfstream Park	Mar. 5, 1988
$30,000 Davona Dale Handicap	Cadillacing	Gulfstream Park	Mar. 5, 1988
$50,000 Buckram Oak Handicap	Native Mommy	Gulfstream Park	Mar. 5, 1988
$100,000 Swift Stakes (G3)	Aloha Prospector	Aqueduct	Mar. 12, 1988
$75,000 Catskill Stakes	Timmy	Aqueduct	Mar. 23, 1988
$100,000 Mutual Savings Life	Native Mommy	Fair Grounds	Mar. 24, 1988
$100,000 Mutual Savings Derby	Tanzanid	Fair Grounds	Mar. 26, 1988
$100,000 Mutual Savings Gold Cup	Yankee Affair	Fair Grounds	Mar. 27, 1988
$75,000 Distaff Handicap (G3)	Cadillacing	Aqueduct	Apr. 1, 1988
$35,000 Bourbonette Stakes	Darien Miss	Turfway Park (?)	Apr. 2, 1988
$150,000 Shuvee Handicap (G1)	Personal Ensign	Belmont Park	May 15, 1988

$200,000 Hempstead Handicap (G1)	Personal Ensign	Belmont Park	June 11, 1988
$100,000 Nassau County H'cap (G2)	Personal Flag	Belmont Park	June 12, 1988
$150,000 Molly Pitcher H'cap (G2)	Personal Ensign	Monmouth Park	July 4, 1988
$75,000 Astoria Stakes (G3)	Seattle Meteor	Belmont Park	July 13, 1988
$250,000 Whitney Handicap (G1)	Personal Ensign	Saratoga	Aug. 6, 1988
$75,000 Nijana Stakes (G3)	Love You by Heart	Saratoga	Aug. 10, 1988
$100,000 Bernard Baruch H'cap (G1)	My Big Boy	Saratoga	Aug. 14, 1988
$200,000 Spinaway Stakes (G1)	Seattle Meteor	Saratoga	Aug. 29, 1988
$100,000 Gazelle Handicap (G1)	Classic Crown	Belmont Park	Aug. 31, 1988
$100,000 Longfellow H'cap (G2)	Triteamtri	Monmouth Park	Sept. 3, 1988
$75,000 Hudson Handicap	Tinchen's Prince	Belmont Park	Sept. 7, 1988
$100,000 Maskette Stakes (G1)	Personal Ensign	Belmont Park	Sept. 10, 1988
$60,000 Violet Handicap (G3)	Graceful Darby	Meadowlands	Sept. 10, 1988
$100,000 Fall Highweight H'cap (G2)	Parlay Me	Belmont Park	Sept. 17, 1988
$75,000 Queen Charlotte H'cap (G3)	Graceful Darby	Meadowlands	Oct. 1, 1988
$200,000 Vosburgh Stakes (G1)	Mining	Belmont Park	Oct. 9, 1988
$300,000 Beldame Stakes (G1)	Personal Ensign	Belmont Park	Oct. 16, 1988
$100,000 Queen Elizabeth (G2)	Love You by Heart	Keeneland	Oct. 29, 1988
$50,000 Pocahontas Stakes	Solid Eight	Churchill Downs	Oct. 30, 1988
$1,000,000 Breeder's Cup Distaff (G1)	Personal Ensign	Churchill Downs	Nov. 5, 1988
$50,000 Abrogate Handicap	Littlebitapleasure	Churchill Downs	Nov. 5, 1988
$40,000 Palm Beach Stakes	Shy Tom	Gulfstream Park	Jan. 15, 1989
$40,000 Joe Namath Handicap	Vana Turns	Gulfstream Park	Jan. 20, 1989
$50,000 Super Bowl Handicap	Prospector's Halo	Gulfstream Park	Jan. 21, 1989
$75,000 Hutcheson Stakes (G3)	Dixieland Brass	Gulfstream Park	Jan. 28, 1989
$50,000 Suwanee River H'cap (G3)	Love You by Heart	Gulfstream Park	Feb. 4, 1989
$100,000 Fountain of Youth (G2)	Dixieland Brass	Gulfstream Park	Feb. 18, 1989
$50,000 Golden Grass Stakes	Feather Ridge	Gulfstream Park	Feb. 20, 1989
$50,000 Fort Lauderdale Handicap	Regal Brek	Gulfstream Park	Mar. 1, 1989
$50,000 Buckram Oak Handicap	Native Mommy	Gulfstream Park	Mar. 4, 1989
$100,000 Poinciana Handicap	Plate Queen	Hialeah	Mar. 29, 1989
$100,000 Week of Fame Ladies	Native Mommy	Fair Grounds	Mar. 30, 1989
$50,000 Appalachian Stakes	To the Lighthouse	Keeneland	Apr. 7, 1989
$50,000 Transylvania Stakes	Shy Tom	Keeneland	Apr. 8, 1989
$50,000 Fort Harrod Stakes	Yankee Affair	Keeneland	Apr. 13, 1989
$50,000 Commonwealth Breeders' Cup	Sewickley	Keeneland	Apr. 14, 1989
$250,000 Blue Grass Stakes (G1)	Western Playboy	Keeneland	Apr. 15, 1989
$75,000 Thor. Club of America (G3)	Plate Queen	Keeneland	Apr. 19, 1989
$75,000 Vineland Handicap (G3)	Blossoming Beauty	Garden State Park	May 27, 1989
$100,000 Tom Fool Stakes (G2)	Sewickley	Belmont Park	July 15, 1989
$75,000 Tremont Stakes (G3)	Eternal Flight	Belmont Park	July 19, 1989
$50,000 Colleen Stakes	Chrissy's Secret	Monmouth Park	July 25, 1989
$100,000 Fall Highweight H'cap (G2)	Sewickley	Belmont Park	Sept. 16, 1989
$200,000 Vosburgh Stakes (G1)	Sewickley	Belmont Park	Oct. 8, 1989
$200,000 Theatrical Handicap	Iron Courage	Gulfstream Park	Nov. 3, 1989
$1,000,000 Breeders' Cup Juvenile Filly (G1)	Go for Wand	Gulfstream Park	Nov. 4, 1989
$100,000 Tempted Stakes	Worth Avenue	Aqueduct	Dec. 10, 1989
$50,000 Meadowbrook Farm Stakes	Southern Tradition	Gulfstream Park	Jan. 17, 1990
$75,000 Hutcheson Stakes (G3)	Housebuster	Gulfstream Park	Feb. 10, 1990
$25,000 Davona Dale Stakes	Windansea	Fair Grounds	Mar. 11, 1990
$50,000 Olympic Handicap	Beau Genius	Gulfstream Park	Mar. 14, 1990
$50,000 Transylvania Stakes	Izvestia	Keeneland	Apr. 7, 1990
$75,000 Beaumont Stakes (G3)	Go for Wand	Keeneland	Apr. 10, 1990
$100,000 Elkhorn Stakes (G2)	Ten Keys	Keeneland	Apr. 14, 1990
$75,000 Forerunner Stakes (G3)	Izvestia	Keeneland	Apr. 20, 1990
$200,000 Ashland Stakes (G1)	Go for Wand	Keeneland	Apr. 21, 1990

$250,000 Sam Houston Stakes	Slow Fuse	Dueling Grounds	Apr. 22, 1990
$150,000 Dixie Handicap	Two Moccasins	Pimlico	May 17, 1990
$50,000 Governor's Stakes	Jenny's Playmate	Arlington Park	June 3, 1990
$40,000 Emerald Isle Stakes	Charming Ballerina	Arlington Park	June 9, 1990
$200,000 Mother Goose Stakes (G1)	Go for Wand	Belmont Park	June 10, 1990
$50,000 Manila Stakes	Super Abound	Arlington Park	July 2, 1990
$50,000 Colfax Maid Stakes	Bungalow	Arlington Park	July 3, 1990
$50,000 Mary Todd Stakes	Bungalow	Balmoral	July 17, 1990
$75,000 Tremont Stakes (G3)	Hansel	Belmont Park	July 21, 1990
$100,000 Test Stakes (G1)	Go for Wand	Saratoga	Aug. 2, 1990
$200,000 Alabama Stakes (G1)	Go for Wand	Saratoga	Aug. 11, 1990
$100,000 Maskette Stakes (G1)	Go for Wand	Belmont Park	Sept. 2, 1990
$250,000 Secretariat Stakes (G1)	Super Abound	Arlington Park	Sept. 3, 1990
$75,000 Arlington Matron (G3)	Degenerate Gal	Arlington Park	Sept. 8, 1990
$75,000 Arlington Oaks (G3)	Overturned	Arlington Park	Sept. 16, 1990
$250,000 Beldame Stakes (G1)	Go for Wand	Belmont Park	Oct. 7, 1990
$100,000 Fayette Handicap (G2)	Lac Ouimet	Keeneland	Oct. 19, 1990
$50,000 The Very One Handicap	Rigamajig	Gulfstream Park	Feb. 10, 1991
$60,000 Vineland Handicap (G3)	Christiecat	Garden State Park	May 25, 1991
$100,000 Tremont Breeders' Cup Stakes (G3)	Salt Lake	Belmont Park	July 5, 1991
$80,000 New York Stallion Stakes	Rush Chairman Bill	Aqueduct	Oct. 25, 1992
$75,000 Young American Stakes (G2)	Mischievous Music	Meadowlands	Oct. 30, 1992
$350,000 Brooklyn Handicap (G1)	Chief Honcho	Aqueduct	Nov. 21, 1992
$80,000 New York Stallion Stakes	Rush Chairman Bill	Aqueduct	Nov. 28, 1992
$75,000 Tropical Park H'cap (G3)	Barkerville	Calder	Jan. 2, 1993
$50,000 Forward Gal Breeders' Cup (G2)	Sun Runner	Gulfstream Park	Feb. 3, 1993
$75,000 Hutcheson Stakes (G2)	Hidden Trick	Gulfstream Park	Feb. 6, 1993
$25,000 Risen Star Stakes	Dixieland Heat	Fair Grounds	Mar. 6, 1993
$300,000 Louisiana Derby (G3)	Dixieland Heat	Fair Grounds	Mar. 20, 1993
$100,000 Fleur de Lis Handicap (G3)	Quilma Churchill Downs		June 5, 1993
$100,000 Louisville Handicap	Stark South	Churchill Downs	June 12, 1993
$100,000 Adirondack Stakes (G2)	Astas Foxy Lady	Saratoga	Aug. 12, 1993
$60,000 Audobon Oaks	Lady Tasso	Ellis Park	Aug. 22, 1993
$100,000 Pelleteri Handicap	Dixieland Heat	Fair Grounds	Mar. 25, 1995
$60,000 Fairway Fun Stakes	Fit to Lead	Turfway Park	Apr. 2, 1995
$500,000 Blue Grass Stakes (G2)	Wild Syn	Keeneland	Apr. 15, 1995
$40,000 Office Wife Stakes	Go Go Jack	Arlington Park	July 9, 1995
$40,000 Mister Gus Stakes	Manilaman	Arlington Park	July 30, 1995
$25,000 Cardinal Br Cup Handicap	Michislew	Fairmont Park	Aug. 15, 1995
$45,000 Teleprompter Stakes	Golden Gear	Arlington Park	Aug. 27, 1995
$75,000 Turfway Championship	Bound by Honor	Turfway Park	Sept. 9, 1995
$58,000 The Minstrel Stakes	Cinch	Keeneland	Oct. 18, 1995
$100,000 River City Handicap	Homing Pigeon	Churchill Downs	Nov. 12, 1995
$35,000 F.W. Gaudin Mem. H'cap	Once a Sailor	Fair Grounds	Dec. 17, 1995
$40,000 Sugar Bowl Handicap	Valid Expectations	Fair Grounds	Dec. 31, 1995
$40,000 Colonel Power Stakes	Once a Sailor	Fair Grounds	Jan. 20, 1996
$500,000 Illinois Derby (G2)	Natural Selection	Sportsman's Park	May 11, 1996
$150,000 Pucker Up Stakes (G2)	Ms. Mostly	Arlington Park	June 29, 1996
$30,000 Miss Oceana Stakes	Southern Playgirl	Arlington Park	Aug. 18, 1996
$150,000 Arlington-Was Lass (G2)	Southern Playgirl	Arlington Park	Sept. 29, 1996
$250,000 Alcibades Stakes (G2)	Southern Playgirl	Keeneland	Oct. 10, 1996
$40,000 Louisiana Handicap	Bucks Nephew	Fair Grounds	Dec. 29, 1996
$60,000 Diplomat Way Handicap	Bucks Nephew	Fair Grounds	Jan. 26, 1997
$60,000 Tiffany Lass Stakes	Dancing Water	Fair Grounds	Feb. 2, 1997
$250,000 Miami Beach Sprint H'cap	Vivace	Calder	June 21, 1997
$150,000 Spirit of Fighter Handicap	Tarzena	Calder	Aug. 2, 1997

$250,000 Princess Rooney Handicap	Vivace	Calder	Oct. 4, 1997
$100,000 Mecke Stakes	East of Easy	Calder	Nov. 22, 1997
$28,000 Maggies Pistol Handicap	Vivace	Calder	Dec. 1, 1997
$200,000 Bnnie Miss Stakes (G2)	Banshee Breeze	Gulfstream Park	Mar. 16, 1998
$30,000 Primal Stakes	Crafty Sandi	Calder	June 21, 1998
$65,000 A.P. Indy Stakes	Ayrial Delight	Keeneland	Oct. 18, 1998
$60,000 Holiday Inaugural Stakes	Freddie Frisson	Turfway Park	Nov. 29, 1998
$60,000 Turfway Prevue	Kimberlilte Pipe	Turfway Park	Dec. 12, 1998
$65,000 Spinning World Stakes	Ayrial Delight	Keeneland	Apr. 18, 1999

Randy Romero's Quarter Horse Statistics

Starts	1sts	2nds	3rds	Earnings
587	97	41	74	$332,503

Index